PROSPECT HEIGHTS PUBLIC LIBRARY

3 1530 00115 9820

D0847707

Prospect Heights Public Library
12 N. Elm St.
Prospect Heights, IL 60070-1499

The Signers of the Declaration of Independence

THE SIGNERS OF THE DECLARATION OF INDEPENDENCE

A Biographical and Genealogical Reference

by Della Gray Barthelmas

with a foreword by Frank Borman

McFarland & Company, Inc., Publishers
Jefferson, North Carolina, and London

Prospect Heights Public Library
12 N. Elm St.
Prospect Heights, IL 60070-1499

Front cover portraits (from top, left to right): Thomas McKean (Delaware), Samuel Chase (Maryland), John Adams (Massachusetts), Joseph Worth Hewes (North Carolina), George Read (Delaware)

Portraits that appear in this book are reproduced from the collections of the Library of Congress

British Library Cataloguing-in-Publication data are available

Library of Congress Cataloguing-in-Publication Data

Barthelmas, Della Gray, 1920–
      The signers of the Declaration of Independence : a biographical and genealogical reference / by Della Gray Barthelmas ; with a foreword by Frank Borman.
            p.   cm.
      Includes bibliographical references (p.) and index.
      ISBN 0-7864-0318-7 (library binding : 50# alkaline paper) ∞
      1. United States. Declaration of Independence — Signers — Biography.   2. United States. Declaration of Independence — Signers — Genealogy.   3. United States — History — Revolution, 1775–1783 — Biography.   I. Title.
E221.B37   1997
973.3'13'0922 — dc21   97-11663
                                                                          CIP

©1997 Della Gray Barthelmas. All rights reserved

No part of this book, specifically including the index, may be reproduced or transmitted in any form or by any means, electronic or mechanical, including photocopying or recording, or by any information storage and retrieval system, without permission in writing from the publisher.

Manufactured in the United States of America

McFarland & Company, Inc., Publishers
  Box 611, Jefferson, North Carolina 28640

TABLE OF CONTENTS

FOREWORD

Della Gray Barthelmas has done a remarkable job in chronicling the lives of the signers of the Declaration of Independence. Through extensive research she has assembled facts of personal and historical significance on each of these remarkable men. In the process she has provided the reader with valuable insight into the events that led to our country's independence. Read this book to learn, but also read it to enjoy for it is well done and thoroughly absorbing.

COLONEL FRANK BORMAN
Las Cruces, New Mexico

PREFACE

More than two centuries after its conclusion, the Revolutionary War remains probably the most thoroughly taught topic in American history, and no event from the Revolutionary period is as well known as the creation of the Declaration of Independence in 1776. The words of this world-changing document are familiar both within and beyond the United States, but many of the names bravely signed below those words have been forgotten in the passage of time. A few loom large in the national memory for their later accomplishments — future presidents and statesmen such as Thomas Jefferson and Benjamin Franklin, for example — but the others who helped draft the Declaration and risked their lives by signing it deserve a better fate than obscurity. This book has been written to reveal the 56 signers (as well as Secretary Charles Thomson, who attended all meetings and witnessed the original broadside with John Hancock but did not sign it) as the individuals they were.

It is interesting to note the diverse backgrounds of the signers. Several of them were members of very wealthy families in the American colonies. Eight were foreign born. The character and convictions of these men were formed early, some under the guidance of guardians and headmasters of their schools. When their fathers died, eleven of the signers were under the age of fifteen; another nine were under the age of twenty. Some were sent to England to be educated as early as age eleven and did not return home until they were grown.

All of the signers of the Declaration of Independence began their adult lives as loyal British subjects. Some had held British government posts in their home colonies. Gradually their philosophies changed under the increasingly restrictive practices of English control.

Samuel Adams was one of the earliest advocates for independence, as revealed by a paper written at Harvard College in 1743. Stephen Hopkins expressed his strong views to Benjamin Franklin at the Albany Convention of 1754, where Franklin presented his Plan of Union. His plan was considered premature; however, the convention was one early step toward independence.

England's pressing financial needs brought about their oppressive administration, greed, and lack of sympathetic understanding of the colonists. Open resistance began with the Port Bill of 1760. It was followed in 1761 by the trial of the Writs of Assistance in Boston, which tested the legality of Crown officers' authority to enter the houses of inhabitants at their discretion.

In 1764, the British government claimed they had a right to make laws and to levy taxes on the colonists without their consent or representation. In February Lord George Grenville proposed his stamp act plan. In debate a supporter of the bill asked: "Will these Americans, planted by our care and nourished by our indulgence, as well as protected by our arms, grudge to contribute their mite to relieve us from heavy burdens?"

Colonel Barre, who had resided in America and was familiar with its history answered: "Planted by your care?—no! Your oppression planted them in America. Nourished by your indulgence?—they grew by your neglect. Protected by your arms?—they themselves have nobly taken up arms in your defense."

Benjamin Franklin was in England and wrote to his friend and neighbor Charles Thomson, "The sun of liberty is set. The Americans must light the lamps of industry and economy." Thomson, in reply, wrote "Be assured we shall light torches of quite another sort," thus predicting revolutionary events to follow.

Some of the colonists were not seriously affected by the Stamp Act, and in 1765 few were entertaining the idea of separation. At this time, only a small percentage of the population wanted independence. The movement grew slowly as fear and distrust between colonists, friends, and within families prevented them from exchanging views. The line between loyalist and patriot divided many families. Benjamin Franklin's son William became the loyalist governor of New Jersey and was lost to him forever; Francis Lewis's only daughter married a loyalist and moved to England; Dorothy Camber, daughter of Thomas Camber, a loyalist, married George Walton and supported his patriotic causes.

Most of the new patriots were de-

scendants of people who had left their homes in England for a happier existence, others were immigrants. Oppressive acts became laws and hostilities grew causing previously loyal British subjects to become "traitors" or patriotic Americans.

Having pledged their lives, fortunes, and sacred honor to the great cause, the signers were absent from their homes for long periods of time. While these courageous men applied themselves to the task of uniting the colonies and forming a government, their families were dealing with adversity at home. They were often in fear of Indian attacks. The invading British troops completely destroyed the homes and plantations of those who had been identified as signers of the Declaration of Independence, forcing them to live with relatives and friends. The families of the signers also deserve the highest honors that can be bestowed upon them.

Several biographies of the signers have been written, beginning with John Sanderson's 1827 *Biographies of the Signers to the Declaration of Independence*, written when Charles Carroll of Carrollton was still living. In 1848, Benson John Lossing published his *Lives of the Signers to the Declaration of Independence*. There have been several more recent books, but none have given much attention to the genealogy of the signers or their wives. That missing element is one of the primary distinguishing features of the present work.

Each chapter of this book contains two sections. The first section contains information about the signer's education, career, military and political involvement, and other services rendered during the Revolutionary period, 1774–1789. The second section contains additional information about the signer, including a description of, in most cases, his birth-place, personality, personal appearance, and final resting place, and a genealogy. In the genealogy, "I." presents informa-tion about the signer, his children, and his wife and her family. Each successive roman numeral goes back one generation in the signer's paternal lineage, traces his maternal lineage, and when applicable presents information about other wives of the paternal ancestor. This personal information has been separated from the body of the chapter, which focuses on each signer's public life, to make it more useful to historians and genealogists.

Chapter 1

JOHN
ADAMS

1735–1826

MASSACHUSETTS

John Adams

JOHN ADAMS, teacher, lawyer, statesman, vice president, and president of the United States, learned to read under his father's instruction before he was sent to Dame Belcher's school where she taught reading, writing, and arithmetic. He then attended the Latin School, at the time being taught by the schoolmaster Joseph Cleverly. John disliked Cleverly, so his father consented to another teacher. He entered Harvard College at fourteen and was graduated in 1755. Due to his family's prominence and wealth, he was rated fourteenth in a class of twenty-four. It is not known how he ranked academically.

After graduating, he became a teacher of the "circuit" grammar school for about a year. He described his teaching as "instructing a large number of little runtlings, just capable of lisping A, B, C, and troubling the master." He pondered entering a career in theology or medicine, but decided to become a lawyer and studied in the law office of James Putnam at Worcester. He was presented by Jeremiah Gridley for admission to the Boston Bar on November 6, 1758, and immediately began to practice law. During his first ten years of professional life, he was a selectman, assessor, and overseer of the poor in the town of Braintree.

In 1765, under the pseudonym of Humphrey Ploughjogger, he wrote weekly articles and essays for the *Boston Gazette* concerning public affairs. His writings were produced at random, with no preconceived plan and were published as *A Dissertation on the Canon and Feudal Law*. Also in 1765, Adams wrote his *Resolutions for Braintree* to protest the Stamp Act, and became associated with Jeremiah Gridley and James Otis, Jr. In

1769, a customs official struck Otis on the head with a cutlass and he became insane. Otis was killed by lightning at Andover, Massachusetts, on May 23, 1783. Adams opposed the Stamp Act because the colonists had not consented to it. However, he disapproved of the riots in which his cousin, Samuel Adams, was involved.

While living in Boston in 1768, John Adams' important court cases included John Hancock's smuggling charge, and the Corbet case on a charge of impressment and manslaughter. Following the March 5, 1770, event known as the Boston Massacre, he and Josiah Quincy were the defense counsel for Captain Thomas Preston and the six British soldiers indicted with him. The so-called massacre was actually a riot caused by a mob of about fifty Boston men and boys who threw snowballs at the British sentinel in front of the customs house. Captain Preston and several soldiers came to his aid. Shots were fired by the soldiers. Five men were killed and several others were wounded. Their trial on a charge of manslaughter began on October 24, 1770. Captain Preston and six of the soldiers were acquitted, but two soldiers were found guilty and were branded on the hand and dismissed from the army.

Political events drew John Adams further into public life and he became firmly identified with the patriotic cause. When the First Continental Congress was organized in 1774, he was chosen by the Provincial Assembly as one of the five delegates from Massachusetts. John Adams' journey to Philadelphia with others of the Massachusetts delegation was an informative prelude to the Continental Congress. They visited places he had never seen and met several political leaders in Hartford, New Haven, Milford and

Stratford, Connecticut. They stayed a few days in New York and Adams was impressed by the wealthy New Yorkers and their huge estates. After a visit to Princeton, the delegates continued on to Philadelphia.

The First Continental Congress convened on September 5, 1774, and twelve colonies were represented. Georgians had not experienced many infringements of their rights and did not send a delegation. Except for John Adams' observations of the delegates and his notes concerning the business that transpired on the first day of the Congress, there is no record of what took place.

He signed the Articles of Association on October 20, 1774. During this first Continental Congress, John Adams persuaded the delegates to organize the Sons of Liberty who were, at that time, besieging the British at Boston. It was he who nominated George Washington, a Virginia delegate, to be commander in chief of the Army. Samuel Adams seconded his motion. When Congress adjourned he returned to Braintree and was reelected to the Provincial Congress.

He devoted himself to the measures toward resistance to Great Britain and continued to contribute to the public press under the pen name of Novanglus, under which he reviewed the policies of Massachusetts governors Bernard and Hutchinson. Soon after the Battle of Bunker Hill on June 17, 1775, Adams wrote in a letter, "The die is now cast. I have passed the Rubicon. Sink or swim, live or die, survive or perish with my country is my unalterable determination."

On May 10, 1775, he was again in Philadelphia when the Second Continental Congress convened. John Adams was an eloquent orator, and a hard working member of the Congress. He worked from seven in the morning until eleven at night, though he was frequently ill. During the first week of December 1775, Adams requested a leave to visit his family. He spent Christmas Day with his family, then went to Cambridge to inspect General Washington's army. By the end of December, he began a cold, eighteen-day horseback trip back to Philadelphia making several military and patriotic stops along the way. Delegates to the Second Continental Congress had grown anxious, and he too was eager for independence. The war had spread from Massachusetts to New Hampshire. Norfolk, Virginia, had been burned by the order of Lord Dunmore, and Virginia wanted to declare independence. The middle colonies of South Carolina, Pennsylvania, Delaware, and New York were unhappy, but still did not want separation from Great Britain.

He returned to Congress February 9, 1776. During that month, he wrote *Thoughts on Government* to counteract Thomas Paine's *Common Sense*. He then wrote a preamble, which James Duane (1733–1797) called a "machine for the fabrication of independence." Adams himself thought it was independence.

When on June 7, 1776, Richard Henry Lee placed Virginia's resolution for independence before the Congress, John Adams seconded the motion. It was agreed they would wait three weeks to allow the Assemblies of the reluctant colonies to reconsider and give their permission to the delegates to vote for independence. Committees were appointed on June 11, 1776, to prepare a declaration of independence and a plan of treaties for trade with foreign countries. John Adams was appointed to both committees.

On June 13, he was placed on the

newly created Board of War. On July 1, John Adams, Samuel Adams, and Richard Henry Lee met to review their plans for getting the resolution passed.

John Dickinson, a Quaker and leader of the opposition to independence, was first to speak during the debates. He spoke eloquently in favor of reconciliation with Great Britain. John Adams then made what has been described as the most notable speech of his life, reviewing all the causes making independence inevitable and describing the advantages of an immediate declaration.

The committee for writing the Declaration of Independence comprised John Adams, Thomas Jefferson, Robert Livingston (brother of signer Philip Livingston) and Roger Sherman. Adams contributed little or nothing of importance to the writing of the Declaration of Independence but he defended and supported its passage through Congress on July 2.

On July 4, 1776, after the vote in favor of adoption, he stated:

> It will be the most memorable epoch in the history of America. It ought to be solemnized with pomp and parade, with shows, games, guns, bells, bonfires, from one end of this continent to the other, and from this time forevermore. You will think me transported with enthusiasm, but I am not. I am well aware of the toil and blood and treasure that it will cost us to maintain this Declaration and support and defend these states, yet through all the gloom I can see the ravishing light and glory. I can see that the end is worth more than all the means, and that posterity will triumph in this day's transactions, even although we shall rue it, which I trust to God we shall not.

He signed the Declaration of Independence on August 2, 1776, and re-

mained in Congress until 1777, when he was appointed minister to France to assist in obtaining a treaty of alliance with France. On February 13, 1778, John Adams and his ten-year-old son, John Quincy Adams, boarded the frigate *Boston*. Arriving in Paris on April 8, he found that the treaty had been signed on February 6, 1778, and that Benjamin Franklin had been commissioned ambassador. He did, however, provide valuable service in arranging and systematizing the American business accounts. He was recalled in the spring of 1779 and helped draft Massachusetts' new constitution.

Later in 1779, he returned to France as a member of the commission charged with the authority to negotiate a treaty with Great Britain. On September 3, 1783, John Adams, John Jay, and Benjamin Franklin signed the Treaty of Paris, ending the Revolutionary War.

During the negotiations, he secured a treaty with Holland recognizing American independence and the promise of financial support. In 1785, with peace assured, he was appointed the first American minister to Great Britain. After three years of efforts without success in obtaining an acceptable commercial treaty, he resigned in 1788. Arriving home he was elected to the last Congress under the Articles of Confederation but never took his seat.

Adams was sworn in on April 21, 1789, as the first vice president of the United States, a post he characterized as "the most insignificant office that ever the invention of man contrived or his imagination conceived." He was reelected to the vice presidency in 1792.

In 1796, John Adams was elected to the presidency with only three more electoral votes than Thomas Jefferson, who became his vice president. His four years as president were effective but stormy and not very happy years for him.

Of particular interest was the XYZ Affair which caused much anger throughout the country. President Adams had sent ministers to France to negotiate a peace treaty, and they reported that they had been offered the treaty if the United States would pay a bribe to Talleyrand, the French minister. The French diplomats insisted the United States lend the French government $10,000,000. War was not declared but many battles occurred at sea between French and American ships. President Adams was determined to keep the peace and again asked Talleyrand for a treaty. Talleyrand was now ready to negotiate, as he feared the United States might join forces with England. Adams believed that keeping the country out of war with France was the most important achievement of his administration.

In the election of 1800, President Adams lost to Thomas Jefferson by a vote of seventy-three to sixty-five. They had always had very different basic political beliefs, but had been friends. They now became completely estranged. John Adams was so angry about his defeat that he refused to stay in Washington for Thomas Jefferson's inauguration. He left Washington on the morning of March 4, 1801, for his home in Quincy, Massachusetts. He lived in retirement for twenty-five years, during which time he observed the political career of his son and did much writing.

In January 1812, he wrote a letter to Thomas Jefferson. With political issues set aside, their friendship blossomed and continued to the end of their lives. President Jefferson died at about two in the afternoon and President Adams died at about six in the evening of July 4, 1826,

the fiftieth anniversary of the vote accepting the broadside draft of the Declaration of Independence.

A thirty-one inch bust of President John Adams, by sculptor Daniel Chester French, is displayed in the Senate Chamber Gallery of the United States Capitol Building.

Additional Information

A grandson, Charles Francis Adams, 1807–1886, was nineteen years old when President John Adams died. He described his grandfather as "scarcely exceeding middle height, but of a stout, well-knit frame, denoting vigor and long life, yet as he grew old, inclining more and more to corpulence. His head was large and round, with a wide forehead and expanded brow."

Thomas Jefferson's opinion of President Adams, written in 1787, was:

> He is vain, irritable, and a bad calculator of the force and probable effect of the motives which govern men. This is all the ill which can possibly be said of him. He is as disinterested as the being who made him; he is profound in his views and accurate in his judgement, except where knowledge of the world is necessary to form a judgement. He is so amiable, that I pronounce you will love him if ever you become acquainted with him. He would be, as he was, a great man in Congress.

Benjamin Franklin wrote of John Adams, "He was always an honest man, often a great man, and sometimes positively mad."

About the time John Adams began his professional career, he counseled himself in his diary to "let no trifling diversion decoy you from your books; no girl, no gun, no cards, no flutes, no violin, no dress, no tobacco, no laziness…" His keen insight and characterizations of his fellow signers give critical information about some of the signers of whom little is known. His pen was a sometimes cruel, tactless, but honest instrument — even his dear wife Abigail feared it.

President Adams died on the evening of July 4, 1826. He was interred in a basement crypt of the United First Parish Church at Quincy, Massachusetts.

In 1900, the John Adams Chapter of the Daughters of the American Revolution installed a memorial plaque at the entrance to the crypt. He was elected to the Hall of Fame at New York University in 1901. In 1924, the Massachusetts Society of the Sons of the American Revolution dedicated a bust of him in the colonnade of the New York University Hall of Fame. In 1952, his home in Quincy, Massachusetts, was designated as a historic site.

Genealogy

I. John Adams, Jr., October 19, 1735–July 4, 1826, was born at Quincy, Massachusetts. He married on October 15, 1764, his cousin Abigail Smith, and they had five children.

His children were: John Quincy 1767; Susannah 1768; Charles 1770; Thomas Boyleston 1772; Elizabeth 1777.

SMITH

Abigail Quincy Smith, November 23, 1744–October 18, 1818, was the daughter of the Reverend William Smith, Jr., of Charlestown, Massachusetts, born February 2, 1706/7, and died at Weymouth, September 17, 1783. He married at Braintree, October 16, 1740, Elizabeth Quincy,

baptized at Braintree on December 17, 1721, and died at Weymouth October 1, 1775. The Reverend William Smith, Jr., graduated from Harvard College in 1725 and was ordained at Weymouth. Elizabeth Quincy was the daughter of Colonel John Quincy, born at Boston July 21, 1689, died at Braintree July 13, 1767. John Quincy married on October 6, 1715, at Hingham, Elizabeth Norton, born at Hingham March 15, 1695/6.

John Quincy was the son of Daniel Quincy, born at Braintree February 7, 1650, and died at Boston August 10, 1690. On November 9, 1682, Daniel Quincy married Anna Shepard, born at Charlestown September 8, 1663, died at Braintree July 24, 1708. Elizabeth Norton was the daughter of the Reverend John Norton, born ca. 1651 and died at Hingham October 1716, who married at Boston, November 29, 1678, Mary Mason who died at Braintree in June 1740. She was the daughter of Arthur Mason, 1630–1707/8, and Joanna Parker, 1635–1704/5, who were married at Boston July 5, 1655. Daniel Quincy was a member of the Artillery Company in 1675.

Edmund Quincy, baptized at Achurch, County Northamptonshire, England, on March 15, 1627/8, died at Braintree, January 7, 1697/8. He married first, at Braintree, July 26, 1648, Joanna Hoar, baptized at St. Michael's, Gloucester, England, June 1624. Joanna died at Braintree, Massachusetts, on May 16, 1680; Joanna was the daughter of Charles Hoar, alderman of Gloucester who died in 1638, and Joanna Hincksman, who died at Braintree, December 21, 1661. Edmund Quincy married second, Elizabeth (Gookin) Eliot, daughter of Daniel Gookin and widow of the Reverend John Eliot, Jr. Edmund Quincy born 1627/8 was the son of Edmund Quincy, baptized in 1602 and died 1635, who married in England on July 14, 1623, Judith Pares. Judith married second Moses Paine, and married third, Robert Hall. She died November 29, 1654.

Edmund Quincy, 1602–1635, arrived in America on September 4, 1633, with the Reverend John Cotton from Wigsthorpe, County Northampton, England. He had a land grant at Braintree, Massachusetts, in 1635, and died the same year. He was the son of Edmund Quincy, 1559–1627/8, of Wigsthorpe, Northamptonshire, England, who married on October 14, 1593, Ann Palmer.

The Reverend William Smith, Jr., was the son of Captain William Smith, ca. 1666–1730. Captain Smith married at Charleston, about 1700, Abigail Fowle, born August 7, 1679, daughter of Isaac and Beriah (Bright) Fowle. Beriah was born September 22, 1651, and was the youngest daughter of Henry and Ann (Goldstone) Bright who were married at Watertown in 1634. Henry Bright was the son of Henry Bright of Bury St., Edmunds. He was at Charleston in 1630 and probably came from Ipswich in Suffolk in the Winthrop Fleet. Ann Goldstone was age eighteen at her marriage to Henry Bright; she was the daughter of Henry Goldstone, baptized July 17, 1591, and died July 25, 1638. Henry and Ann Goldstone came to America on the *Elizabeth* in 1634, he at age forty-three, and Ann at age forty-five. She was baptized May 16, 1615, at Wickham Skeith, Suffolk, and died at Watertown April 26, 1670, age seventy-nine. Henry Goldstone was the son of the Reverend William Goldstone, vicar of Bedington, County Suffolk, England. Henry Bright probably came from Ipswich in County Suffolk.

Isaac Fowle, 1648–October 15, 1718, of Charlestown, was the son of George Fowle of Concord, a freeman March 14, 1639, and removed to Charlestown where Isaac was born. George Fowle died September 19, 1682, age seventy-two; Mary Fowle died February 15, 1677, age sixty-three. George was baptized January 27, 1610, at Wittersham, Kent County, England, probably a son of Myles Fowle, born ca. 1562 and buried at Tenterden, Kent, on January 22, 1620.

Captain William Smith, 1666/7–1730, was the son of Thomas Smith, butcher, who lived at Charleston. He married about 1663, Susanna Boyleston, September 30, 1642–August 8, 1711, daughter of Thomas Boyleston, 1615–1653. Thomas Boyleston came, at age twenty, from London on the *Defense* in 1635. Captain William Smith was the son of Thomas Smith who was baptized at St. Dionis, Backchurch, London, February 12, 1614/5. He lived at Watertown, married about 1639, Sarah whose surname is unknown, and died in 1653. Sarah married second, John Chinery and died September 14, 1704.

BOYLESTON

II. Deacon John Adams, February 8, 1692–May 25, 1761, married at Brookline, Massachusetts, November 23, 1734, Susanna Boyleston, March 5, 1708/9, and died at Quincy April 17, 1797, daughter of Peter Boyleston, ca. 1673–September 10, 1743. Susanna (Boyleston) Adams was the daughter of Peter Boyleston who married about 1704, Ann White, 1685–1772, daughter of Benjamin White, born ca. 1626 and died at Brookline January 9, 1722/3. Benjamin White married at Ipswich, January 21, 1681/2, Susanna Cogswell, born at Ipswich January 5, 1657/8, and died post 1701. Susanna Cogswell was the daughter of William and Susanna (Hawkes) Cogswell; she was born in 1633 and died about 1696 at Charlestown. Benjamin White was the son of John and Frances (Jackson) White of Brookline, Massachusetts.

Peter Boyleston was the son of Thomas Boyleston, Jr., of Watertown who married on December 13, 1655, Mary Gardner, baptized April 9, 1648, and died at Brookline July 8, 1722. Mary Gardner was the daughter of Thomas Gardner of Roxbury.

Thomas Gardner was born in England and was a freeman in 1646. He married on July 4, 1641, Lucy Smith whose ancestry is unknown. She died November 4, 1687, at Roxbury. He died there July 15, 1689. He was probably the son of Thomas Gardner, Sr., of Roxbury who died in 1638 and "our aged sister Gardner" who was buried October 7, 1658.

Thomas Boyleston, Jr., January 26, 1644/5–ca. 1695, lived at Muddy River, Boston. He was a surgeon in King Philip's War. He was the son of Thomas Boyleston, Sr., baptized at St. Dionis Backchurch February 12, 1614/5, who came on the *Defense* in 1635, age twenty, and lived at Watertown. He was a cloth-worker from London. He married about 1639, Sarah, who married second, John Chinery, and died September 14, 1704. Thomas Boyleston died at Watertown October 4, 1653. He was the son of Edward Boyleston, citizen and pewterer of Litchfield, England, who died at Newton Solney, Derbyshire, between September 12 and 14, 1592. Edward Boyleston's wife of unknown name died before September 12, 1592.

BASS

III. Joseph Adams, December 24, 1654–February 2, 1736/7, married first on February 20, 1682, Mary Chapin, 1662–1687, daughter of Josiah Chapin. He married second, in 1688, Hannah Bass, born at Braintree June 22, 1667, died there October 24, 1705. Hannah was the daughter of John Bass, baptized September 18, 1630, at Saffron Walden, Essex, England, and died at Braintree September 12, 1716.

John Bass married at Braintree, February 3, 1657/8, Ruth Alden, ca. 1640–October 12, 1674. He was the son of Samuel Bass who married Ann Savell at Saffron Walden on April 25, 1625; John Bass died at Braintree December 30, 1694.

Samuel Bass was the first deacon at Braintree in 1640 and for fifty years thereafter, dying at the age of ninety-three. At the time of his death, he had one hundred sixty-two descendants.

Ann Savell/Savill, was baptized at Saffron Walden April 26, 1601, and died at Braintree, Massachusetts, September 5, 1693. She was the daughter of William Savell of Saffron Walden.

Ruth Alden was the third daughter of John and Priscilla (Mullins) Alden, who were married at Plymouth in 1623; both were *Mayflower* passengers. Priscilla Mullins was the daughter of William Mullins, 1578–February 21, 1621, and Alice Atwood, who died a few days before her husband. William Mullins made a nuncupative will, dated at Plymouth February 21, 1620/1.

John Alden was born about 1600 and died at Duxbury, Massachusetts, on September 12, 1687. He was not a member of the Reverend John Robinson's congregation at Leyden, Holland, but was hired as a cooper at Southampton, England, with the privilege of returning to England on the *Mayflower* if he wished. He possibly had a familial connection with

Christopher Jones, master of the *Mayflower*.

Joseph Adams married third, Elizabeth, ancestry unknown, who died February 14, 1739, age seventy-one.

BAXTER

IV. Joseph Adams, Sr., born in England, ca. 1626 and died December 6, 1694; his will was dated July 18, 1694. He married, November 29, 1650, Abigail Baxter, September 1634–August 27, 1692, daughter of Gregory Baxter born in England 1606–June 21, 1659, who married in 1632, Margaret Paddy who died February 13, 1662. Gregory Baxter came from the vicinity of Rowtown, England. He came on the *Mary and John* of 1630 and was of Roxbury in 1630 but removed to Braintree in 1640. He was a freeman March 6, 1631/2 and a member of the church the same year. Margaret Paddy's

brother, William Paddy, was treasurer for the Plymouth Colony, 1640–1653.

SQUIRES

V. Henry Adams, ca. 1583–1646, married in England, October 19, 1609, Edith Squires, 1587–1673, daughter of Henry Squires, 1563–post 1649, of Charlton Mackell and King Weston who was married about 1586, wife's name unknown. Henry Adams came from Devonshire or from Braintree in County Essex in 1632, and had a land grant for ten persons in February 1641. He died or was buried October 8, 1646; his will was probated June 8, 1647.

VI. Henry Adams, ca. 1531 and died at Barton, St. David, shortly before August 12, 1596. His wife Rose was buried at Barton, St. David, on September 20, 1598.

Chapter 2

SAMUEL ADAMS

1722–1803

MASSACHUSETTS

SAMUEL ADAMS, political leader and patriot, probably received his elementary education at the Boston Grammar School. He entered Harvard College in 1736, where he studied Latin, Greek, and the classics. He was graduated in 1740, and studied law to please his father, though studying for the ministry would have pleased both his parents. He returned to Harvard in 1743 to receive the degree of master of arts, writing for his thesis, "Whether It Be Lawful to Resist the Supreme Magistrate, if the Commonwealth Cannot Be Otherwise Preserved." Samuel Adams, Sr., was of sufficient wealth and prominence that Samuel was rated fifth, socially, in his class of twenty-two at Harvard.

Adams first entered the counting house of a merchant, Thomas Cushing, but left after a few months. His father then advanced him £1,000 to establish a business, but he lent half of the money to a friend who did not repay it. Of the other half, it can only be said that his business did not succeed. He began working in his father's brewery in 1743.

In 1747, Samuel Adams participated in founding the political club which was called The Whipping Post by their adversaries. He became a member of several other local organizations and by 1763 was politically influential.

Upon the death of his father in 1748, and of his mother in 1749, he inherited one-third of their estate which included a house on Purchase Street and the brewery. The estate was gradually dissipated, and he nearly lost his home several times. He was tax collector from 1756 to 1764 and in 1764 owed the town of Boston £8,000 in uncollected taxes.

He had considerable writing ability, and in 1764 he was asked to draft instructions from the town of Boston to its representatives. His public service career now began in earnest. Of particular interest to Samuel Adams were the actions of Thomas Hutchinson, chief justice, lieutenant governor, and a member of the Council. When the Stamp Act was enacted on March 22, 1764, and the Sugar Act followed in May, Governor Hutchinson became opposed to the radicals' schemes to defeat application of George Grenville's Stamp Act. The colonists simply continued to do business without the prescribed stamps.

John Adams observed that Samuel had the most thorough understanding of liberty of anyone concerned in its cause. The radicals denounced the Hutchinsonians as "enemies of liberty," as sympathizers of the British oppression. Governor Hutchinson's brother-in-law, Andrew Oliver, became the stamp distributor at Boston, and during the 1765 riots, Oliver was burned in effigy at the Liberty Tree. Governor Hutchinson's town house was gutted by the mob, and his family was forced to flee. On September 27, 1765, Samuel Adams became a member of the Assembly. He was an active member of the colonial legislature until 1774. In 1767 he opposed the Townshend Acts. It is likely, even at that early date, that Samuel Adams had grasped the idea of independence from Great Britain.

At the First Continental Congress, Adams was immediately placed on a committee to prepare the reply to a message sent in by Massachusetts Governor Bernard, in which he asserted the supreme authority of the British Parliament over the American colonies. Within the same month, October, Samuel Adams submitted a response to

Bernard, as well as the Massachusetts Resolves. The resolves expressed loyalty to the king, but refused to aid in the execution of the Stamp Act. These papers were in Adams' own handwriting. He also drew up a resolution that was passed by the Massachusetts House criticizing the governor for using money from the Provincial Treasury to pay additional troops at the castle in Boston, without the consent of the House. It was about this time, in letters he sent to England, that he developed an idea which he had previously suggested, of a nonimportation scheme. Plans had not been completed for cutting off British imports, but in the fall of 1768, two regiments of British troops arrived in Boston to assist the governor in his efforts to enforce their laws.

By 1770, Samuel Adams' patriotic followers, calling themselves the Sons of Liberty began to agitate the British soldiers. The soldiers fired on a group of Bostonians, killing five men and wounding seven others. Some soldiers were arrested but most were acquitted, and the governor agreed to withdraw one regiment from the town. These men of the Boston Massacre were defended by Samuel Adams' second cousin, John Adams, who would later be president of the United States.

Samuel Adams was an avid political writer, and as clerk of the House, he drafted most of their official papers. Privately, he wrote numerous letters to prominent people in England and in America. He wrote many articles for the *Boston Gazette* and other journals, which he signed using Candidus, Vindex, Poplicola, and other pseudonyms. These articles won numerous supporters for the radicals' movement, and he, in general, was the leader against reconciliation with

Great Britain. He led the struggle against the Townshend Acts which were repealed April 7, 1770. Following their repeal, for a time conflicts with England subsided. The merchants abandoned the nonimportation association. John Hancock, who had been accused of being "led by the nose" by Adams, quarreled with him and resumed his mercantile business. Samuel Adams' popularity and influence waned, but he turned to the press to point out such facts as that Governor Hutchinson's salary was being paid by the king, not by the Massachusetts General Court. In 1771, Lieutenant Governor Hutchinson had succeeded Bernard as governor of Massachusetts. Adams pointed out that the colonists were gradually "being made slaves unaware."

On November 2, 1772, the Boston Town Meeting, on Adams' motion, appointed a Committee of Correspondence to state the rights of the colonists and the Province. Samuel Adams was the author of the Declaration of Rights which was presented to the town on November 20, 1772.

Governor Hutchinson had become alarmed at Adams' renewed popularity, and in 1771 he said of Samuel Adams, "I doubt whether there is a greater incendiary in the King's dominion or a man of greater malignity of heart." He hired writers to answer Adams' newspaper articles. Governor Hutchinson might have had more influence had not the six famous Hutchinson Letters, written during 1768–1769 to an English official, been published. Benjamin Franklin had acquired the originals of these letters, in which Hutchinson requested troops and urged curtailment of liberties in the colonies, and sent them to an American friend so that they might be read by the proper persons. He asked that they not be printed or copied. They were read in secret session and later printed for the various Committees of Correspondence by authority of Governor Hutchinson. The ensuing scandal cost Benjamin Franklin his position as postmaster general.

On May 10, 1773, Lord North's Tea Act was passed by Parliament. On November 2, 1773, the North End Caucus, with the Boston Committee of Correspondence present by request, voted "that the tea shipped by the East India Company shall not be landed." The following day, a committee of the Sons of Liberty of which Adams was a member, requested the consignees of the tea to resign. They did not, and on November 5, a Boston town meeting adopted Samuel Adams' draft declaring that anyone who aided in landing or selling tea to be an enemy of America.

The *Dartmouth*, the first tea ship, arrived November 28, 1773. On November 29, at an informal meeting held at Faneuil Hall, Adams made a motion and it was resolved that the tea "shall be returned to the place from which it came at all events." Many meetings were held during the following two weeks. Under customs law, the tea had to be landed, or confiscated, by December 16. A meeting was held, with about seven thousand persons attending, filling the Old South Church, the adjoining streets, and the Boston Common. Adams presided over the meeting from ten in the morning until six in the evening. Finally a messenger came, bearing Governor Hutchinson's refusal to have the ship return to England.

Samuel Adams said, "This meeting can do nothing more to save the country." This was perhaps a prearranged signal, for several men dressed as Mohawk Indians immediately went to the wharf

and threw the cargo of tea into the harbor. "Tea Parties" occurred in other colonies as well. As a result, King George, his adviser Lord North, and Parliament, retaliated by passing the Boston Port Act and the port was closed at the end of March 1774. Six weeks later the Boston Committee retaliated with a recommendation to all the colonies to suspend trade with Great Britain. During the Massachusetts General Court in July 1774, Samuel Adams moved to appoint delegates to a Continental Congress "to deliberate and determine upon all measures," and he was chosen as one of their five delegates. On October 20, 1774, he signed the Articles of Association. He resigned from the Massachusetts General Court.

In Philadelphia Joseph Galloway was Speaker of the Pennsylvania Assembly, and was now a leader in Congress and of the party which wanted reconciliation with Great Britain. Galloway thought Samuel Adams managed all the correspondence between Philadelphia and Boston. He wrote:

> These were under the management of Samuel Adams. He eats little, drinks little, sleeps little, thinks much, and is most decisive and indefatigable in the pursuit of his objects. It was this man, who, by his superior application, managed at once the faction in Congress at Philadelphia and the factions in New England.

In Boston General Gage had been observing the patriotic activities of Samuel Adams and John Hancock, and he was aware that the colonists were storing ammunition at Lexington and Concord. On the night of April 18-19, 1775, General Gage removed his troops to seize the ammunition and he hoped to capture Adams and Hancock as well. For some time the British soldiers had been kept under the watchful eye of the first American intelligence net of about thirty men who patrolled the streets at night to watch the Tories. On the evening of April 18, 1775, Adams and Hancock were staying in the home of the Reverend Jonas Clark at Lexington. Paul Revere rode to Lexington to warn them of the regulars' approach. They escaped across fields to Woburn. The British troops arrived at dawn and the Battle of Lexington began.

On May 10, 1775, the Second Continental Congress convened. Perhaps the most important act of this Congress was the appointment of George Washington as commander in chief of the army. John Adams nominated him; Samuel Adams seconded his motion.

Adams signed John Dickinson's Olive Branch Petition to King George III on July 8, 1775. When the Continental Congress met on September 5, 1775, the war had begun, and Samuel Adams was fully in favor of declaring independence. Though the committees were debating and working day and night, the middle colonies had not yet accepted the idea. In November 1775, Congress formed the first American Navy.

On January 1, 1776, Lord Dunmore, the Royal Governor of Virginia, attacked and burned Norfolk. In April, the delegates from North Carolina were instructed to vote for independence. In May, the delegates from Virginia were instructed by their constituency to present a formal proposal to Congress to separate from Great Britain. On June 7, Richard Henry Lee offered to Congress Virginia's resolution for independence.

Lee and Samuel Adams became friends. Edward Rutledge of South Carolina suggested a delay of three weeks to allow hesitating delegates time to receive instructions from their home colonies to vote for independence. During those three weeks, Adams worked long hours in personal conferences to assure passage of Lee's resolution.

Samuel Adams voted in favor of independence on July 2, and signed the engrossed copy of the Declaration of Independence on August 2, 1776. He made a notable speech before the Second Continental Congress on the eve of that signing.

Adams remained in Congress until 1781, serving on many committees, notably the one which drafted the Articles of Confederation which he signed on November 15, 1777. He was a delegate to the convention called in 1788 to ratify the federal Constitution. He also assisted in drafting the Massachusetts Constitution in 1779-1780. He was a Senator and member of the Council in the new government; and was elected lieutenant governor, 1789–1793. He became governor of Massachusetts after John Hancock's death, and was subsequently elected governor, 1794–1797.

Additional Information

Though well educated and of a wealthy family, Adams never found a vocation in which he became successful. He did not wish to be a clergyman, businessman, or lawyer. He was a dreamer and generous to the detriment of his family. His business ventures all failed, his inheritance was gradually lost, he got in debt and nearly lost his Purchase Street home several times. Adams was a political genius. John Adams, his second cousin thirteen years his junior, called him "a universal good character, unless it should be admitted that he is too attentive to the public, and not enough to himself and his family."

Samuel Adams was of medium height, muscular build, gray eyes, and he had a pleasant and genial manner. He was a devout Puritan, but was a most revolutionary agitator.

William Bentley wrote in his diary the day after Samuel Adams died, "He was feared by his enemies, but too secret to be loved by his friends. He did not put confidence in them, while he was of importance to them." Samuel Adams died on Sunday, October 2, 1803, and was buried near the site of the Boston Massacre. A bronze metal plate mounted on a boulder marks his grave, close to the curb on Tremont Street in Boston. The inscription is simply, "This marks the grave of Samuel Adams." Nearby is a metal flagholder placed there by the Sons of the American Revolution.

In 1873, the State of Massachusetts honored him by placing his bronze statue in Statuary Hall, in the Capitol Building, Washington, D.C.

Genealogy

I. Samuel Adams, September 27, 1722–October 2, 1803, was born at Purchase Street, Boston, one of the twelve children of Samuel and Mary (Fifield) Adams. He married first, in 1749, Elizabeth Checkley, who died in 1757, leaving one son and one daughter. He married second, December 6, 1764, Elizabeth Wells.

His children were: Samuel, 1750; Samuel again, 1751; Joseph, 1753; Mary, 1754; Hannah, 1756.

CHECKLEY
Elizabeth Checkley, ca. 1725–1757,

was the first wife of Samuel Adams, signer of the Declaration of Independence. They were married in 1749. Elizabeth Checkley was the daughter of the Reverend Samuel Checkley, February 11, 1696–December 1, 1769, who graduated from Harvard College in 1715. He was ordained in 1719 and became the first minister at the new South Church in 1719. The Reverend Checkley married on January 5, 1721, Elizabeth Rolfe, born December 15, 1679, daughter of the Reverend Benjamin Rolfe of Haverhill, Massachusetts. The Reverend Benjamin Rolfe was born September 13, 1662, and graduated from Harvard College in 1684. He married Mehitable Atwater on March 12, 1693; was chaplain of forces at Falmouth in 1689, second minister of Haverhill, ordained 1694. He was killed by Indians August 29, 1708. The Reverend Rolfe was the son of Benjamin Rolfe of Newbury, a weaver, who married on November 3, 1659, Appia (maiden name unknown). He became a freeman in 1659. He was the son of John Rolfe and grandson of Henry Rolfe and his wife Honour Rolfe. Henry and Honour Rolfe were of Whiteparish, Wiltshire, England. Honour Rolfe died in 1656.

The Reverend Samuel Checkley was the son of Samuel Checkley, October 14, 1653–January 4, 1739, of Boston and Roxbury, who married Mary Scottow, 1653–1721, daughter of Joshua Scottow, born in England in 1615, who came to Boston in 1634 with his mother Thomasine, widow of Thomas Scottow. He was a captain and magistrate at Scarborough, Maine, in 1676, and died January 20, 1698. He was the son of William Checkley of Preston Capes Parish, Daventry, in the west of Northamptonshire, England.

FIFIELD
II. Samuel Adams, May 6, 1689–1748,

maltster, married in 1715, Mary Fifield, born ca. 1695 and still living in 1748. They had twelve children. Samuel Adams was a justice of the peace, deacon in Old South Church, a member of the Massachusetts Bay Assembly, and a wealthy landowner and civic leader. He was the son of Captain John Adams. Mary Fifield, May 8, 1694–post 1748, was the daughter of Richard Fifield, baptized November 6, 1665, who married about 1690 Mary Thurston, February 24, 1667–1701, daughter of Benjamin Thurston, b. July 8, 1640, and Elizabeth Walker, who were married December 12, 1669. Benjamin Thurston, baptized January 13, 1601, was the son of John Thurston of Salem in 1638. John Thurston came to America on the *Mary Ann* of Yarmouth in 1637, age thirty-six, and had a land grant in 1640. He was a freeman in 1643. His wife Margaret died May 9, 1662.

Richard Fifield was the son of Giles Fifield, 1624–post 1660, of Hampton, New Hampshire, and Boston. He married, June 17, 1652, Mary Perkins, baptized December 15, 1639, and died in November 1683, daughter of Abraham Perkins, 1603–1683. Abraham Perkins was of Hampton and married ca. 1639 at Ipswich, Mary Whethy, 1618–May 29, 1706. He was a freeman May 13, 1640. His will was dated August 22, 1683, and proved September 18, 1683. Abraham Perkins was the son of Isaac Perkins, baptized December 28, 1571, who married first, Alice, surname unknown, who was buried June 22, 1603. He married second, by mid–1605, Alice Kebbel, buried August 20, 1613. Isaac Perkins was the son of Thomas Perkins of Hillmorton, who was the son of Henry and Mary Perkins.

WEBB

III. Captain John Adams, twin with Bethia, and third son of Joseph Adams, Sr., was born December 3, 1661, and died January 20, 1712. He was a merchant, married first about 1683, Hannah Webb, September 5, 1665–1694, a daughter of Christopher Webb, Jr., 1630–May 30, 1694, who married January 18, 1656, Hannah Scott, 1634–1718, perhaps daughter of the first Benjamin Scott. Christopher Webb was representative for Braintree, Massachusetts, in 1689-90. He was the son of Christopher Webb, 1588–June 1671, a freeman at Braintree in 1645, whose wife was Humility. He was the son of Alexander Webb of England.

Captain John Adams married second, Hannah Checkley, daughter of Anthony and Hannah (Wheelwright) Checkley. Hannah was born December 19, 1674, and was the daughter of the Reverend John Wheelwright, born in Saleby, Lincolnshire, England, in 1594, son of Robert and Katherine (Mawer) Wheelwright.

Anthony Checkley married second wife, Lydia (Scottow) Gibbs, widow of Benjamin Gibbs and daughter of Joshua Scottow. He was attorney general in 1689, and died October 18, 1708. Anthony Checkley was the son of William Checkley of Preston Capes Parish, Northamptonshire, England. (See the genealogy of Elizabeth Checkley, wife of signer Samuel Adams, for more about the Checkley family.)

IV. Joseph Adams, Sr., 1626–1694. (To continue the Adams genealogy, see Chapter 1.)

Chapter 3

JOSIAH
BARTLETT

1729–1795

NEW HAMPSHIRE

Josiah Bartlett

JOSIAH BARTLETT, physician, patriot, chief justice, and governor of New Hampshire, was probably educated in the circuit schools and acquired his knowledge of Greek and Latin under the private tutoring of the Reverend Doctor John Webster, a relative. At the age of sixteen, he began the study of medicine at Amesbury in the office of Dr. James Ordway who had married Tirzah Titcomb Bartlett, widow of his Uncle Thomas Bartlett. In addition he used the libraries of neighboring towns to augment his medical knowledge, and at twenty-one began to practice medicine at Kingston, New Hampshire, residing with the Reverend Joseph Secombe. He quickly acquired a large practice as an all around country doctor.

Bartlett gained recognition because of his work with patients who had diphtheria which he successfully treated with Peruvian bark (quinine). Although he was suspended by the New England Medical Society for the use of this new treatment, he was soon reinstated. He relied greatly on observation and experimentation and introduced a number of medical reforms.

In 1757, Bartlett became town selectman. He became interested in public affairs and his fellow citizens, recognizing his intelligence and integrity, chose him to represent Kingston in the Provincial Assembly in 1765. During the progressive controversies between the colonies and Great Britain, he allied himself with the people and maintained his position vigorously. He raised the Seventh Militia Regiment, and in the Stamp Act controversy he was liaison between the Provincial Assembly and Royal Governor Benning Wentworth.

He was appointed in 1767, by Royal Governor John Wentworth, as a justice of the peace and soon thereafter as a colonel of the militia. He opposed the Townshend Acts.

Bartlett had been recognized as an active patriot in 1774 and was appointed to the Committee of Correspondence of the Provincial Assembly, then to the Assembly's revolutionary successor, the first Provincial Congress. He was chosen to be one of the two delegates from New Hampshire to the First Continental Congress but was unable to accept this position since his home had been burned in May of 1774, probably because of his patriotic activities.

In January 1774, Royal Governor Benning Wentworth had appointed him colonel in the militia. In May 1774, he became a member of the Committee of Safety. In December of that year, he became an "accessory after the fact" in the disposition of gunpowder captured at Fort William and Mary in Newcastle. In February 1775, Royal Governor Benning Wentworth dismissed him from both his appointed offices for open opposition to the Crown.

In 1775-1776, Bartlett was again chosen as a delegate to the Continental Congress. He was the first to vote in favor of adopting the Declaration of Independence, and signed the engrossed copy on August 2, 1776. He was reelected in 1777, but soon resigned and turned his attention to matters in New Hampshire. After organizing regiments for the impending attack from Montreal, he accompanied General Stark to Bennington to furnish New Hampshire troops with medical and other supplies. In 1779 he was a colonel in the militia.

Bartlett was once again in the Continental Congress in 1778-1779, and as the states were called, was honored to be the first to vote for the Proposed Articles of Confederation. He was reelected to the Continental Congress on March 14, 1778, took his seat on May 21, was reelected August 19, but withdrew October 31 to take care of private affairs.

In 1778, he attended the Constitutional Convention at Philadelphia, and returning to New Hampshire he exerted his influence at the state convention called to ratify the United States Constitution. He became chief justice in 1788, and succeeded Matthew Thornton as judge of the common pleas, 1779–1782. In 1782, he became associate justice of the Superior Court, and in 1788 was named chief justice. Under his influence and membership at the State Convention, on June 21, 1788, New Hampshire became the ninth state by ratifying the federal Constitution. He was elected to the United States Senate in 1789, but declined to serve.

In 1790, Bartlett was elected chief executive. His popularity is revealed by the election returns: he received 7,385 of the 9,854 votes cast. In June 1793, the newly amended Constitution changed the title of chief executive to governor. He therefore became the first governor of New Hampshire. At the close of his term in 1794, he withdrew from politics due to ill health.

In 1790, he received the honorary degree of doctor of medicine from Dartmouth College. In 1791, he secured a charter from the legislature to establish the New Hampshire Medical Society. The society was organized with a constitution and bylaws drafted in his own handwriting. He was elected its first president.

Additional Information

Bartlett's colleagues described him as tall, well built, with auburn hair. His manner was dignified, kind, and compassionate. His mode of living was unpretentious. He was reared a Calvinist, but he turned to the Universalist Church. Bartlett died May 19, 1795, at Kingston, New Hampshire, and was buried in the Universalist Church Cemetery.

A memorial ledger marks the graves of Josiah and Mary Bartlett. Near the foot of the sarcophagus on the right is a seven-inch in diameter medallion of the Sons of the American Revolution. On the left is a seven-inch in diameter medallion presented by the Daughters of the American Revolution, Sally Plimber Chapter.

A copy of Bartlett's original oil portrait, painted by Jonathon Trumbull, Jr., hangs in the State House at Concord, New Hampshire. A bronze statue of Bartlett was unveiled on July 4, 1888, in the public square at Amesbury, Massachusetts. His home, located on the Plains in Kingston, is an historic landmark.

Genealogy

I. Josiah Bartlett, November 21, 1729–May 19, 1795, was born at Amesbury, Massachusetts, the seventh son of Stephen and Hannah (Webster) Bartlett. He married, on January 15, 1754, Mary Bartlett, daughter of his uncle, Deacon Joseph and his second wife Sarah (Hoyt) Bartlett. They lived at Kingston, New Hampshire, and to them were born twelve children of whom three sons became doctors. Seven of their grandsons also became physicians.

His children were: Mary (Marey), 1754; Lois, 1756; Miriam, 1758; Rhoda, 1760; Ezra, 1760; Hannah, 1762; Levi, 1763; Josiah, 1765; an unnamed child, 1767; Sarah (Sally), 1773; Hannah again, 1776.

BARTLETT

Mary Bartlett, ca. 1734–1789, was the daughter of Deacon Joseph and Sarah (Hoyt) Bartlett, of Newington, New Hampshire.

Deacon Joseph Bartlett, November 18, 1686–1754, was the fifth son of Richard Bartlett, 1649–1724, of Newbury. He was a soldier taken prisoner at the assault on Haverhill August 29, 1708. His commander, Captain Wainwright, was killed by Indians, and Bartlett was held in captivity for four years.

Joseph Bartlett married first, December 5, 1717, a Miss Tewksbury by whom he had no children; married second on April 27, 1721, Sarah Hoyt, born May 6, 1686. Sarah Hoyt was the daughter of Deacon David Hoyt, April 22, 1651–1704, and his second wife, Sarah Wilson.

David Hoyt married first, Mary Wells, daughter of Thomas Wells; she died in 1676. He married second, Sarah Wilson, who died in 1689. He married third on February 29, 1704, Abigail (Cook) Pomeroy, daughter of Nathaniel Cook and widow of Joshua Pomeroy, removed to Deerfield and became a deacon. In Deerfield, he, his wife Abigail, and four children were captured by Indians and taken to Canada. His three-year-old daughter Abigail was killed on the journey, and he died of hunger near the Lower Cohos.

David Hoyt was the son of Nicholas and Susanna (Joyce) Hoyt of Windsor, Connecticut. Nicholas Hoyt was probably son of Simon and Deborah (Stowers) Hoyt who were first at Charlestown in 1629. He was a freeman May 18, 1631, and at Scituate, 1633–1636. Simon and Deborah removed to Windsor in 1639, and were at Fairfield in 1650. Simon Hoyt died at Stamford in 1659.

WEBSTER

II. Stephen Bartlett, April 21, 1691–April 20, 1773, was the seventh son of Richard of Newbury, 1648–1724. He married on December 18, 1712, at Salisbury, Essex County, Massachusetts, Hannah Webster, born October 5, 1692, daughter of John and Bridgett (Huggins) Webster of Hampton who were married March 9, 1681. John Huggins died in 1670 and Bridgett Huggins married second, Israel Clifford of Hampton. Her will was dated August 23, 1685. She died May 7, 1695.

John Webster, Jr., 1632–December 6, 1677, was a blacksmith; took the oath of fidelity in 1678; lived at Haverhill but returned to Newbury. He married June 13, 1653, Ann Batt, daughter of Nicholas Batt, a linen weaver. Nicholas Batt and his wife Lucy came to Newbury from Southampton, England, on the *James* arriving in Boston June 3, 1635. He died December 6, 1677, and Lucy died January 26, 1679.

John Webster, Jr., was the son of John Webster, Sr., ca. 1600–1645, who came from Suffolk, England, in 1634, having married in England ca. 1627, Mary Shatswell, 1607–April 28, 1694, sister of John Shatswell of Ipswich. She was the daughter of John (1574–) and Judith (1578–1648) Shatswell of England. Mary Webster married second, as his second wife, October 29, 1650, John Emery, Sr., September 29, 1598–November 3, 1683, of Newbury. John Webster, Sr., became a freeman March 4, 1635.

EMERY

III. Richard Bartlett, February 21, 1648/9–April 17, 1724, married first, November 18, 1673, at Newbury, Massachusetts, Hannah Emery, April 25, 1654–May 1, 1705, daughter of John and Mary (Webster) Emery, Jr., and granddaughter of John and Mary (Shatswell) Webster. Mary (Webster) Emery was born in 1630 in England. Richard Bartlett's will was probated in 1693. John Emery, Jr., was the son of John Emery, Sr., and his first wife Mary.

John Emery, Sr., came to America with his brother Anthony. He was born at Romney, Hants, England, September 29, 1598; sailed from Southampton on April 3, 1635, on the *James*, William Cooper master, arriving at Boston June 3, 1635. He settled at Newbury and became a freeman June 2, 1641, and on December 2, 1642, was one of the ninety-one freeholders of the town. His first wife died in 1649 and he married second, on October 29, 1649, Mary Shatswell Webster, widow of John Webster, Sr. He was brought up before the court of Ipswich on March 16, 1663, on charges of entertaining Quakers and travelers. On May 5, the case was referred to the next court. He was a selectman, fence viewer, and grand juryman in 1666; trial juror in 1672. John Emery, Sr., born 1598, died April 1672, was the son of John Emery who resided in Romney, Hants, England, with his wife Agnes. They probably died there.

WELLS

IV. Richard Bartlett, October 31, 1621–1698, married before 1645, Abigail Wells, ca. 1625–March 8, 1686/7. They lived first at Oldtown in Newbury, Massachusetts, where he died in 1698, age seventy-six. He had been four years a deputy to the General Court. His will was dated April 19, 1695, and was probated July 18, 1698.

V. Richard Bartlett, shoemaker, died at Newbury May 25, 1647. He married in England, Johan, surname unknown, and was at Newbury in 1637.

This Bartlett family traces its ancestry back to Adam de Barttelot, who was buried in 1100 A.D., at Stopham, England. He came to England with William the Conqueror, fought at the Battle of Hastings, and received land grants at Stopham, Sussex, England.

Chapter 4

CARTER
BRAXTON

1736–1797

VIRGINIA

Carter Braxton

CARTER BRAXTON, planter and statesman, completed his studies at the College of William and Mary in 1755. He continued his educationin England from 1758 until the autumn of 1760.

In 1761, he was sent to the House of Burgesses from King William County to which he had moved. There he served from 1761 to 1775 with the exception of a brief period in the 1770s. He was also high sheriff for a time in the early 1770s, just before the arrival of Lord Dunmore, the royal governor.

Braxton was present in the House of Burgesses in 1765, when Patrick Henry's resolutions were passed defining the rights of the colony and condemning the Stamp Act. He was also a member in 1769, when Lord Botetourt dissolved the assembly. He united with others in signing the Virginia Resolves and the Virginia Association, a nonimportation agreement. He was on three of the six standing committees appointed by the assembly at the next session.

Braxton was a member of the first Colonial Convention at Williamsburg on April 20, 1775, the day after the battles at Lexington and Concord. Royal Governor Lord Dunmore confiscated the gunpowder in the Williamsburg magazine and placed it on board a British warship. Several militia units prepared to retaliate but were calmed by Peyton Randolph and George Washington.

Patrick Henry refused to be pacified and led a group of Hanover County militia into Williamsburg, demanding return of the gunpowder or payment for it. Before any hostilities occurred, Braxton, speaking for Patrick Henry, met with his father-in-law Richard Corbin, receiver general of the colony, and convinced him to pay for the gunpowder, thus averting an open conflict. He attended the last Virginia House of Burgesses convention under royal authority.

In 1775, Braxton was in the convention at Richmond, Virginia, and served on the Committee of Safety. At the sudden death of Peyton Randolph in October 1775, he was selected to fill the vacancy at the Continental Congress. He took his seat on February 23, 1776. On April 14, 1776, he expressed his belief that "Independence is in truth a delusive bait which men inconsiderably catch at, without knowing the hook to which it is affixed." During the debates preceding the vote for independence on July 2, Braxton was opposed to separation from England. However, he voted in favor of independence and signed the engrossed copy of the Declaration of Independence on August 2, 1776. He was not reappointed to the Continental Congress, probably due to his having advocated a conservative form of government for Virginia and expressing little faith in democracy. He supported Thomas Jefferson's Bill for Establishing Religious Freedom.

During the first General Assembly of the State of Virginia, Braxton and Thomas Jefferson received a vote of thanks from the Assembly "for the diligence, ability, and integrity with which they executed the important trust reposed in them as two of the delegates of the County [King William] in the General Congress."

Braxton was active and influential in the Virginia Legislature from 1777 to 1785. From January 1786 until 1791, he was a member of the Council of State. In May 1794, he was again elected to this office and served until October 6, 1797, four days before his death.

The Revolutionary War brought

financial hardships to Braxton. At its beginning he had invested heavily in shipping. The British captured most of his vessels and ravaged some of his plantations and extensive land holdings. Commercial setbacks in later years ruined him.

Additional Information

Dr. Benjamin Rush recorded that Carter Braxton was agreeable, a sensible speaker, and an accomplished gentleman, but was strongly prejudiced against New Englanders.

Braxton's homes were Elsing Green and Chericoke. His brother, George, built Chericoke for him during his absence in 1758–1759. Braxton died of paralysis at Elsing Green on October 10, 1797, and was buried in a family plot near Chericoke.

A large granite monument in the Hollywood Cemetery at Richmond, Virginia, honors many of his descendants and ancestors including George Braxton, the emigrant.

Genealogy

I. Carter Braxton was born September 10, 1736, at Newington Plantation, Livingston, Virginia. His mother died when he was seven days old. He married first, July 16, 1755, Judith Robinson of Hewick, Middlesex County, Virginia. Judith died in December 1757 at the birth of their second daughter.

His children were: (by first wife) Mary, 1756; Judith, 1757; (by second wife) Elizabeth, 1761; George, 1762; Corbin, 1764; Carter, 1765; Ann, 1767; Richard, 1769; Alicia Corbin, 1770; Richard again,

1772; Richard again, 1773; Robert Carter, 1775; unnamed child, 1777; Lucy Fitzhugh, 1778, Lucy Carter, 1780; John Tayloe, 1781; William Fitzhugh, 1783; Carter again, 1787; Eliza Griffin, 1787.

ROBINSON
Judith Robinson, d. December 1757, was the daughter of Christopher and Judith (Beverley)(Griffin)(Beverley) Robinson of Hewick, Middlesex County, Virginia. Judith Robinson's mother was Mary Berkeley, daughter of Colonel Edmund Berkeley of Barn Elms, Middlesex County, Virginia.

CORBIN
Braxton married Elizabeth Corbin in May 1761, daughter of Colonel Richard and Elizabeth (Tayloe) Corbin of Lanesville, Virginia. By Elizabeth Corbin, Braxton had sixteen children, six of whom died young.

Colonel Richard Corbin, 1708–1787, of Lanesville, King and Queen County, Virginia, eldest son of Colonel Gawin and Jane (Lane-Wilson) Corbin of Pecaton and Lanesville, married in July 1737 his cousin Elizabeth Tayloe, born May 28, 1721, daughter of the Honorable John and Elizabeth (Gwynn Lyde) Tayloe of The Old House at Richmond. Colonel Richard Corbin was educated in England; he was a strong supporter of the Episcopal Church; burgess from Middlesex 1749; president of the King's Council in 1750; and receiver general of the colony 1754–1776. Colonel Richard Corbin was the son of Colonel Gawin Corbin of Pecaton, Westmoreland County and Lanesville, King and Queen County, Virginia, who was born in 1650 and died 1744. Colonel Gawin Corbin was educated in England and was a firm supporter of the Established Church; naval officer of the Rappahannock; a burgess; and an influential member of the King's Council and later its president. He made a will dated November 1, 1739, probated February 12, 1744, leaving large estates in Virginia: Pecatone in Westmoreland; Buckingham House in Middlesex; Lanesville in King and Queen; and many acres in other counties. He married first, Catherine (Wormley) daughter of the Honorable Ralph and Catherine (Lunsford-Jennings) Wormley. He married second, Jane (Lane) Wilson, widow of the Honorable Willis Wilson, and daughter and heiress of the Honorable John Lane of Lanesville, King and Queen County, Virginia. He married third, Martha Bassett, daughter of the Honorable William and Joanna (Burwell) Bassett of Eltham, New Kent County, Virginia.

Gawin Corbin was the son of the Honorable Henry Corbin of Buckingham House, Middlesex County, born 1629 at Hall End, Warwick County, England. He died January 2, 1676, at Buckingham House, in Middlesex County, Virginia. He came to the Virginia Colony in 1650. He first resided in the parish of Stratton Manor, King and Queen County, which was named after the Corbins' home in Stratton, Cornwall County, England. He was registrar from 1663 to 1667, and was one of the vestrymen appointed to write to England for a minister for the parish. He was an influential member of the King's Council; burgess from Lancaster County in 1657, 1659, and 1660. He married, in England, July 25, 1645, Alice Eltonhead of Eltonhead, in Lancaster County, England.

The Honorable Henry Corbin was the son of Thomas Corbin of Hall End, Warwick County, England, who was born May 24, 1594, at Hall End and died in June 1637 at Hall End. He married, in

1620, Winifred Grosvenor of Sutton Colfield, Warwick County, England. The Grosvenors were descended from Sir Gilbert Grosvenor, who came into England with William the Conqueror. Thomas Corbin was a descendant in the seventeenth generation from Robert Corbion/Corbin whose son Robert gave lands to the Abbey of Talesworth, in the reign of Henry II of England, 1154–1161.

CARTER

II. George Braxton, Jr., of Newington Plantation, Livingston, Virginia, died before 1755. On January 16, 1732/3, he married Mary Carter, daughter of Robert "King" Carter and his third wife, Elizabeth (Landon) Willis, widow of the Honorable Wilson Willis and daughter of Thomas Landon of Grednal, Hereford County, England. George Braxton received large land grants from King George II. He was a member of the House of Burgesses in 1718, 1723, 1726, and 1734. He held lands in common with William Brooke, his son George Braxton, Humphrey Brooke, Sr. (his son-in-law), and Ambrose Madison (grandfather of U. S. president James Madison). By his wife Mary Carter he had four children: Mary, who married first, the Honorable Robert Carter Burwell of Isle of Wight County, Virginia, and second Colonel Nathaniel Burwell; Elizabeth, who married Humphrey Brooke, Sr.; Colonel George Braxton, who married Mary Blair, daughter of the Honorable John Blair, president of the College of William and Mary; and Carter Braxton.

Robert Carter of Corotoman, Lancaster County, Virginia, was born 1663 and died August 4, 1732. He was called "King" Carter because of his wealth and prominence. He served as a burgess, 1695–1699; as Speaker of the House;

Treasurer of the Colony, 1694–1732, and was an influential member on the King's Council, 1699–1732, and as its president; and as acting governor, 1726–1727. His estate consisted of 300,000 acres of land, 1,000 slaves, and £10,100. Robert Carter was an active member of the Established Church and served as vestryman of Christ Church, Lancaster County, Virginia, which he built. He is buried just outside that church. He married first, Judith Armistead who died in 1699, daughter of Colonel John and Judith (Bowles) Armistead of Hesse, Gloucester County, Virginia. Colonel John Armistead was son of William Armistead, the emigrant. He served as high sheriff in 1765; a burgess in 1685; of King's Council 1688; justice and lieutenant colonel of horse 1680. He married Judith (her uncertain surname may have been Bowles, Beverley, or Hane). Their daughter Judith died in 1699, having married Col. Robert Carter of Corotoman, son of Colonel John and Sarah (Ludlow) Carter. William Armistead came to the colony about 1635. He was the son of Anthony and Frances (Thompson) Armistead of Kirk Deighton, York County, England, baptized in All Saints' Church August 3, 1610. He died before 1660.

William Armistead received a patent for 450 acres of land in Elizabeth City County in 1636, also a patent for lands in Gloucester County, Virginia. He married, in England, Anne whose surname is unknown. The family came originally from Hesse-Darmstadt or their forefathers came with the Norsemen and settled in England.

Colonel John Carter of England and Virginia was the son of the Honorable William Carter of Casstown, Hereford County, England, born in 1620, died 1699 at Corotoman, Lancaster County,

Virginia. He came to Virginia Colony in 1649, settled in lower Norfolk, which he represented as burgess in 1649, then moved to Lancaster County and built the ancestral home of Corotoman. He served as a burgess from Lancaster County 1653–1658: was an influential member of the King's Council 1658-59; commander against the Rappahannock Indians, 1654; Colonel of Lancaster 1656; and a liberal supporter of the Established Church. He gave the first church which stood on the land where Christ Church was later built and was a vestryman. He made his will in 1669. He married first, Jane Glyn, daughter of Morgan Glyn of England; second, Eleanor (Eltonhead) Brocas, widow of the Honorable William Brocas and daughter of Richard and Ann (Sutton) Eltonhead of England; third, Anne Carter, daughter of Cleave Carter of England; fourth, Sarah Ludlow, daughter of Gabriel Ludlow of Dinton; and fifth, Elizabeth Sherley of Gloucester County, Virginia. Col. John Carter was great-grandfather, not only to Carter Braxton but to signer Benjamin Harrison, and was great-great-grandfather of signer Thomas Nelson.

PAULIN

III. George Braxton, Sr., the emigrant, of England and Virginia, came to the colony about 1690 from London. He was of an ancient family seated in Lancaster County, England, in the neighborhood of Chester. Braxton's home on the Mattapony River was Mantua. He married Elizabeth Paulin, daughter of Thomas and Elizabeth Paulin. Braxton's will, dated June 30, 1725, left a tract of 578 acres on the Mattapony River, in King William County, to his daughter Elizabeth Brooke and her heirs. Elizabeth was the wife of Humphrey Brooke, Sr.

Thomas Paulin was a justice of Old

Rappahannock in 1688. On February 25, 1699, he was one of the county officers in King and Queen County. He was listed in the Quit Rents of Norfolk County in 1704. Thomas Paulin is buried at Mattapony Church in King and Queen County, Virginia.

William Cox was granted 150 acres in Henrico County due to transporting three persons: Thomas Braxton, Richard Bird, and Richard Hewes. Whether Thomas Braxton was father, brother, or no relation to George Braxton III above was not determined. However, Thomas Braxton is also buried at Mattapony Church in King and Queen County, Virginia.

Chapter 5

CHARLES CARROLL

1737–1832

MARYLAND

CHARLES CARROLL, landowner, lawyer, patriot, began his education at Jesuits' College of Bohemian Manor, in Maryland. Biographers disagree on the date, probably 1748, when his Roman Catholic father took him to French Flanders where he entered the College of St. Omer to study the classics under the Jesuits. In 1753, he began studies at another Jesuit seminary at Rheims, and after a year there, entered the College of Louis de Grand, where he was graduated at seventeen. His father went to France to see him, probably about 1756. He studied law at Bourges for one year and moved to Paris. In 1757, Carroll moved to London to continue his study of law at the Inner Temple, Cambridge, where he remained until 1765.

Carroll returned to Maryland, a well-educated, polished gentleman, at the age of twenty-eight. His father gave him a tract of 10,000 acres located at the mouth of the Monocacy River in Frederick County, and he set about developing his estate which became known as Carrollton Manor. At this time a Roman Catholic could not practice law.

He had returned to Maryland at the height of the Stamp Act controversies, and immediately aligned himself with the colonists and urged resistance to British oppression. He knew that the repeal of the Stamp Act was not the end of their problems with the mother country. The main disagreement at the time was the right of the government of the colony to tax the people for the purpose of paying their officers and the support of the clergy.

Well known Tory lawyer Charles Dulaney favored the right of the government to tax the colonies. Carroll wrote a series of articles for the *Maryland Gazette* under the name of The First Citizen and identified himself as a "finished scholar and polished gentleman." Dulaney exhibited great ability during their war of words but the colonists adhered to Charles Carroll's beliefs.

After the repeal of the Stamp Act in 1766, Great Britain had levied a tax on tea and other important products. In Massachusetts, the Boston Tea Party took place on December 16, 1773. When a second cargo of tea arrived in Chesapeake Bay, Marylanders followed the Massachusetts example and did not allow the ship to land its cargo. Carroll's opinion was solicited on how to handle the matter, and he answered, "Gentlemen, set fire to the vessel and burn her, with her cargo, to the water's edge." With sails set, and colors flying, the ship floated, a sheet of fire, down the bay amid shouts of people who had gathered along the shore to observe it.

The law barring Roman Catholics from political activities lapsed in 1773. Carroll became a member of the Committee of Correspondence and the Committee of Safety. He was a delegate from Anne Arundel County to the revolutionary convention which met December 7, 1775, at Annapolis. In 1776, he was appointed a member of the convention which framed the constitution of Maryland as an independent state, and after its adoption he was chosen a member of the state senate.

On February 15, 1776, the Continental Congress appointed Carroll, Samuel Chase, Benjamin Franklin, and the Right Reverend John Carroll to visit Canada "to promote or form a union" between Canada and the colonies. Carroll was not then a member of the Congress, but was chosen because he was a Catholic and spoke French. During their return in May, they visited General Philip Schuyler who advised them that more men, supplies, and money were needed for organizing his Canadian Campaign. The Committee agreed to submit his requests in their report to the Congress. They submitted their report to the Continental Congress on June 12, 1776. Carroll wrote a journal of their failed mission.

In June 1776, he was appointed a member of the convention with Samuel Chase and William Paca which framed the constitution of Maryland as an independent state. After its adoption he was chosen as a member of the Maryland State Senate.

On July 19, 1776, he was chosen as a delegate from Maryland to the Continental Congress and was reelected in 1777. Carroll was not in Congress in time to vote for independence, but he signed the engrossed copy of the Declaration of Independence on August 2, 1776.

He was a member of the Board of War, and served on the committee which was sent to Valley Forge to investigate complaints against General Washington. Members of the Conway Cabal, who were engaged in covert activity trying to displace Washington in an attempt to make General Gates commander in chief, also served on the Board of War. Charles Carroll was solicited by these plotters. However, Carroll was a strong supporter of Washington.

He was elected to the Constitutional Convention in 1787, but declined the election. However, when the Constitution came before the Maryland senate for adoption, he allied himself with those in favor of adoption, and remained a Federalist throughout his lifetime.

Carroll resigned from the Continental Congress in 1778. At that time he was opposed to the confiscation of loyalists' property.

In 1788, he was elected the first United States senator from Maryland after its adoption of the federal constitution and cast his affirmative vote to ratify the federal Constitution. His term expired in 1793, but he returned to serve in the Maryland Senate until 1801; thereafter he held no other political office.

Carroll was a member of the Potomac Company, which had plans for a waterway to Ohio. He was also a member of the Chesapeake and Ohio Canal Company which was organized in 1823, and was a member of the first board of directors of the Baltimore and Ohio Railroad. He laid its cornerstone on July 4, 1828.

In 1901, the State of Maryland honored Charles Carroll by placing his statue in Statuary Hall, in the Capitol Building, Washington, D.C.

Additional Information

Charles Carroll was probably the wealthiest man in America, and he was much more fortunate than most of the signers because the British did not destroy his home and property. His home, Doughoregan Manor, is an impressive mansion, 300 feet long. It was built in 1727 by his father. His tomb is in the chapel located in the right wing of the mansion. Carroll was a man of small stature and had been frail as a child, but lived to the age of ninety-five.

Genealogy

I. Charles Carroll of Carrollton, September 19, 1737–November 14, 1832, was the son of Charles and Elizabeth (Brooke) Carroll. He married his first cousin, Mary Darnall, on June 5, 1768, and they had one son and one daughter. He married second, Margaret Tilghman, 1742–March 14, 1817, daughter of the Honorable Matthew Tilghman.

His children were: (by first wife) Charles, 1775–1861; Mary; Catherine; (by second wife) none.

DARNALL

Charles Carroll married Mary Darnall, b. March 19, 1749, who was the daughter of Henry and Rachel (Brooke) Darnall, Jr., of Portland Manor.

TILGHMAN

Margaret Tilghman, 1742–March 14, 1817, second wife of Charles Carroll, was the daughter of the Honorable Matthew Tilghman, 1717/8–1790, and Anna Lloyd, ca. 1723–1794, his first cousin. Matthew Tilghman was the son of Richard Tilghman, 1672–1738/9, and grandson of Philemon Lloyd, 1646–1685.

BROOKE

II. Charles Carroll, 1702–1782, married on March 22, 1728, Elizabeth Brooke, 1702–March 12, 1761, daughter of Clement Brooke, 1676–1737, and Jane Sewall. Clement Brooke was the son of Mayor Thomas Brooke of Battlecreek, Calvert County, Maryland, and his wife Eleanor (Hatton) Brooke. Eleanor was a daughter of Richard and Margaret Hatton, secretary of the province. Jane Sewall was the daughter of Major Nicholas and Susanna (Burgess) Sewall. Nicholas Sewall was Mayor of Mattapony, St. Mary's County, Maryland. He was born in England in 1655 and died in 1737. His will was probated May 9, 1737. Susanna Burgess was the daughter of Colonel

William and Sophia (Ewell) Burgess. Nicholas Sewall was the son of Henry Sewall, who came to America in 1660 and settled at Mattapony. He was commissioned by Lord Baltimore in 1661 as principal secretary of Maryland; he died in 1665. He was the son of Richard Sewall who married Mary Dugdale, only daughter of Sir William, garter king and historian of Warwickshire. Richard Sewall was the son of Henry Sewall, who was born about 1544 and died before April 8, 1628, and was alderman and mayor of Coventry in 1589 and in 1606. He married in 1575, Margaret Grazebrook, daughter of Avery and Margaret Keene Grazebrook of Middleton, County Warwick. Henry Sewall, born about 1544, was son of William Sewall of Coventry, born about 1520, who married about 1540, Matilda Horne, daughter of Reginald Horne of Pikesley.

Thomas Brooke, Sr., married Eleanor Hatton. He was the son of Governor Robert Brooke who married first, Mary, daughter of Thomas Baker, of Battel, Sussex, and his wife, Mary Engham, daughter of Thomas Engham, and granddaughter of Robert de Honeywood.

DARNALL

III. Charles Carroll (O'Carroll), 1660–July 20, 1720, the emigrant, was born at Litterlouna, Kings County, Ireland, the son of Daniel Carroll. He studied law and settled in London, where he was secretary to Lord Powis, minister of King James II. He received a commission as agent for Lord Baltimore in Maryland, and arrived in Maryland on October l, 1688. He acquired large tracts of land in good locations both by grant and by purchase from Indians. He went to England in 1715, and while there, Lord Baltimore died and he acted as attorney of the Baltimore estates both in England and Maryland. On his return to Maryland, he set up in the practice of law. He married first, Martha, daughter of Anthony Underwood, who died the following year. He married second, in 1693, Mary Darnall, daughter of Henry Darnall, Sr., and his wife Eleanor Hatton. They had ten children.

Chapter 6

SAMUEL
CHASE

1741–1811

MARYLAND

SAMUEL CHASE, lawyer, patriot, justice of the U.S. Supreme Court, was educated in the classics by his father, until he was eighteen. In 1759, he began the study of law in the offices of Hammond and Hall at Annapolis. He was admitted to practice in the Mayor's Court in 1761, in Chancery, and certain of the county courts in 1763.

In 1761, Chase was chosen a member of the Provincial Assembly. He was, from the start, distinguished for his opposition to the royal governor and the court party. On one occasion, he voted for a measure which reduced his father's income as a clergyman by one-half.

He took part in the riots that were staged by The Sons of Liberty when, in 1765, the Stamp Act was enacted. The mayor and aldermen of Annapolis called him "a busy, restless incendiary, a ringleader of mobs, a foul-mouthed and inflaming son of discord." He characterized his critics as "despicable tools of power, emerged from obscurity and basking in proprietary sunshine."

From 1764 to 1784, Chase was a member of the Maryland General Assembly. In 1774, he was a member of the Maryland Committee of Correspondence, and became a delegate to the first Continental Congress. The next year he was a member of the Maryland Convention and attended both congresses at Philadelphia. He supported the nonimportation agreement against Great Britain, feeling the measure would force Great Britain into bankruptcy or submission.

On February 15, 1776, he, with Benjamin Franklin, Charles Carroll, and the Right Reverend John Carroll were appointed a commission to go to Canada to win the Canadian government over to the American cause. They reached Montreal on April 29, and were well received by Commander in Chief Arnold, and the town gave them food and entertainment. The members of the commission soon realized they had neither the military strength nor financial resources to persuade the Canadians. The mission failed and they left on May 11, to inform Congress. They arrived in New York on the evening of May 26, and were in Philadelphia by the end of the month.

Chase proceeded at once to Maryland and resumed his work to bring about the rescinding of Maryland's previous instructions, so that their delegates might vote in favor of independence. Finally Maryland advised them to vote for independence and Chase rode the 150 miles in two days to be in Philadelphia for the vote.

On the morning of July 1, the unanimous vote of Maryland's delegation was read before Congress. Chase signed the engrossed copy of the Declaration of Independence on August 2, 1776.

He was thereafter reappointed until the end of 1778. In 1777, he served on twenty-one congressional committees, and in 1778, on thirty. One of these, possibly the most important, was with Richard Henry Lee of Virginia and Gouverneur Morris (half-brother of Lewis Morris) of New York, to write a circular to discredit the British peace proposals of 1778. Chase was said to have written the document.

At the close of 1778, he resumed the practice of law at Annapolis, Maryland. Governor William Paca sent him to England in 1783, to recover from two fugitive loyalists Maryland's holdings ($650,000) in stock of the Bank of England. He remained in England a year, but the matter was tied up in Chancery

Proceedings. The matter was concluded several years later by William Pinckney, Chase's one-time protégé.

In 1785 he attended the trade convention that met at Mount Vernon to draft the compact of that year between Maryland and Virginia regarding navigation on the Potomac River. He moved to Baltimore in 1786, and in 1788 became chief justice of the Criminal Court, followed in 1791 by the post of chief judge of the General Court of Maryland. Chase was one of eleven Marylanders who cast negative votes at the ratifying convention, in opposition to adoption of the U. S. Constitution. He was a member of a committee at the convention which proposed amendments to it.

In January 1796, President Washington nominated Chase to the U. S. Supreme Court. His intellectual abilities and performance on the bench were notable. However, his judgeship was marred by an impeachment and trial. The immediate cause of the impeachment was an intemperate charge to a Baltimore grand jury on May 2, 1803. On May 13, 1803, President Thomas Jefferson wrote Nicholson, a Maryland member of the House, suggesting impeachment. On March 12, 1804, the House complied under the leadership of John Randolph, by a vote of seventy-three to thirty-two. Eight articles were presented against him, but only two dealt with the grand jury's charge. The other six concerned Chase's "hanging judge" conduct in 1800 during two trials, one for treason, the other for sedition. Although Thomas Jefferson exerted a great deal of secret pressure, on March 5, 1805, Samuel Chase was acquitted and remained on the bench until his death. Among his counsel were Luther Martin and Joseph Hopkinson, son of signer Francis Hopkinson.

Chase was a Federalist, but was democratic in his sentiments. An ardent lover of liberty, he has been described as "the torch that lighted up the revolutionary flame in Maryland."

Samuel Chase died in Washington, D.C., and is buried at Old St. Paul's Cemetery in Baltimore, Maryland.

At the entrance to Old St. Paul's Cemetery is a plaque honoring several famous Maryland citizens, including Samuel Chase. The plaque was erected in September 1914 by the National Star Spangled Banner Centennial Committee.

Genealogy

I. Samuel Chase, April 17, 1741–June 19, 1811, was born in Somerset County, Maryland. He married first, on May 2, 1762, Ann Baldwin, with whom he had two sons and two daughters. He married second, in 1781, Hannah (Kitty) Giles, 1759–1848, of Kentbury, England, who survived him. Chase was guardian of his half-brothers and half-sisters after the death of his father.

His children were: (by first wife) Matilda, 1763; Thomas, 1764; Nancy, 1768; Frances, 1770; Ann, 1771; Samuel, 1773; Thomas, again, 1774; (by second wife) Elizabeth, after 1784; Mary, after 1784.

BALDWIN
Ann Baldwin, d. 1776, was the daughter of Thomas Baldwin, gentleman, of Anne Arundel County and his wife Agnes. Baldwin died in 1762, soon after his imprisonment for debt.

WALKER
II. The Reverend Thomas Chase, ca. 1703–1779, married Matilda Walker, who died before 1744. She was the daughter of

Thomas Walker, who died in 1744. He was a farmer and innkeeper of Somerset County Maryland. His wife was Sarah Maddox, b. 1681/2, the daughter of Lazarus Maddox, ca. 1656–1716/7. Lazarus Maddox was born in Northampton County, Virginia, and was brought by his stepfather and family to Maryland. His father was Alexander Maddox, d. 1659/60. His mother, Eleanor, d. 1694, married second, John Bozman, and third, James Caine. Lazarus Maddox married, before February 1679/80, Sarah and resided at Manokin Hundred, Somerset County, Maryland.

Alexander Maddox, d. c1659/60, emigrated from London, England, to Virginia by 1645.

The Reverend Thomas Chase married second, Ann Birch, who died in 1772. Ann was the daughter of Thomas Birch, a surgeon and male midwife of England. The Reverend Chase was born in England, and attended St. John's and Sidney Sussex colleges, Cambridge University. He immigrated to the West Indies to practice medicine, but returned to England where he was ordained an Anglican priest in February 1738/9. He was licensed to preach February 12, 1738/9, and immigrated to Maryland to become Rector of Somerset Parish, Somerset County, May 1739–February 1744/5; then rector of St. Paul's Parish, Baltimore County, 1745–1779.

TOWNLEY

III. The Reverend Richard Chase, died 1742, who married Margaret Frances Townley. Margaret was the daughter of Jeremiah Townley, a merchant, of London. The Reverend Chase emigrated from St. Andrews, London, to America in 1734. He was chaplain to Charles Calvert (the fifth Lord Baltimore); rector of the Parishes of Westminster and All Hollows in Anne Arundel County; and Christ Church in Calvert County, Maryland.

IV. Samuel Chase, of Westminster and Maidenhead, England. He was a freeman of London, England; a member of the Honorable Company of Tylers and Brickmakers, and owned considerable property in Westminster and Maidenhead.

Chapter 7

ABRAHAM CLARK

1726–1794

NEW JERSEY

ABRAHAM CLARK, surveyor, lawyer, farmer, patriot, "received a meager education in the English branches." He was studious and had a natural ability for mathematics. He became a surveyor and real estate agent, then informally mastered law as a way of arbitrating and settling land disputes. Clark gave free legal advice, although he was probably never admitted to the bar. He became known as "the poor man's counselor." Under the royal government, he was high sheriff of Essex County, New Jersey, and also served as clerk of the Colonial Assembly.

In December 1774, he allied himself with the patriots and became a member of the New Jersey Committee of Safety and was subsequently its secretary. He sat in New Jersey's first Provincial Congress in May 1775, which drafted the first state constitution.

Clark had been outspoken in favor of separation from Great Britain. He was on the Committee of Safety and on June 22, 1776, he was appointed a delegate to the Second Constitutional Congress where he sat until 1778. On July 1, 1776, he predicted that the independence movement had progressed so far "that we must now be a free and independent state, or a conquered country." The following day he voted in favor of independence, and signed the engrossed copy of the Declaration of Independence on August 2, 1776. He was again in the Continental Congress from 1780 to the end of the war.

He raised supplies for Washington's army and was nearly always present in Congress to vote on important issues. In December 1777, he was pleased when General Washington selected Valley Forge for his winter quarters, so there could be some protection of shipping on the Delaware River and other interests in Pennsylvania and New Jersey.

In 1784, the New Jersey legislature passed "An Act for Regulating and Shortening the Proceedings of the Courts of Law." This was popularly known as Clark's Law, and he had been quoted as saying, "If it succeeds, it will tear off the ruffles from the lawyers' wrists."

Clark was a member of the New Jersey legislature from 1783 to 1787; attended the Annapolis Convention of 1786; and was elected to the 1787 Convention in Philadelphia for framing the Constitution but illness prevented his attending. He was elected to the second and third United States Congresses, 1791–1794, as a member of the House of Representatives. He served as commissioner to settle New Jersey's accounts with the federal government.

Early in 1794, Clark introduced a resolution to suspend all relations with England until all articles of the Treaty of Paris were carried out. It was passed in the House, but was narrowly defeated by the Senate.

On July 4, 1848, the citizens of Rahway, New Jersey, provided a 10 foot monument in the Rahway Cemetery to honor Clark.

Genealogy

I. Abraham Clark, February 15, 1726–September 15, 1794, was born at Roselle, New Jersey, the only child of Thomas and Hannah (Winans) Clark. He married Sarah Hatfield, in 1748; they had ten children. Two of Mr. Clark's sons entered the army and were captured and confined on the *Jersey* prison ship. They were subjected to cruel treatment. As a result, Mr. Clark suffered permanent mental distress.

On September 15, 1794, he suffered a sunstroke while observing the building of a bridge on his farm and died two hours later. He was buried in the cemetery of the Presbyterian Church at Rahway, where he had been a long time member.

His children were: Aaron, 1750; Thomas, ca. 1753; Abraham, ca. 1755; Hannah, ca. 1757; Andrew, 1759; Sarah, 1761; Cavalier, ca. 1763; Elizabeth, ca. 1765; Abraham, 1767; Abigail, 1773; Mary, ?1772.

HATFIELD

Sarah Hatfield, 1728–June 2, 1804, was the eldest daughter of Isaac Hatfield, 1667–1709/10, and Sarah Price who died November 22, 1783. Sarah Price was the daughter of Benjamin and Mary Price. Isaac and Sarah Hatfield were married before 1698. Isaac was the son of Matthias Hatfield, weaver, who may have come, under the patronage of Cornelius Melyn, to Staten Island, New York. He married Maria, daughter of Cornelius Melyn, at New Haven, probably on August 25, 1664. Matthias Hatfield was a juryman at Elizabethtown, New Jersey, on May 10, 1668. He died before April 22, 1693.

WINANS

II. Thomas Clark, born 1701, married Hannah Winans, probably about 1724, daughter of Samuel Winans, Sr., 1670–1747, and his wife Zerviah, 1684–1737.

Samuel Winans was the son of John Winans, ca. 1640–December 1694, who married at New Haven, August 8, 1664, Susanna Melyn, June 14, 1645–ca. 1688. Susanna was the daughter of Cornelius Melyn, 1600–1662, and his wife Jannetje Adriaens, 1604–1681, whom he married in 1627, at Amsterdam. John Winans came from Holland, and was one of the eighty Associates who founded Elizabethtown, New Jersey, in 1664-65.

Cornelius Melyn came from Holland to New Netherlands in 1638, returned to Holland for his wife and children, and came back in 1641 with an order granting him most of Staten Island. He was president of the Council of Eight, moved to New Amsterdam, but returned to Staten Island in 1649. After an Indian massacre in 1655, he settled at New Haven, Connecticut, and took the oath of fidelity at New Haven with twenty-nine others, on February 7, 1657.

DUEHURST

III. Thomas Clark was born at Elizabethtown, New Jersey in 1670. He married, in 1692, Margaret Duehurst, whose dates and parents are unknown (possibly she was a daughter or granddaughter of Henry Dewhurst, age thirty-five, who arrived on the *Defense* in 1635). He was the son of Richard Clark and his wife Elizabeth, whose surname is not known.

IV. Richard Clark, 1613–1697, emigrated from England to Barbados, 1634–1651, and to Southampton, Long Island, New York, about 1650/1 and was at Southold, Long Island, in 1667. He was in the Indian War in 1657. A shipbuilder and planter, he was living at Southold in 1675 with his wife, Elizabeth, one daughter, and five sons. Soon after this, they moved to Elizabethtown, New Jersey, where Thomas Clark and his brother, Benjamin, were born. Richard Clark's will was dated May 1, 1697. Elizabeth Clark was born about 1660/1 and died in 1724.

Chapter 8

GEORGE CLYMER

1739–1813

PENNSYLVANIA

GEORGE CLYMER, merchant, patriot, orphaned at the age of seven, was the ward of his wealthy uncle, William Coleman. He received a thorough English education and had the use of his uncle's large library. He then attended the College of Philadelphia in 1757-58. In 1759, he became a clerk in the accounting room of his uncle's mercantile business. His diligence and competence soon earned him a partnership in the firm. When Coleman died, he left the mercantile business and most of his large estate to Clymer. He married the daughter of Reese Meredith, another Philadelphia merchant, and joined his father- and brother-in law in a partnership, establishing the firm of Merediths and Clymer. His father-in-law died in 1778; he continued the business with his brother-in-law until 1782.

Clymer embraced the patriot causes early. He attended meetings, and became a captain of volunteers in General Cadwalader's brigade. He was chairman of a committee of the Philadelphia Tea Party of October 16, 1773, which forced the resignation of British-appointed East India Company merchants.

Early in 1775, he and Michael Hillegas were appointed the first joint treasurers of the United Colonies. They served until August 6, 1776. Clymer became a member of the Council of Safety of Philadelphia on June 30, 1775. He supported colonial loans and exchanged his "hard coin" for continental currency.

On July 20, 1776, when three of the Pennsylvania delegates to the Continental Congress declined to vote for the Declaration of Independence and withdrew from their seats, Clymer was appointed to succeed one of them. He happily affixed his signature to the engrossed copy of the Declaration of Independence on August 2, 1776.

In September 1776, he and Richard Stockton of New Jersey were sent to inspect the northern army at Ticonderoga. As a result of their report on the demands and conditions of the Army, Congress was moved to give broader powers to General George Washington.

When in December 1776, the British drove the United Colonies' government to Baltimore, he was left in Philadelphia in company with Robert Morris and George Walton, as a committee for congressional business and to protect Philadelphia.

He was reelected to the Continental Congress on March 12, 1777, and served on the boards of war and of the treasury. These duties proved so strenuous after three months that he found it necessary to withdraw for a time. By July he returned and was, with Philip Livingston and Elbridge Gerry, a commission sent to Washington's headquarters at Valley Forge on July 11, 1777, to investigate alleged abuses within the commissary department.

Mr. Clymer continued to serve in Congress until after September 14, 1777, although not reelected. As commissioner of prisoners he received the captive Hessians and sent those who could travel to Allentown.

After the British victory at the Battle of Brandywine, September 11, 1777, some of the British were told where Clymer lived by local Tories. They ransacked his home, destroyed all his furniture, and took whatever they could use. His family had left and were unhurt.

Clymer was one of three who were commissioned on December 11, 1777, to go to Fort Pitt to quiet the Indians who, inspired by the British, were committing vicious attacks on the frontier. Their mission was successful and they received the thanks of Congress.

In the autumn of 1780, he was elected to Congress for the third time, and continued as an attentive and active member until 1782. He assisted Robert Morris and others in establishing the Bank of Philadelphia in 1782, which was the first national bank. He was made one of its first directors. Clymer was almost continuously a member or chairman of special and standing committees, particularly those dealing with finance and commerce. His service in the Confederation Congress ended in 1783. In 1785, he was elected a member of the Pennsylvania House of Representatives.

In 1785, George Clymer and Edward Rutledge were appointed by Congress to visit the southern states to urge prompt contribution of their assessed quota of funds for the public treasury. Soon he was called to the Pennsylvania legislature where the criminal code was modified and the penitentiary system introduced. Clymer was given much credit for the improvement of Pennsylvania's system of punishment.

He was elected on December 12, 1787, as a member of the convention that framed the United States Constitution, of which he was a signer. In November 1788, he was elected to the first United States Congress (1789–1791). He supported President Washington, but favored liberal naturalization and a pro–French and Jeffersonian economic policy. He declined reelection, but was appointed by President Washington to be supervisor of revenue for the State of Pennsylvania. During this tour of duty, the Whiskey Rebellion occurred (1794). When the trouble passed, he resigned.

As a member of the commission appointed by President Washington in 1796, he went to Georgia with colonels Hawkins and Pickens and they successfully negotiated a treaty with the Cherokee and Creek tribes.

Clymer retired from public life on July 31, 1796, after which he promoted many community interests. He was the first president of the Philadelphia Bank and of the Academy of Fine Arts. In 1805, he became vice president of the Pennsylvania Agricultural Society. He retained these offices for the rest of his life.

The Pennsylvania Constitution Commemoration Committee placed a bronze plaque at his grave in 1937, to honor his signing of the federal Constitution on September 17, 1787.

Genealogy

I. George Clymer, March 16, 1739–January 23, 1813, was the son of Christopher and Deborah (Fitzwater) Clymer. His mother died when he was eleven months old, and his father when he was seven. He became the ward of his uncle, William Coleman, a merchant friend of Benjamin Franklin. He married at Christ Church in Philadelphia, on March 18, 1765, Elizabeth Meredith. Clymer died at Sommerseat at Morrisville, Bucks County, Pennsylvania, and was buried in the Friends Meeting House Cemetery at Trenton, New Jersey. A small gravestone marks his resting place. The Sons of the American Revolution placed bronze flag holders at the grave.

His children were: William Coleman, 1766; Henry, 1767; John Meredith, 1769; Margaret, 1772; Elizabeth, 1774; Julian, 1780; George, ca. 1782.

MEREDITH
Elizabeth Meredith, date of birth

unknown, died in February 1815, in Northumberland County, Pennsylvania. She was the daughter of Reese and Martha (Carpenter) Meredith, who were married on March 23, 1738. Martha died August 26, 1769. Reese Meredith was born in Wales in 1708, and graduated from Oxford in 1728. He presented a certificate February 1730, from Leominster Meeting in Hereford. He became a prominent shipping merchant in Philadelphia and died there November 17, 1778.

Meredith owned a ship *The Black Prince* and he hosted George Washington when he was in Philadelphia. Martha Carpenter was the daughter of John Carpenter, May 5, 1690–1724, who married in 1710, Ann Hoskin, daughter of Richard and Esther (Clymer) Hoskins. Richard Hoskins was a merchant who came via Barbados.

John Carpenter was the son of Samuel Carpenter, 1650–April 10, 1714, who was born in England and came to Philadelphia via Barbados, bearing a certificate dated June 23, 1683. He married at Friends Meeting House on October 12, 1684, at Philadelphia, Hannah Hardiman. Hannah's certificate from the Friends Meeting House of Haverford West, South Wales, was dated August 2, 1683, and received at Philadelphia, November 4, 1684. It was signed by Abraham and Jane Hardiman. Jane Hardiman was Hannah

(Hardiman) Carpenter's mother. Hannah was an eminent minister among Friends and traveled extensively "in the service of Truth." She died May 24, 1728, at the age of eighty-two. Burke's *General Armory* lists the arms of the Carpenter family of Barbados. Their arms were granted in Ireland, June 11, 1647.

Reese Meredith, 1708–1778, was the son of Reese Meredith of Radnor, Wales.

FITZWATER

II. Christopher Clymer was born at Philadelphia on August 11, 1711, and was buried July 27, 1746, at Christ Church burial ground. He married, probably about 1737, Deborah Fitzwater who died and was buried in Friends Burial Ground, May 6, 1740. She was the daughter of George Fitzwater, who came in 1682 with his parents, Thomas and Mary Fitzwater of Hamworth, Middlesex, England. They came with William Penn on his first visit to Pennsylvania.

III. Richard Clymer, date of birth unknown, was buried August 14, 1734, in Christ Church burial ground. His wife Elizabeth died in 1733, buried at Christ Church burial ground in July 1733. They came from Bristol, England, before July 30, 1710.

IV. Christopher Clymer of Bristol, England, whose wife was Catherine, maiden name unknown.

Chapter 9

WILLIAM ELLERY

1727–1820

RHODE ISLAND

William Ellery

WILLIAM ELLERY, merchant, judge, state senator, deputy governor, and patriot, was carefully prepared for his entry into Harvard by his father. He was graduated from Harvard in 1747, and soon became a merchant at Newport. He became a Master Mason in the First Lodge of Boston on October 25, 1748.

Ellery was one of the founders of Rhode Island College in 1764, and one of its incorporators. He served as naval officer of the colony for a time and was clerk of the General Assembly in 1769 and 1770.

Ellery was admitted to the bar in 1770, twenty-three years after his graduation from Harvard. He practiced law with success at Newport for several years, but public service required much of his attention. At the outbreak of the Revolutionary War, he became a member of the Committee of Safety, the Committee of Inspection, Committee of Military Defenses, and was also on a committee to bear a memorial to General Washington who was then at Cambridge.

In March 1776, he was appointed as a delegate to the Continental Congress to succeed Samuel Ward, deceased. He took his seat on May 14, 1776, and signed the Declaration of Independence on August 2, 1776, with the greatest number of the signers.

With a touch of grim humor, Ellery took a seat near Thomson's table to observe the faces of his fellow signers as they appended their names to "what might be their death warrant," but saw, as he recorded, only "undaunted resolution." Ellery signed the Articles of Confederation on November 15, 1777. He served on many committees and kept his seat in the Continental Congress until 1779.

In 1778, the British took possession of Newport, Rhode Island, and Ellery took part in a failed effort to drive them out. As a known patriot leader, he was an object of their wrath. They were unable to capture him, but burned his home and destroyed much of his property.

Ellery returned to Congress in 1781 and again from 1783 to 1785. He became a notable speaker, and was an active member of the Board of the Admiralty. The last of his services in the Continental Congress, working with Rufus King, was an effort to end slavery throughout the United States.

He became a judge, then chief justice of the Superior Court of Rhode Island, Commissioner of loans, April 18, 1786–January 1, 1790. In 1790, he was appointed Collector of Revenue at Newport, by President Washington, a position he held until his death.

Additional Information

Ellery's post–Revolutionary War life was probably happier than that of some of his fellow signers, and he appeared to have rebuilt his fortune. His nature was genial and kindly. He had a broad knowledge of literature, English, French, and Latin, and was an avid letter writer.

Ellery died at his home, sitting in his chair, while reading Cicero's *De Officiis*. He was buried in the Common Ground Cemetery at Newport, Rhode Island. A memorial ledger marks his grave; it was restored in 1965 by the Rhode Island State Society of the Daughters of the American Revolution.

Genealogy

I. William Ellery, December 22, 1727–February 15, 1820, was born and died at Newport, Rhode Island. He was the eldest son of William and Abigail (Wilkinson) Ellery. He married first, on October 11, 1750, Ann Remington. He married second, on June 28, 1767, Abigail Carey, his second cousin. Ellery had seventeen children: seven by his first wife, ten by his second wife. Six of the children died at age six or under.

His children were: (by first wife) Elizabeth, 1751; Lucy, 1752; Ann, 1755; William, 1757; Almy, 1759; William again, 1761; Edmund Trowbridge, 1763; (by second wife) Abigail, 1768; John Wilkins, 1770; Abigail again, 1772; Ruth Champlin, 1773; Susan Kent, 1775; Philadelphia, 1776; Nathan Carey, 1778; Ruth Champlin again, 1779; Mehitable Redwood, 1784; George Wanton, 1789.

REMINGTON

Ann Remington, February 19, 1724–September 7, 1764, first wife of William Ellery, Jr., was the daughter of the Honorable Jonathon Remington, July 27, 1677–1745. Remington was graduated from Harvard College in 1696, and became a judge of the Superior Court; he lived in Cambridge, Massachusetts. He was the son of Jonathon Remington, 1639–April 21, 1700, of Cambridge. He was a selectman, town clerk, and treasurer. His wife was Martha Belcher, July 26, 1644–July 16, 1711, whom he married on July 13, 1664. Martha was the daughter of Andrew Belcher, of Sudbury in 1639, a taverner, who was in the artillery company in 1642. He died June 16, 1680.

Andrew Belcher was the son of Thomas and Ann (Solme) Belcher of London. Thomas was a clothworker, bound January 9, 1604, and made free on May 8, 1612. Ann Solme was the daughter of Andrew Solme of Sandon, in Essex. Thomas Belcher was a son of Robert

Belcher of Kingswood in County Essex, a weaver. Andrew Belcher's wife was Elizabeth Danforth, ca. 1619–June 16, before 1680, daughter of Nicholas and Elizabeth (Symmes) Danforth of Cambridge, married in England. The Danforths came from Framingham, County Suffolk, in 1634. Nicholas Danforth was a freeman March 3, 1636, and died in April 1638.

Jonathon Remington, 1639–1700, was the son of John Remington, of Newbury in 1637, a freeman May 22, 1639. John Remington was a lieutenant in a military company formed in 1645 with Denison, Bradstreet, and others. His wife was Elizabeth who died in December 1657. He married second, at Roxbury, Rhoda Gore, widow of John Gore. He died and was buried on June 8, 1667.

CAREY

Abigail Carey, November 10, 1742–July 17, 1793, was the second wife of William Ellery, Jr. She was his second cousin, daughter of Colonel Nathaniel and Elizabeth (Wanton) Carey/Cary who were married September 6, 1739. Elizabeth Wanton was baptized October 25, 1719, daughter of George Wanton, who married on November 15, 1715, Abigail Ellery, born February 24, 1698, daughter of Benjamin and Abigail (Wilkins) Ellery.

II. William Ellery, Sr., October 3, 1701–March 15, 1764, was the son of the Honorable Benjamin and Abigail (Wilkins) Ellery. He was graduated from Harvard College in 1722; married January 3, 1722, Elizabeth Almy, at Newport, Rhode Island. Ellery, as the eldest son, inherited a major part of his father's estate. He was a deputy and assistant in the Colonial Assembly; judge of the county court, and deputy governor of Rhode Island. His obituary notice was in the

Newport Mercury of March 1764. He was buried in the Common Ground Cemetery at Newport, Rhode Island.

ALMY

Elizabeth Almy, August 1, 1703–July 13, 1783, born at Portsmouth, Rhode Island, was the daughter of Colonel Job Almy, October 10, 1675–December 21, 1743, and Ann Lawton, who were married about 1699. Ann Lawton, born April 28, 1678, was the daughter of Isaac Lawton of Portsmouth, Rhode Island, and his second wife Elizabeth Tallman, who were married March 3, 1674. Isaac Lawton, December 11, 1650, was the son of George Lawton of Portsmouth, who died October 5, 1693. Isaac married third, October 11, 1701, Naomi (Hunt)(Lawton), widow of his brother George. Elizabeth Tallman married Isaac Lawton March 3, 1674 and died May 20, 1701. She was the daughter of Peter Tallman, March 22, 1658–July 6, 1726, and Ann Wright Walstone who died 1731. Ann was the daughter of Benjamin and Joane Wright. Peter Tallman was a freeman at Newport, Rhode Island, in 1665.

Job Almy married second, Abigail Gardner, no children. He was the son of Christopher Almy, 1632–1712/3, and Elizabeth Cornell who were married in 1661. Elizabeth Cornell was the granddaughter of Thomas Cornell of Boston in 1639, who moved to Portsmouth, Rhode Island, about 1654, and became a freeman in 1655, His wife was Elizabeth Fiscock.

Christopher Almy was an assistant in 1690. He was born about 1632 in England, the son of William Almy 1601–1764, who was at Lynn, Massachusetts in 1631 or before. William Almy went home but returned in the Abigail in 1635, age 35, with his wife Audrey (Barlow), age

32, and children Annis 8 and Christopher 3.

On April 3, 1637, Edmund Freeman and nine associates, all previously residents of Lynn (Saugus), received a grant to erect a plantation, Sandwich Massachusetts. One of Freeman's nine associates was William Almy who "left town early." Almy was a freeman of Portsmouth, Rhode Island, in 1655.

GOLD

III. The Honorable Benjamin Ellery, September 6, 1669–July 26, 1746, was the son of William and Hannah (Vincent) Ellery. He married, at Gloucester Massachusetts, on July 30, 1696, Abigail Wilkins, daughter of John and Anstis (Gold) Bissett, of Bristol, Rhode Island, from Wilts in England. He settled at Bristol following his marriage, but moved to Newport and became a successful merchant. He owned the ferry. He was Speaker of the House of Deputies and was an assistant and a judge of the County Court. Ellery was a member of the Second Congressional Society of Newport. In December 1733, he headed the subscription for building a new church and his contribution of £200 was the largest. In 1793, he was moderator of the Society and was a member of the Newport Town Council. Benjamin Ellery's will disposed of a large landed estate, including lands inherited from his father at Gloucester.

WILKINS

Abigail Wilkins, born at Boston in 1677, died December 15, 1742. She was the daughter of John and Anstis (Gold) (Bisset) Wilkins.

John Wilkins was born in Wiltshire, England. He served an apprenticeship for the trade of glassmaker and came to

Boston and set up to work at his trade. He removed to Bristol, Rhode Island, where he was one of the original proprietors. In Boston he had married Anstis (Gold) Bissett, a widow. His will dated January 3, 1703/4, stated he was between sixty and seventy years of age.

He made bequests to "her Most Excellent Majesty Queen Ann, over England," his wife Anstes son Samuel, and three daughters — Mary Ginkins, Abigail Ellery, and Mehitable Wilkins. Also, to his grandson, William Ellery, one-fourth part of his stock remaining after Anstis' death. Queen Ann, Samuel Wilkins, and son-in-law, Benjamin Ellery, were his executors.

Anstis Gold Bissett Wilkins, 1638–October 31, 1711, was born in England. Her first husband and all her family died during the plague in London. She came to Nantasket in Massachusetts Bay, where her brother had been well settled for years, having received his estate from his Uncle Stone. Benjamin Ellery was the son of Sergeant William Ellery, born ca. 1643.

VINCENT

IV. Sergeant William Ellery, ca. 1643–1696, the emigrant, married at Gloucester, Massachusetts, on October 8, 1663, Hannah Vinson (or Vincent). He was living at Salem in 1668, was a freeman in 1672, representative in 1689, and died December 9, 1696. Ellery called himself about thirty years of age in a deposition made November 21, 1673. He was a merchant, and his signature was Ellerey; however, some records spell the name Illary. In England the name is written Hillary, Illary, and Ellery. William Ellery married second, on June 13, 1676, Mary, daughter of John Coit.

Hannah Vincent, born before 1643, died December 24, 1675. She was the daughter of William Vincent and his first wife, Sarah, who died February 4, 1660. Vincent was a freeman at Gloucester May 10, 1643. He was selectman in 1646, and later moved to New London, Connecticut. He married second, June 10, 1661, Rachel Cooke, who died February 15, 1707.

Chapter 10

WILLIAM FLOYD

1734–1821

NEW YORK

WILLIAM FLOYD, farmer, landed proprietor, patriot, received a very limited formal education. He became a landed proprietor in 1753, following the death of his father. Floyd was intelligent and possessed a strong character. The connections of his wealthy family soon enabled him to be effective in the civic and military affairs of Suffolk County, New York. He was made an officer in the militia in 1760.

Having allied himself with the patriots, Floyd was elected as one of New York's twelve delegates to the First Continental Congress and took his seat on September 5, 1774. He served during sessions in 1774–1777 and 1778–1783, except for an absence in 1780. His activities in Congress were neither brilliant nor aggressive; he took no part in the debates and did not make speeches. He did, however, serve on many committees, and his sound judgment commanded the respect of his fellow congressmen.

He was elected to the Second Continental Congress and had, during 1775, become a colonel in the Suffolk County Militia. On July 8, 1775, he signed the Olive Branch Petition. He was a member of the important committees on clothing in 1776.

On October 20, 1774, Floyd signed the Articles of Association. He was elected to the second Continental Congress. When the British first attacked Long Island, Floyd led the militia and drove them off.

New York had no delegates present at the Continental Congress on July 2, 1776, when the vote for independence occurred. However, Floyd was one of the four New York delegates who had the honor of signing the engrossed copy of the Declaration of Independence on August 2, 1776.

On July 19, 1776, the British invaders confiscated his home. His family escaped across the sound to Connecticut. The home was used by the British cavalry as a barracks for seven years, and his livestock was used to feed enemy soldiers. Floyd served on the boards of treasury and admiralty in 1779.

From 1777 to 1783, while serving in the Continental Congress, he also was appointed New York state senator representing Long Island, although his property was being held by the British. In 1783, he returned to his farm and became a major-general of the Long Island militia. After leaving the Confederation Congress in 1783, Floyd served a notable term in the New York State Senate, where he worked for the adoption of a conservative and stable financial policy. In June 1788, Floyd was named as a delegate to the Poughkeepsie Convention where the United States Constitution would be voted upon.

Floyd served in the first United States Congress, 1789–1791, but declined reelection. He was a delegate to the New York Constitutional Convention in 1801, and was a presidential elector many times, 1792–1820. He was also a firm supporter of Thomas Jefferson in 1801 in his race against Aaron Burr.

Floyd was an unsuccessful candidate for lieutenant governor of New York in 1795. In 1808, he was a New York State senator. In 1820, he was a presidential elector for the last time.

He had purchased a tract of undeveloped land in 1783, located on the headwaters of the Mohawk (now in Oneida County), and moved there in 1802 or 1803. During the year 1787, Floyd had received, under dates February 15 and April 12, eleven separate Certificates of Location for lots in township 8, consisting of a total of 11,158 acres. These were in the tract purchased from the Oneida and Tuscarora Indians.

Genealogy

I. William Floyd, December 17, 1734–August 4, 1821, was born at Mastic Long Island, New York, the eldest son of Nicholl and Tabitha (Smith) Floyd. He married first, on April 20 or 23, 1760, Hannah Jones. He married second, on May 16, 1784, Joanna Strong. By his two wives, William Floyd had thirteen children. He was a practical man who pursued his goals methodically. He had a frank, independent manner which discouraged intimacy but he was well liked and enjoyed the respect of his contemporaries.

Floyd died at the age of eighty-seven, and is buried in the Westernville Methodist-Presbyterian cemetery. His gravestone was erected in 1904 by the General William Floyd Chapter of the Daughters of the American Revolution. The monument also honors both of his wives.

His children were: (by first wife) Ann, 1760; Eliza, ca. 1762; Nicoll, 1762; Mary, 1764; Catherine, 1767; (by second wife) Anna, 1786; Eliza, 1789. Perhaps his remaining eight children died in infancy, names not found.

JONES
Hannah Jones, 1740–May 16, 1781, was the daughter of William Jones of Southampton, Long Island, New York. She was one of the refugees from Mastic to Middleton, Connecticut, in July 1776. Her gravestone in Mortimer Cemetery at Middleton states:

In Memory of Mrs. Hannah Floyd, the Consort of Mr. William Floyd of Long Island, Who Departed This Life May 16, 1781, In The 41st Year of Her Age.

STRONG
Joanna Strong (1740–1826), born at Setauket, Long Island, was daughter of Benajah Strong, born at Northampton, September 24, 1682. Benajah was the son of Thomas Strong, 1636–October 3, 1689, who took the Oath of Fidelity on February 8, 1679.

Thomas Strong married first in 1660, Mary Hewett who died on February 20, 1671. She was the daughter of the Reverend Ephriam Huet/Hewett/Hulett. He married second in October 1671, Rachel Holton, daughter of Deacon William Holton of Hartford, who came in the *Francis* from Ipswich in 1634 and died August 12, 1691. Rachel (Holton Strong), married second, May 16, 1698, Nathan Bradley.

Thomas Strong was the son of the Reverend John Strong, 1613–April 14, 1699, who was born at Chard, Somerset, England, and died at Northampton, Massachusetts. He married first, about 1632, Margery Deane, daughter of Walter Deane. Margery probably died about 1635 in New England. The Reverend Strong married second, Abigail Ford, 1619–July 6, 1688, who with her parents, Thomas Ford and Elizabeth Chard, came on the *Mary and John* in 1630. Thomas Ford had married first, on December 13, 1610, at Powerstock, Dorset, England, Joane Way who was buried May 10, 1615. He married second, June 19, 1616, at Bridgport, Elizabeth Chard who was the widow of Aaron Cooke. Aaron Cooke was buried at Thorncombe, Dorset on December 28, 1615. Elizabeth Chard Cook Ford died April 18, 1643, at Windsor,

Connecticut. Thomas Ford married
third, Ann Steel Scott, 1589–1676, widow
of Thomas Scott. Thomas Ford, 1589–
1676, was the son of William Ford of
Forde Green who married in 1569, Alice
Harlbutt of Loyd, Stafford, England. The
Ford line has been traced to John de
Forde who died in 1315, son of Simon
de Forde of Abbey Field and his wife
Agnes.

SMITH

II. Nicholl Floyd, who died about
1753, married before 1734, Tabitha
Smith, born February 18, 1704, daughter
of Jonathon and Elizabeth (Platt)
(Schuyler) Smith.

NICHOLL

III. Richard Floyd, May 12, 1665–
1738, of Setauket, Suffolk County, New
York, married May 12, 1686, Margaret
Nicholl, May 30, 1662–February 1, 1718,
daughter of Matthias Nicholl of Setauket, Long Island. Margaret died at
Brookhaven in her fifty-seventh year.
Matthias Nicoll/Nicholl, March 26,
1626–December 22, 1687 (armorial descent), was the son and heir of Matthew

Nicholl of Plympton, Devon, England.
He was admitted to the bar, at Lincoln's
Inn, November 27, 1649, and came to
New York in 1664, as the first English
colonial secretary. His wife was Abigail
Johns. Matthias (Matthew) Nicholl, February 22, 1589–August 19, 1631, married
Martha Oakes. He was born at the Parish
of Mildred, Poultney, County Buckingham. His will was proved October 10,
1631; in that will he described himself as
a "preacher of God's word to the town
of Plymouth, Devon." Nicholl graduated
from New College, Oxford, May 5, 1614,
with a Bachelor of Divinity degree. He
was the son of John Nicholl who was
buried October 17, 1639, of the town of
Buckingham and Cliffords Inn, London.
John Nicholl married Johanna Grafton,
daughter and heiress of John Grafton of
London who was buried February 23,
1621.

IV. Richard Floyd, 1626–1706, married in 1645, Susanna, 1626–1706, surname unknown; they both died age
eighty. Richard Floyd came from Brec-
knockshire, Wales, in 1650, and was one
of the fifty-five original proprietors of
Brookhaven, Suffolk County, New York.

Chapter 11

BENJAMIN FRANKLIN
1706–1790

PENNSYLVANIA

BENJAMIN FRANKLIN, printer, author, publisher, businessman, diplomat, inventor, philosopher, statesman, was one of history's most accomplished self-taught men. It is likely that his father, Josiah Franklin, taught him to read. He said he could not remember when he could not read, and he was reading the Bible at five. At eight he was sent to the Boston Grammar School, later called Boston Latin School. The expense was too great and after one year he was transferred to George Brownell's school for writing and arithmetic; he failed arithmetic. Years later he would teach himself arithmetic and some geometry.

At ten he expressed a desire to go to sea, but his father put him to work in his own candle-making shop for two years. He disliked the work and his father felt his love of books might make him suited to a career as a printer. Benjamin's brother James had just returned from England after completing his apprenticeship, bringing with him a press and type to set up a printing business in Boston. Josiah paid James £12 for Benjamin's room and board. Under parental pressure Benjamin signed indentures that made him an apprentice to James until he was twenty.

Benjamin made good progress and had access to more and better books, and Matthew Adams, a local tradesman, invited him to use his library. Occasionally James asked him to write ballads. One which sold well was "The Lighthouse Tragedy," which described a recent event.

After a time James realized that Benjamin was more talented and intelligent than he and became jealous. The brothers were not getting along and when taking issues to their father, Josiah sided with Benjamin. In August 1721, James Franklin began printing the *New England Courant* and soon printed an article which offended the Colonial Assembly. He was censured and imprisoned for a month by Speaker's warrant because he would not disclose the author's name. They decreed that the *New England Courant* could not be published by James Franklin. It was decided that the paper would be published by Benjamin Franklin and his apprentice papers were returned to him.

Between April 4, 1722, and September 24, 1722, Benjamin printed a series of cleverly written articles under the pseudonym of Mrs. Silence Dogood, who described herself as the widow of a country parson. Mrs. Dogood said that she intended to present readers with one article each fortnight "which I presume will add somewhat to their entertainment." They were slipped under the door of the print shop at night, and all were published in the *New England Courant*. Eventually, Benjamin confessed to being the author of the Mrs. Dogood's letters.

Unwilling to suffer the tyranny of his brother James any longer, Benjamin ran away in 1722. On September 29, 1723, James Franklin placed this notice in the *Courant*: "James Franklin, Printer in Queen Street, wants a likely lad for an apprentice." Benjamin did not tell his family he was leaving, but borrowed a small amount of money from his friend Collins. He boarded a sloop for New York, hoping to work for William Bradford, the only printer in town. Bradford sent him on to Philadelphia where his son had just lost his assistant. He rested in New York, found his own way across the Hudson, walked part of the way across New Jersey, and arrived in Philadelphia on a Sunday in October.

In Philadelphia he was directed to the Crooked Billet in Water Street, where he dined and spent the night. Next morning he went directly to Andrew Bradford's but Bradford could not give him work. Instead he offered to lodge him until he found work. On Bradford's advice, Benjamin visited Samuel Keimer who had recently arrived and intended to establish a printing shop and bookstore. Keimer had no workmen and he immediately hired Franklin.

Franklin loved Philadelphia and enjoyed working with his eccentric employer. His pay was good, the work was easy, and he had time to study. Keimer did not want him lodging with his competitor, Bradford, and arranged lodging with John and Sarah Read. Soon Benjamin had a circle of friends, mostly young men apprenticed to printers, particularly James Ralph. All were somewhat cultivated and they gathered evenings and Sundays to discuss affairs of the world and other subjects.

Governor William Keith and his aide-de-camp, Colonel French came to Keimer's shop to meet Franklin. The governor had recently talked with Captain Holmes, who had just married Franklin's sister Mary. Holmes had written to Franklin urging him to return home. Franklin replied by refusing, giving good reasons in a well-constructed letter, and Holmes showed the letter to Keith, who decided to become acquainted with Franklin. He wanted Franklin to establish a print shop, but sent him to Boston to ask for the financial aid of Franklin's father, Josiah. In April 1724, Franklin left for Boston. His parents had had no news of him since he had left seven months earlier. They forgave him and gave their permission for him to leave again. He was carrying a long, persuasive letter written by Governor Keith, but Josiah Franklin declined as he was convinced there was something suspicious about the idea. He told Benjamin to come back when he was twenty-one.

Governor Keith encouraged Franklin to go to England to finish his education as a printer and to procure machinery and supplies. The governor did not see Franklin for several days before he and his friend James Ralph boarded the *London Hope* at Newcastle but promised him that letters of recommendation and credit would be sent aboard before their departure.

The *London Hope* was a small packet boat and the crossing was a difficult one. Their food was poor and storms caused the ship to veer off course. On board, Benjamin met the Quaker merchant Thomas Denham, who took a special interest in him. They arrived at Gravesend on Christmas Eve, 1724, and took lodging at a tavern. Franklin learned that he had no letters of introduction or credit from Governor Keith. He was out of work, had no English friends, no definite plans, and Ralph was dependent upon him.

Franklin entered the employ of Samuel Palmer, who employed fifty workmen. His wages were high and he could, with Ralph as a guide, attend theaters, dances, lectures on science, and sermons. Finally, Ralph moved to the country to teach and to write poetry. Franklin wrote Ralph a letter that criticized his poetry and Ralph was offended. He broke off the friendship, owing Benjamin £27. While at Palmer's, Benjamin wrote a pamphlet, *A Dissertation on Liberty and Necessity, Pleasure and Pain*, which he later regretted writing.

He left Palmer's and went to Watts, a more famous printer, and moved his lodgings closer to Watts. Thomas Denham returned to London to attend to his mercantile business and was nearly ready to return to Philadelphia. He offered Franklin a position as clerk in his establishment where he would learn accounts and become expert at selling. His pay would be £52 per year, and Denham promised to advance him later. He boarded the *Berkshire* on July 2, 1726, happy to be returning to Philadelphia. He arrived in Philadelphia on October 11, 1726.

In the summer of 1726, Franklin began keeping a journal. In 1727, he formed the Junto, a debating club. Franklin's mercantile career was short-lived, for an epidemic swept through Philadelphia in February 1727 and both he and Denham became ill. Denham died and Franklin thought he would too. Exhausted from his illness, he was once again alone without a job or money, and Denham had neglected to make a promised will.

He returned to Samuel Keimer's printing shop where there were now five workmen who all needed training. Resentful of the manner in which Franklin had left for London, Keimer invented an opportunity and dismissed Franklin, but not until the five workmen had been trained. Franklin had become close friends of the men and one of them, Hugh Meredith, proposed founding a printing shop with Meredith's father furnishing the money in a joint partnership.

Equipment had to be ordered from England and Franklin needed work in the meantime. Keimer received an order for printing the paper money of New Jersey and, of necessity, turned to Benjamin Franklin for assistance. To accomplish his task, Franklin built the first copperplate press.

In 1728, Franklin and Meredith set up their shop on High Street, sharing a house with a glazier. In the spring of 1728, through a Junto member, they acquired the Quaker clientele who had a large work related to their society to be printed. In 1729, they bought the *Pennsylvania Gazette* that had been founded by Keimer in 1728. Their first issue was published on October 2, 1729. It quickly became profitable (in 1821 it was renamed the *Saturday Evening Post*).

In 1729, he drafted the Articles of Belief and Acts of Religion, which contained a creed aimed at achieving his own "moral perfection." To further this aim he listed thirteen virtues: temperance, silence, order, resolution, frugality, industry, sincerity, justice, moderation, cleanliness, tranquillity, chastity, and humility, and recorded his progress for many years.

Franklin wrote articles for the *American Weekly Mercury* which he signed Busy Body. He bought out Hugh Meredith by borrowing money from Junto members and forming a partnership with them which was dissolved on July 14, 1730.

Having married in 1730, he set up shop in part of his home where his wife helped in selling books and stationery. From this shop, his mother-in-law also sold salves, ointments, and other products. He enlarged his shop and sold goods that he could advertise in the *Gazette* and became a general trader as well as a printer and publisher.

By 1731 his *Pennsylvania Gazette* was a success, and he invested in or was partners with gazettes in South Carolina and Rhode Island; later there would be others. Early in 1731, he became a Freemason. In that year he was instrumental in founding the first circulating library in America, with the special support of the Junto. He initiated the establishment of a city police and a public works program for paving, cleaning, and lighting of city streets.

Benjamin Franklin began writing

Poor Richard's Almanack in December 1732, and continued to publish it annually until 1757. *Poor Richard's Almanack* was translated into French and eventually gained international fame.

About 1733, Franklin began teaching himself to read French, Spanish, Italian, and Latin. He was undoubtedly more "educated" than his contemporaries who had graduated from various colleges.

He organized the first fire department in America in 1736. In that year he became clerk of the Pennsylvania Assembly; and was a member for Philadelphia, 1751–1764. He was deputy postmaster at Philadelphia, 1737–1753, jointly with William Hunter, 1753–1774. In this post he visited many of the colonies, increased the efficiency and frequency of mail deliveries and made the post office a financial success. He also established the first dead letter office.

In 1743, Franklin founded the American Philosophical Society which was incorporated in 1780. For membership, he selected the most intelligent men in his Junto as well as other distinguished men of his acquaintance. He wrote articles in his *Pennsylvania Gazette* to promote an academy for the education of youth, which opened in 1751 and was incorporated in 1753. He was appointed its first president and drew up its constitution. Under his leadership the Pennsylvania Hospital was chartered in 1751.

In 1746, Franklin had become intensely interested in electricity after Peter Collison, a London merchant, sent an "electric tube" to the Philadelphia library. He was so fascinated with the tube that he spent all his spare time experimenting with it. He said, "I never was before engaged in any study that so totally engrossed my attention." Four months later, he sent Collison a complete report of his experiments.

In 1747, he published a pamphlet, *Plain Truth*, which suggested a voluntary association of the people. The Assembly did not act upon it, and he held a lottery and with the proceeds saw to it that a fort was erected on the Delaware River to protect Philadelphia. Along with other volunteers, he took his turns of duty.

He retired from business in 1748, forming a partnership with his employee, David Hall, who would pay him £1,000 per year. The partnership lasted eighteen years. Franklin continued to write *Poor Richard's Almanack* as well as some other articles.

On December 25, 1750, Franklin wrote a letter to his brother John about an electrical experiment that had nearly proved fatal. Two days before Christmas Franklin prepared to kill a turkey by electrical shock. He had casually continued to hold the chain between two battery jars. He wrote that though he did not hear the crack or see the flash, those who did said the flash was bright and the crack was as loud as a pistol. Later Franklin saw a round swelling on his hand where the electricity entered his body and his breastbone was sore for a week.

Following his kite experiment in 1752, he invented the lightning rod, installing the first one on his own roof. It had a bell which would ring when charged. He refused to apply for a patent, though his friends urged him to do so. He felt everyone should be free to use it. A detailed description of his lightning rod, then called an electrical conductor, appeared in *Poor Richard's Almanack* of 1753.

It was for his letters on electricity that he received degrees from Yale and Harvard in 1753, and in 1756 received a degree of master of arts from William and Mary. Also in 1756, Governor Denny, returning from London, presented him with a diploma of Membership of the Royal Society of Science in London.

In 1754, he was sent to represent Pennsylvania at the Albany, New York, conference which was called to unite the colonies in the war against the French and Indians. He presented his Plan of Union, but the Assemblies did not adopt it.

In 1755, the governor appointed Franklin to take charge of the defense of the western frontier. Measures for creating a militia were passed by the assembly, and Benjamin Franklin left at the end of December with 300 volunteer militiamen. He took his son William with him to help with his administration. Arriving at Gnadenhutten, which had just been pillaged, they found fresh tracks left by Indians. Franklin immediately had a fort built of earth and wood, which they named Fort Allen. On his return to Philadelphia he was called colonel and had his own regiment.

In 1757, the General Assembly of the Province of Pennsylvania sent Franklin to London as its counsel in a taxation dispute with the Penn family, whom the colony's charter designated as its proprietors. He took William Franklin with him as his secretary. He arrived in London on July 26 and was the Assembly's resident agent in England for five years. They lodged with Mrs. Margaret Stevenson, at 7 Craven Street, by the Thames, where they occupied four rooms. Franklin felt that no solutions could be had from the Penns, who were "virtuous, hypocritical, unintelligent, and above all, obstinate." Lord George Grenville, president of the King's Council, wished to talk with him, having heard of his devotion to the Crown and of the services he had rendered to Braddock.

After asking him some questions about the American situation, Grenville lectured Franklin about the nature of the American constitution. He said their laws were drawn up by judges learned in laws, considered, debated, and sometimes amended in Council, and signed by the king, and, "They are then, so far as they relate to you, the law of the land, for the King is the legislator of the colonies." Shocked, Franklin tried to see if he might find help from the new prime minister, William Pitt, but an order forbade him all access to Pitt.

Franklin became seriously ill in September 1757, and was thereafter plagued by colds during his entire stay in England. At the end of November 1757, his health improved, and he readied himself for the long struggle he knew was ahead.

The Penns heard of Franklin's uncomplimentary assessment of them, and Franklin began to write the Assembly asking, in vain, to be recalled. His stay in England had made it obvious that the Assembly wished an open fight with the Penns. One of Franklin's main efforts was to have the king bring Pennsylvania back under royal government. He did not achieve this goal, but ultimately he was able to negotiate a compromise acceptable to both the Penns and the Assembly.

In 1758, Benjamin and William Franklin traveled into the countryside of England to restore Benjamin's health and calm his nerves. He also wanted to renew family connections and the trip became something of a genealogical expedition.

In May he went to Cambridge and conducted some scientific experiments on evaporation with John Hadley. At that time evaporation was a great mystery and no one knew why it had a cooling effect. In 1760, they made a trip in England and went into Wales. During August and September 1761, they made a tour of Flanders and Holland. They returned to London for the coronation of George III, following the sudden death of George II on September 25, 1760.

In April 1762, Franklin went to Oxford to receive a doctor of laws degree which honored him at the same time it honored William with his degree of master of arts.

He returned to Philadelphia in 1762 on the *Caroline* in company with nine other ships under protection of the war frigate *Scarborough*. He was publicly thanked by the General Assembly, and given $20,000 as compensation for his services.

William did not return with him, as he had met Elizabeth Downs of the West Indies, who would soon become his wife. William had been appointed royal governor of New Jersey and arrived in America with his wife on February 19, 1763.

In 1764, the Assembly again sent Franklin to England to obtain recall of the Penn Charter. In February Lord Greenville's Stamp Act was passed and Franklin loudly and boldly protested against it. Lord Howe was sympathetic but expressed his regret that they did not share in the protection of British power. Franklin informed him that he need not be concerned on the colonies' account as the Americans were fully able to take care of themselves.

Franklin was asked to remain as agent, and he also became the colonial agent in London for Georgia in 1768; New Jersey in 1769; and Massachusetts in 1770. He attended Parliament in matters concerning American colonial affairs.

During the February 1766 debates on the repeal of the Stamp Act, he was called before the House of Commons for questioning. One hundred seventy-four questions were put to him, some by opponents and some by friends of the Stamp Act. His replies, brief and to the point, were aimed at showing that the tax was contrary to custom and administratively impractical, both on account of the circumstances of the country and due to the opposition of the people. The Stamp Act was repealed within the year.

Franklin became involved in the Hutchinson Letters Scandal in 1773-74. These letters were written by Thomas Hutchinson, then chief justice of Massachusetts, to a British official, in which he requested troops and urged abridgment of American liberties. Franklin obtained the original letters and sent them to a friend in the colonies late in 1772, requesting that he not have them published but rather show them in the original to key individuals. In June 1773, Samuel Adams nonetheless had the letters published. As a result, on January 31, 1774, Franklin received a letter from the postmaster general informing him his position had been taken away because of his pro-colonial activities which were considered disloyal to the Crown.

Franklin sailed from England on March 20, 1775, on the *Pennsylvania Packet*, and arrived Philadelphia on May 6. He was unanimously elected by the Pennsylvania Assembly to be one of its representatives in Congress. He wrote to William on May 7, urging him to resign as royal governor of New Jersey and turn to agriculture. William did not resign, and when Congress dispersed in August 1775, Benjamin visited him at his home in Perth Amboy. At the end of the visit, King George had a loyal servant in William; Benjamin Franklin had lost his son.

On July 26, 1775, Congress elected

Franklin postmaster general for a year. His salary was $1,000, and he had the power of naming all his employees. On September 5, 1775, Congress met again, and Franklin was elected to the most important committees: for powder manufacture, September 18; development of American commerce, September 22. He was chosen to inspect Washington's army at Cambridge, aided by B. Harris and Thomas Lynch. They left Philadelphia on October 4, and arrived at headquarters on October 17. On their return to Philadelphia, the delegates made a favorable report.

On November 9, 1775, he was elected to the Assembly of Pennsylvania where the majority were either his enemies or liberals who were against independence. He had become an alderman of Philadelphia in August; on January 26, the Philosophical Society of America once more elected him president. After November 29, 1775, new duties were assigned to him. A Committee of Secret Correspondence was formed in Congress, and Franklin took part in it although it was clearly treason against the Crown. It was certain he would be hanged if the revolution failed.

Benjamin Franklin aided adventurer Thomas Paine — a Quaker, a Mason, his employee, and a vagabond — who wanted to establish himself in America. This self-taught, eloquent man would unloose the most violent of revolutionary passions in the American people. On January 10, 1776, he published his pamphlet *Common Sense* in Robert Bell's new *Pennsylvania Magazine.*

Common Sense denounced monarchy, heredity, and all that formed the basis of contemporary civilization. Four editions of the pamphlet were sold out in one month. It was distributed throughout the colonies and crystallized revolutionary sentiments.

Franklin avoided attending meetings of the assembly and did not join them in swearing an oath to the king. In February 1776, he requested to be excused from his functions. He also resigned as alderman.

He was sent, with Charles Carroll and Samuel Chase, on an unsuccessful mission to Canada to persuade them to join the colonies (see Chapter 6 for information on Samuel Chase). Franklin was an adviser to General Washington; organized the post office and became the first postmaster general of the United States; and was appointed to the committee to draft the Declaration of Independence. It was he who calmed Thomas Jefferson while changes to the Declaration were being made.

He signed the Declaration of Independence on August 2, 1776. On that day, Adams, Jefferson, and Franklin were appointed a committee to create a seal for the United States. They suggested that *E Pluribus Unum* (Out of many, one) be adopted as the motto for the great seal. Their task was not completed and two more committees also failed to adopt a seal. In 1783, based on the three committee reports, Charles Thomson designed a seal which, with some alteration by Congress, was adopted and made law in September 1783, using the "E Pluribus Unum" motto.

In April 1776, the Committee of Correspondence had sent Silas Deane, a Connecticut merchant and former member of Congress, to France to negotiate a commercial treaty and solicit the assistance they needed. Then, in response to Franklin's letter to Barbeau Dubourg (a friend of Franklin's who was a publisher and who also served as a liason with French ministers), a reply arrived in

September saying his time, influence, and connections were completely at the disposal of the Americans. Dubourg would obtain powder, cannons, officers, and generals.

On September 26, 1776, Congress elected Franklin, Silas Deane, and Arthur Lee to represent America in France. Franklin went happily, although he knew that if their ship were captured he would die. He had broken his ties with William, who was in prison. He took William Temple (William's illegitimate son) with him as secretary and companion. He also took Benjamin Bache, son of his daughter Sarah. He gathered all his ready funds and placed them at the disposal of Congress as a loan.

Franklin sailed on the *Reprisal* in October 1776, arriving in England December 3, 1776. Along the coast of France, the *Reprisal* captured the *Success* from Cork and the *La Vigne* from Hull. At Nantes, France, on December 7, 1776, as the calash carrying Franklin and his two grandsons rolled away, the *Reprisal*, flanked by her two prizes, fired a farewell salute.

A treaty was concluded and signed by Benjamin Franklin and the French minister in February 1778. Now America was acknowledged independent, and the French government openly supported her cause.

In addition to being minister to France, Franklin was the American consul. In these posts, Franklin had friends, and the French loved him. His American colleagues were envious of his ability, fame, and popularity. Arthur Lee tried to discredit him and have him recalled. When John Adams arrived in Paris, for a time he respected Franklin, but came to be jealous and resentful of him. Together with Arthur Lee, Adams tried to undermine all his efforts.

Franklin worked long hours, often sleeping only two or three hours each night. John Adams put his records in such condition that Franklin could not find anything he needed. Adams also believed Franklin was "dabbling in treason" when he hired the spies Bancroft, Alexander, and Carmichael. These men had done a bit of spying for England, but much more for America.

In 1779, Franklin was named minister plenipotentiary. He became solidly established in French Masonry, being a member of the Nine Sisters' Lodge, and was its grand marshal, 1779–1781. This lodge had celebrations and special meetings to honor the United States.

It fell to Franklin to arbitrate disputes between French privateers and American sailors. He had to deal with such men as John Paul Jones, whose privateering interrupted British commerce and kept their coastal towns in fear.

On September 3, 1783, John Adams, Benjamin Franklin, and John Jay signed the Treaty of Paris. It was ratified by the Confederation Congress on January 14, 1784, officially ending the Revolutionary War. In 1785, he signed the Treaty of Amity and Commerce with Prussia.

On December 26, 1783, Franklin reminded Congress of its promise to recall him after the peace was made. He finally left Passy with his grandsons on July 12, 1785. Because of his health, he was carried in one of the king's litters, by mule, to embark from Le Havre-de-Grâce. In England he had a final meeting with his son William, but found the love between them was dead. William gave his American lands to William Temple, and father and son separated politely.

Franklin had feared the voyage home, but soon some of his old energies returned and he began to take water temperatures and study the Gulf Stream. Captain Truxton handled the *London Packet* carefully, the food was excellent, and there was general good humor on board. During the voyage he wrote a treatise on "The Causes and Cures of Smoky Chimneys" and another "Description of a New Stove for Burning Pitcoal and Consuming All Its Smoke."

He recorded his "maritime observations" on subjects such as sailors' diets, use of swimming anchors, and soup dishes connected together to prevent scalding. He included his chart and studies of the Gulf Stream, which he had sent in a letter dated October 29, 1769, to Anthony Todd, secretary of the British post office. He had observed that mail packets often took two weeks longer to pass from London to Rhode Island than the merchant ships. His cousin, Capt. (?Timothy) Folger, of Nantucket Island, while visiting in England, assisted with the engrossing of a chart. "Maritime Observations," an account of this journal, was published by Franklin in *Transactions of the American Philosophical Society II*, 1788.

He was especially proud of his adaptation of his lightning conductor for use at sea. It consisted of the usual rod with a long chain dropped into the sea. He said it was sold at a reasonable price by Nairn Company, London, and told of its success. They were kept in a box, and could be set up in about five minutes, upon the approach of a thunderstorm.

On his arrival in Philadelphia on September 14, 1785, Franklin was greeted by the ringing of bells and cheering citizens crowding the docks. On September 15, Richard Henry Lee, president of the Confederation Congress, was the first to visit him. Then members of the Pennsylvania Assembly came, and were followed by visitors from the University of Pennsylvania

and the American Philosophical Society. On October 26, he was chosen to be president of the Executive Council of Pennsylvania (governor), which office he held until 1788.

He attended the Constitutional Convention in May 1787, but made few contributions. Like Thomas Jefferson, he had never been an orator; his speeches were written down and read. He objected to certain major provisions of the Constitution, arguing for a unicameral legislature and an executive committee in place of a president but finally urged that it be unanimously adopted.

In 1784, what might have been our fourteenth state adopted "Franklin" as its name, in his honor. It was formed from a part of North Carolina and was complete with a governor, legislature, and a justice department. It failed by one vote to be approved by Congress and in 1788 became a part of Tennessee.

During the years 1786–1790, Franklin wrote many pamphlets and letters. His last public act was to petition Congress for the abolition of slavery. The last letter written by Benjamin Franklin, nine days before his death, was to Thomas Jefferson.

In 1862, a statue of Franklin, by Hiram Power, was placed in the Senate wing of the Capitol in Washington, D.C. Benjamin Franklin was elected to the Hall of Fame in 1900, the year in which it was founded. A bust of Franklin was unveiled in the colonnade of the New York University on May 7, 1927.

Franklin's profile appeared on the Franklin–Liberty Bell half dollar, designed by John R. Sinnock, which was minted from 1948 to 1963. His likeness is also on the $100 bill.

On June 27, 1981, the Free and Accepted Masons of Pennsylvania dedicated the Benjamin Franklin statue commemorating 250 years of Freemasonry in Pennsylvania (1731–1981). It is a 14 foot bronze statue weighing 6½ tons, and it overlooks the Philadelphia Masonic Temple.

Additional Information

Franklin had an interest in his ancestry and visited Ecton, Northamptonshire, England, in 1758, where he learned he was the youngest son of the youngest son for five generations of Franklin. He studied the parish registers there which go back to 1555. He also calculated that in twenty-one generations he had 1,048,576 ancestors.

On May 26, 1739, his father sent him a letter giving what he knew and suggested the origin of the Franklins was perhaps France. Josiah's brother, Benjamin, had made an inquiry of a person skilled in heraldry, who told him there were two coats of arms, one belonging to the Franklins of the north, and one to the Franklins of the west. Josiah felt, "It hath hardly been worthwhile to concern ourselves about these things any farther than to tickle the fancy a little."

John Franklin, 1690–1756, Benjamin's brother, did use a crest on his bookplate. Similar arms were used by Benjamin Franklin in 1758.

After Franklin's final return to Philadelphia in 1785, he set up a printing press and type foundry for his grandson, Benjamin Bache. The 1790 United States Census Report lists that business. It does not list Benjamin Franklin himself, unless he is accounted in the home of Richard Bache as one of the four "above age sixteen" males.

For himself and the Baches, he had his three houses on Market Street built over into two with a passageway between them and to the garden. By 1786, he had added a huge library on the same level as his own room, which was much admired by visitors. He had a long mechanical arm for removing books from the top shelves, a letter copier, and his armchair had a mechanical fan.

In 1787, he fell down a flight of stairs in his home. Thereafter, he would not venture farther than the garden. He had many visitors and received letters from his friends in France. As of 1766, at the death of his brother Peter, only he and his youngest sister, Jane Mecom, were living.

Thomas Jefferson came to visit him on completion of his service in France. Jefferson also received the last letter ever written by Benjamin Franklin, just nine days before his death.

His grandsons Benjamin Bache and Temple Franklin were with him at his death which occurred at 11 P.M., April 17, 1790. He was buried at Christ Church Cemetery in Philadelphia. His funeral was attended by an estimated 20,000 people.

James Madison moved that the House of Representatives wear mourning for one month. The National Assembly in Paris also wore mourning for three days. A white marble ledger, made to his own specifications, marks the graves of Benjamin and Deborah Franklin.

Genealogy

I. Benjamin Franklin, January 6, 1706–April 17, 1790, was baptized at Old South Church, Boston, on Sunday, the day of his birth. He was the tenth son and fifteenth of seventeen children of Josiah Franklin. On September 1, 1730, he entered into a common-law union with Deborah Read of Philadelphia, and to them were born two children. Their son Francis Folger, 1732–1736, died of smallpox; their daughter Sarah, 1744–living 1790, married Richard Bache and was the mother of eight children. Franklin's illegitimate son, William, 1730–1813, became royal governor of New Jersey. He is buried at Saint Pancreas, Parish of Saint Marlebone, London, England. Franklin's only descendants are through his daughter, Sarah Franklin Bache.

His children were: William, 1730; Francis Folger, 1732; Sarah, 1744.

READ
Deborah Read, 1705–December 19, 1774, was the daughter of John Read and Sarah White, who came to Pennsylvania sometime before July 26, 1711. She married first, August 5, 1725, John Rogers, a potter, who soon told her he had a wife in England and then left for the West Indies, leaving debts. There were rumors of his death, but a legal marriage was not possible and she entered into a common-law marriage with Benjamin Franklin on September 1, 1730. A John Rogers died in the West Indies in 1745, perhaps her bigamous husband. Deborah could never be persuaded to accompany Benjamin to Europe, as she was terrified at the idea of crossing the ocean. Possibly she had the memory of a difficult crossing as a child. She had many relatives in Philadelphia, (Cash, Guest, Leacocks, North, Wilkinson).

Deborah was very helpful in Franklin's businesses, kept their home economically, and always wrote to him often. In 1774, when she suffered a stroke and could not write, no one told Franklin, thinking to spare him distress. When she died on December 19, 1774, she had not seen her husband for nine years.

John Read, 1677–September 2 or 12, 1724, a carpenter and building contractor, married in 1701, Sarah White, 1675–1761, baptized December 16, 1675. Their marriage bond, issued by the Court of the Bishop of Lichfield on February 3, 1700/1 identifies them: Johanne Read de Civit, Middlesex, Attis 25 Annor, a bachelor. The Bride, Saram White de Birmingham, Attis 20 Annor, a spinster. It states the marriage would be solemnized in the Face of the Parish Church of Hansworth, a suburb of Birmingham. They may have decided to marry elsewhere, as there is no record at Hansworth. Sarah (Saram) White was the daughter of Joseph White and Deborah Cash (she was buried July 17, 1703), whose father was Abraham Cash, born 1623 at Birmingham, England.

John Read was well off but in 1721 he foolishly stood security for William Vanhoesdonck Riddleston, an international confidence man, who bilked Read and others before leaving the colony. In 1724, Read mortgaged his property and died that same year in September, leaving debts.

FOLGER
II. Josiah Franklin, December 23, 1657–January 16, 1745, was born at Ecton, England, and served an apprenticeship under his brother John, a dryer at Banbury, Oxfordshire. He married first, about 1677, at Ecton, England, Ann Child, who died early in 1689, leaving seven children. They had come to America in 1682. Josiah married second, on November 25, 1789, Abiah Folger, August 15, 1667–1752. By Abiah he had ten more children, of whom Benjamin Franklin was the eighth.

Abiah Folger was the daughter of Peter Folger, ca. 1618–1690, who married in 1644, Mary Morrill who died 1704. Mary Morrill was the granddaughter of Isaac Morrill, 1588–December 1661, who married in England about 1625, Sarah Clement, 1600–1673. She died at Roxbury, Massachusetts. Isaac Morrill came on the *Lion*, arriving September 16, 1632.

Mary Morrill was a servant in the Reverend Hugh Peter's home. Peter Folger "bought her service" from the Reverend Peter for £20, and married her in 1644. Peter and Mary Folger lived at Martha's Vineyard for some years, where he was a surveyor and taught school, and he learned to speak the Indian language fluently. His father died in 1660, and he moved to Nantucket, on their invitation, to come there to act as an interpreter and as a miller and weaver. He had a land grant and took charge of the first mill on the island. In July 1673, he was elected clerk of courts and held the office for many years. He wrote a poem occasioned by King Philip's war on April 23, 1676: "A Looking Glass for the Times; Or, The Former Spirit of New England Revived in This Generation." Peter Folger was the son of John Folger who came from Norwich, England, in 1635 with the Reverend Hugh Peter, and settled at Watertown, Massachusetts, where he had a

grant of six acres. He married Meribah Gibbs in England, daughter of John Gibbs. He removed to Martha's Vineyard in 1641 where he died in 1660. Meribah (Gibbs) Folger died before 1664.

WHITE

III. Thomas Franklin, October 23, 1598–1682, was born at Ecton, England, married Jane White, niece of Col. White of Banbury. He was a smith. Thomas and Jane Franklin had nine children.

IV. Henry Franklin, a smith by trade. Nothing is known of him, except that he was born at Ecton, and was the son of Thomas Franklin.

V. Thomas Franklin, born 1540, a blacksmith, of Northamptonshire, England, was imprisoned for a year and a day for his writings. He was living during the reign of Henry VIII, 1491–1547.

The Franklins were seated at Ecton, Northampton, England, before the parish registers began in 1555. The family lived in that same village for at least 300 years, on a freehold of about 30 acres, where they followed the smith's business.

It has been determined that there are no descendants of Thomas Franklin, 1598–1682, who bear the surname of Franklin.

Chapter 12

ELBRIDGE GERRY

1744–1814

MASSACHUSETTS

Elbridge Gerry

ELBRIDGE GERRY, merchant, statesman, governor of Massachusetts, vice president of the United States, was graduated from Harvard College in 1762, placing twenty-ninth in his class of fifty-two. He then entered his father's counting house and eventually became one of the wealthiest and most enterprising merchants in Marblehead, Massachusetts. The Gerrys owned their own vessels, in which they shipped dried codfish to Barbados and Spanish Ports, and returned with bills of exchange and goods.

Elbridge Gerry became a Master Mason in the Philanthropic Lodge, Marblehead, Massachusetts, in 1769. On December 1, 1771, a town meeting was held at Marblehead, brought about by the circular letter to the other colonies and the resolves of Samuel Adams' Boston Committee of Correspondence. Thomas Gerry, Sr., father of the signer, was moderator of the meeting. Elbridge and Thomas Gerry, Jr., were on the committee that crafted the fiery resolves which were adopted. All three of the Gerrys were members of the local Committee of Correspondence, appointed in the December 1 meeting. In May 1772, he was elected representative to the General Court where he met Samuel Adams and immediately fell completely under his influence.

Gerry was reelected to the General Court in May 1773 and immediately was placed on the standing Committee of Correspondence. He and the entire committee resigned in disgust in 1774, after a mob burned to the ground the smallpox isolation hospital which Gerry and other prominent men had built at their own expense. Public opinion protected the culprits from punishment as they had not understood that isolation would help prevent the spread of smallpox.

When the Boston Port Bill began to be enforced, Marblehead became a leading port of entry for patriotic donations. Elbridge Gerry and Colonel Azor Orne agreed to receive and forward these supplies to Boston.

In August 1774, he was elected to an Essex County convention; and in October, to the first Provincial Congress where he was appointed to the Executive Committee of Safety. He was reelected to both positions early in 1775. British spies had learned that the Americans had amassed ammunition which they wanted to confiscate. They also wanted to capture Adams and Hancock and those allied with them. On the night of April 18, 1775, Gerry and two American colonels were in bed at the Menotomy Tavern on the road which the British took to Lexington, when Paul Revere made his famous ride. A detachment of redcoats came to search the house; all three gentlemen escaped in their night clothes and hid in a nearby corn field. On June 16, 1775, the night before the battle of Bunker Hill, he met with General Warren.

Gerry spent the rest of 1775 raising troops, procuring ammunition, and other supplies for the Provincial Army, and collecting materials for fortifications. His business and shipping activities made him a valuable man for these tasks, and he worked with energy, economy, and efficiency.

He refused an appointment as admiralty judge of the province, and continued his work in the supply department until January 25, 1776, when he left Boston with John Adams to go to Philadelphia as a Massachusetts delegate to the Second Continental Congress. Gerry took his seat in the Continental Congress on February 9, 1776, and on the seventeenth he was appointed one of five members of a standing committee for overseeing the Treasury Board.

After the long debates of June 10, 1776, the question of independence was postponed to July 1 to give the middle colonies an opportunity to have authority to vote in favor of independence. Gerry was present on July 2, 1776, for the vote, but left Philadelphia, worn out by his labors. On July 11, he wrote to John and Samuel Adams, requesting that they sign the engrossed copy of the Declaration of Independence for him; however, he signed in his own right when he returned to congress on September 3, 1776.

In January 1776, Gerry was reelected to the Continental Congress and continued in that service until 1785. He signed the Articles of Confederation on November 15, 1777, and was again a member of the Congress in 1782. On March 1, 1783, he was a member of the Confederation Congress.

It should be noted that Gerry's actions in Congress, like those of Robert Treat Paine and others, supported all resolutions against theatrical entertainments, horse racing and other such diversions. He was in agreement with those who recommended days of fasting, humiliation, and prayer.

Gerry's last appearance in Congress was on November 2, 1785. Early in 1786, he took his seat in the Massachusetts House of Representatives to which he had been elected in the spring of 1785. He was appointed to the Federal Convention of 1787 which framed the Constitution of the United States. At the start, he advocated a strong central national government, but he was opposed to the Constitution which was adopted. He believed that both the executive and the legislative branches were granted

powers that were ambiguous and dangerous and he refused to sign it. He published his anti–Federalist beliefs as *Observations on the New Constitution, and on the Federal and State Conventions.*

The Republican Party elected Gerry to the first United States Congress after the Constitution was adopted. He was reelected in 1791, but refused to stand for election in 1793 and retired to his family and farm at Cambridge, Massachusetts.

On June 20, 1797, President John Adams sent him, with Charles C. Pinckney and John Marshall, to try to improve some post-war relations. France demanded a cash payment from the United States, and tried to force the three Americans to pay a personal bribe. They refused, and the XYZ Mission failed. Pinckney and Marshall departed but Gerry remained because Prince Charles de Talleyrand convinced him that France would declare war if he left. He refused to negotiate without full powers, but President Adams published the *XYZ Dispatches* and recalled Gerry. He arrived at Boston on October 1, 1798. President Adams did not name Talleyrand's three agents (Bellamy, Hauteval, and Hottinguer) when he made a formal report to Congress, but simply called them X, Y, and Z.

Gerry was elected governor of Massachusetts in April 1810. During his second administration, his famous "Gerrymander" bill was repealed January 16, 1812. The bill had redistricted of Massachusetts to give the Republicans a number of state senators in excess of their voting strength. In an election of April 1812, ex–Governor Strong defeated Gerry by a majority of 1200 votes in a total of over 100,000. Two weeks after leaving the governorship, on June 8, 1812, the Republican Congressional Caucus nominated him for vice president on the ticket with James Madison. Vice President Gerry took the oath of office on March 4, 1813, at his Cambridge home.

In 1892, a small bust of Gerry was placed in the Senate Chamber of the United States Capitol.

Additional Information

Elbridge Gerry was a small, dapper gentleman, possessed of pleasant manners, but never very popular because of his aristocratic traits. He had no sense of humor, frequently changed his mind on important issues, and was suspicious of the motives of others.

John Adams thought he showed an "obstinacy that will risk great things to secure small ones." However, in his favor, he was a conscientious businessman who paid attention to detail. His patriotism and integrity could never be doubted.

Dr. Benjamin Rush wrote that he was "a genuine friend to republication forms of government." One of Gerry's own statements was "I hold it to be the duty of every citizen, though he may have but one day to live, to devote that day to the good of his country."

In May 1787, he purchased his beautiful estate in Cambridge, Massachusetts, a property which had been confiscated from a loyalist. This home, later named Elmwood, was owned by James Russell Lowell. Mr. Gerry had been well-to-do in 1800, but had suffered losses and left debts which consumed all his estate except the Cambridge home.

On November 23, 1814, in Washington, D.C., he died in his carriage on his way to preside over the Senate. He was seized of a hemorrhage of the lungs and died within twenty minutes. Congress paid his burial expenses, but the House rejected a bill introduced by Senator Christopher Gore and passed by the Senate, for paying the vice president's salary to his widow for the remainder of his term.

Gerry's monument in the Congressional Cemetery at Washington, D.C., bears this inscription:

The Tomb of
ELBRIDGE GERRY
Vice President of the United States
who died suddenly in this city on his
way to the Capitol, as President of the Senate
November 23, 1814,
Aged 70

Genealogy

I. Elbridge Gerry, July 17, 1744–November 23, 1814, was the third son of Thomas and Elizabeth (Greenleaf) Gerry. He married, on January 12, 1786, Ann Thompson of New York, and to them were born three sons and six daughters.

His children were: Catherine, 1787; Eliza, 1790; Ann, 1791; Elbridge, 1793; Thomas Russell, 1794; Helen Maria, 1796; James Thompson, 1797; Eleanor Sandford, 1800; Emily Louisa, 1802.

THOMPSON
Ann Thompson, 1753–1849, wife of Elbridge Gerry, was the last surviving widow of a signer of the Declaration of Independence. She was buried in Old Cemetery in New Haven, Connecticut. Their daughter, Emily Louise (Louisa) died in 1894, and was the last surviving child of a signer.

Ann Thompson was the daughter of New York merchant James Thompson and Catharine Walton, born about 1729, who were married on the night of April 21, 1753. Catharine's sister Mary married in 1749, signer Lewis Morris.

Catharine Walton was the youngest daughter of New York merchant Jacob Walton and his first wife, Maria Beekman. Maria Beekman died before March 1760, and he married second, March 11, 1760, Miss Polly Cruger, daughter of Henry Cruger.

GREENLEAF

II. Thomas Gerry, a mariner, ca. 1710–1774, came from Newton Abbott, Devonshire, England, to America in 1730 as master of a vessel. On December 16, 1734, at Marblehead, Essex County, Massachusetts, he married Elizabeth Greenleaf, June 1, 1716–September 2, 1771. She was the daughter of Enoch and Rebecca (Russell) Greenleaf. Thomas Gerry married second, on May 6, 1773, Elizabeth Leman. He died July 13 (or 17), 1774. Grave records give his birth as March 15, 1702. His marriage record calls him Captain Thomas Gerry of Newton Bushel, Devon, England.

Most of the Gerry births in Devonshire took place at Wolborough and Newton Abbott. The only Thomas Gerry found was christened at Ashwater, Devonshire, on December 14, 1712; the father's name was Leonard Gerry.

Elizabeth Greenleaf, June 1, 1716–September 2, 1771, was the daughter of Enoch and Rebecca (Russell) Greenleaf, and was the mother of all the twelve children of Thomas Gerry. Enoch Greenleaf was born about 1665 and was the son of Enoch and Mary Greenleaf, of Malden, baptized March 20, 1617/8 in England, a dryer. He had an estate from his father in 1663 and removed to Boston.

Enoch Greenleaf was the son of Edmond Greenleaf of Newbury, a dryer,

who came to America in 1635 with his wife Sarah More and their children who were all born in England. He removed to Boston about 1650 and died in 1671.

Sara (Sarah) More was baptized December 13, 1588, at St. Peter's, Maldon, in Essex County, England. Her parents were Enoch and Catherine More who were married November 23, 1585. Catherine died or was buried October 11, 1593. Enoch More was baptized January 19, 1560/1. He was the son of Nicholas and Willamin More. By 1599, Enoch had remarried and moved to Haverhill, County Suffolk, where he had two daughters baptized.

Nicholas More died in 1594. His will was written by his son Samuel as clerk, August 18, 1590, and proved in Chelmsford by Samuel as attorney for his mother, October 22, 1594. Enoch and Nicholas, Jr., were witnesses. Willamin More's will was written in 1603 and proved in 1606.

Sara More and Edmond Greenleaf were married at the church of St. Giles, Langford, near Maldon, England, in July 1611.

Rebecca Russell was the daughter of Samuel, b. ca. 1645, and Elizabeth, b. 1653, (Elbridge) Russell, of Marblehead, Massachusetts, in 1674. Elizabeth was the daughter of Thomas and Rebecca (surname unknown) Elbridge.

Thomas Elbridge, Boston, a merchant and joint grantee of the patents February 29, 1632, to Aldsworth. He was an alderman of Bristol. He was the son of Giles Elbridge, an alderman of Bristol by the president and council of New England for Pemaquid, Maine. He came about 1650 to dispose of that interest. He was associated with the first who owned a fire engine in the metropolis, in 1680. He died in 1682; his wife Rebecca died in 1684.

Chapter 13

BUTTON GWINNETT

1735–1777

GEORGIA

BUTTON GWINNETT, merchant, governor of Georgia, patriot, came from Gloucestershire, England. Nothing is known about his education. Gwinnett's business life had its beginning when he became a partner with his father-in-law in the grocery business. He had an uncle, William Gwinnett, Bristol merchant, who probably influenced his becoming an exporter of goods from Bristol to the American colonies sometime before 1760. He was sole owner of the brig *Nancy*, but his mercantile ventures proved unsuccessful and he was indebted to a Bristol firm. The *Nancy* was seized under an attachment and sold by the sheriff to liquidate his debt.

Before September 1765, he had emigrated with his family to Savannah, Georgia, where he secured a store and was advertising in the *Georgia Gazette*. In October 1765, he purchased St. Catherine's Island, a tract of 36 square miles, off the coast of Georgia near the flourishing port of Sunbury. He set up as a planter and became acquainted with a group of settlers who had come from New England to Sunbury. One of these settlers was Lyman Hall who had migrated from Fairfield County, Connecticut.

Through his friendship with Lyman Hall, Gwinnett developed an interest in politics. In a letter to Roger Sherman, Lyman Hall wrote that he regarded Gwinnett as a "Whig to excess." He was justice of the peace in 1767-68 and in 1769 he was a member of the Georgia Colonial Assembly. During the next five years, however, financial or other problems with his plantation seem to have prevented his further involvement in public service. He moved to St. John's Parish in 1772; in 1773 creditors took his properties.

In January 1776, Gwinnett attended a meeting of the Georgia Council of Safety and was elected as one of the Georgia delegates to the Continental Congress. He arrived in Philadelphia on May 20, 1776, took part in the debates of the Congress, voted in favor of independence on July 2, and signed the Declaration of Independence on August 2, 1776. He arrived back in Savannah in late August.

His ambition was to be a general of the Georgia troops, but failing this he satisfied himself with his election in October 1776 as Speaker of the Georgia Assembly, and his reelection to the Continental Congress. In the months following, he played an important part in drafting the first constitution of Georgia, and in preventing Georgia from being absorbed into South Carolina.

Upon the death of Governor Archibald Bulloch on March 4, 1777, Gwinnett was commissioned president (governor) of the State of Georgia and commander in chief of the Army. On the same day, he was directed by the Council of Safety to draft militia and volunteers for a campaign against the British in which they were to cut off all supplies for the garrison at St. Augustine, Florida. About a week later, Gwinnett received a letter from John Hancock, president of the Continental Congress, then sitting in Baltimore, dated January 8, 1777. It read:

> I have the honour to inclose you a copy of an intercepted letter from the Governour of East-Florida to Lord George Germaine, containing, among other things, the most convincing proof of the treasonable conduct of Mr. George McIntosh of your state. This Gentleman it seems, is a Member of the Congress of Georgia, and under that character is secretly reporting, by every act in his

power, the designs of the British King and Parliament against us. The United States of America have hitherto suffered extremely from the misrepresentations of their enemies, but much more from the baseness and perfidy of their pretended friends. I have it therefore in command from Congress to request, that you will cause the said George McIntosh to be immediately apprehended, and take every other step in this matter which shall appear to you to be necessary for the safety of the United States of America.

The intercepted letter referred to here was from Governor Patrick Tonyn of East Florida, reporting to Lord George Germaine on receiving supplies of rice from the rebel colony of Georgia. Tonyn said that he expected one thousand more barrels to arrive and that Panton (a Georgia Tory) had executed the business and was greatly assisted by George McIntosh "one of the Rebel Congress of Georgia."

Gwinnett's new positions placed him above General Lachlan McIntosh, whose brother was now in disgrace, and he was ordered to arrest George McIntosh for treason and to place him in irons. The McIntosh brothers had been members of Georgia's first Provincial Congress; George had been a member of the Council of Safety, also. It is probable that Gwinnett already had suspicions about George McIntosh.

Button Gwinnett's new appointments were great honors and he was in the public's confidence for his ability and integrity. The McIntoshes were undoubtedly envious of him, and the general was losing the confidence of the people of Georgia.

Following a bungled expedition of Georgia troops upon the British in Florida, an inquiry was held which sustained Gwinnett. General Lachlan McIntosh

proclaimed him "a scoundrel and a lying rascal." The next morning on the outskirts of Savannah, both men were wounded in a duel. Gwinnett died three days later. General McIntosh recovered, was brought to trial, and was acquitted.

In 1818, Gwinnett County, Georgia, was created from parts of Jackson County and the Cherokee lands and was named in his honor. Gwinnett was elected to the Georgia Hall of Fame in 1955.

Additional Information

On December 7, 1824, *The Darien Gazette*, Darien, Georgia, carried a missing persons advertisement by William Roberts, c/o Hope Insurance Company, New York City: "Wanted. Information as to the heirs of Mrs. Ann Beling, daughter of Button Gwinnett and wife of Dr. Peter Belin (or Beline). They with the husband's children were living in Georgia in 1785." Gwinnett was probably named for his godmother, Miss Barbara Button, who never married. She was Anne Eames/Emes' cousin, and a descendant of Sir Thomas Button, an admiral and Arctic explorer. Having inherited wealth, Barbara Button was able to aid her cousin. When she died, Button Gwinnett was twenty years old. She left him £100. Gwinnett died insolvent on May 6, 1777, three days after his duel with General Lachlan McIntosh, of a gangrenous infection in his leg.

John Adams noted, "Hall and Gwinnett are both intelligent and spirited men, who made a powerful addition to our Phalanx." One of Gwinnett's autographs was sold at public auction in 1924 for $14,000; another in 1928 for $28,000. Yet another sold in 1927 for $51,000, but it was also signed by John Hancock, Robert Morris, and others. Most are owned by research libraries, universities, and historical societies.

On July 4, 1848, a monument honoring the Georgia signers of the Declaration of Independence was dedicated at Augusta, Georgia. In 1964, patriotic societies financed and erected a large memorial to Button Gwinnett in Colony Park Cemetery in Savannah, Georgia. The inscription states: "This memorial to Button Gwinnett, born 1735–died 1777, Georgia Signer of the Declaration of Independence, President of Georgia, whose remains buried in this cemetery are believed to be entombed hereunder."

Genealogy

I. Button Gwinnett was born at Down Hatherly, Gloucestershire, England, and was baptized there on April 20, 1735. He was the second son of the Reverend Samuel and Ann (Emes) Gwinnett. He married Ann Bourne on April 19, 1757, and they had four daughters. Three of the births were recorded in the registry of the Collegiate Church in Wolverhampton. The last date of birth recorded was 1762.

His children were: Amelia, 1758; Ann, 1759; Elizabeth, 1762; Ann again, 1764.

BOURNE

Ann Bourne and Button Gwinnett were married on April 19, 1757. She was the daughter of Aaron Bourne, a grocer of Wolverhampton. Her birth and death dates were not found.

EMES/EAMES

II. The Reverend Samuel Gwinnett married Anne Emes or Eames of Twyning. They had, besides Button, two sons baptized at St. Nicholas, Gloucestershire: Robert on August 22, 1731, and Samuel on August 22, 1738. Samuel married Emilia Button.

The Reverend Gwinnett's ancestors were residents of Wales from an early date. Gwinnett was originally the Welsh Gwynedd, the name of the northern part of Wales.

Anne Eames had prominent relatives in Herefordshire, England. The home of the Buttons was in Glamorganshire in Southern Wales.

Chapter 14

LYMAN
HALL

1724–1790

GEORGIA

Lyman Hall

LYMAN HALL, minister, doctor, patriot, governor of Georgia, graduated from Yale in 1747. He studied theology under his uncle Samuel Hall and in June 1749 began to preach at Bridgeport, Connecticut. He was ordained by the Fairfield West Consociation; however, in June 1751 he was dismissed by the Consociation following a hearing on charges of immoral conduct. The charges were proven and confessed by him. The Consociation, confident of his sincere repentance, voted to restore him to good standing in the ministry. He continued to preach for two years, filling vacant pulpits.

Hall gave up his ministry, studied medicine, and set up his practice at Wallingford, Connecticut. About 1754 or 1755 he, with a group of New England Congregationalists, moved to Dorchester near Charleston, South Carolina. By 1756, this entire colony had resettled in the Midway District on the coast of Georgia, where, in 1758, they founded the town of Sunbury in St. John's Parish.

Sunbury was not a healthful place, being at the edge of swamps infested with malaria-bearing mosquitoes. Hall's medical skills were much in demand and soon he bought a plantation.

Georgia was slow to join her sister colonies in the revolutionary movement, but St. John's Parish became the center of a revolutionary group. The royal governor, James Wright, reported that the head of the rebellion was in St. John's Parish, where the trouble was due to the "descendants of New England people of the Puritan independent sect."

When the Provincial Congress of Georgia failed to join the other colonies to protest British laws and acts, St. John's Parish, under Hall's leadership, held a convention and invited the other parishes to join them in sending delegates to the Continental Congress but received no cooperation. St. John's Parish acted alone and in 1775 elected Hall as their delegate. He was admitted to the Congress and although he could not vote, took part in the debates. When Georgia finally was brought to agreement in the revolutionary cause, Hall retained his seat in the Continental Congress. As a Georgia delegate, with Button Gwinnett and George Walton, he voted for independence on July 2 and signed the Declaration of Independence on August 2, 1776.

When Savannah fell in December 1778 and the British subjugated the Georgia coast, Hall's home and rice plantation were destroyed. He took his family to visit relatives in Wallingford, Connecticut. He returned to Georgia in 1782, settled in Savannah, and resumed his medical practice.

Dr. Hall was elected governor in 1783 and served one term during which the northern border of Georgia was adjusted, the public debt arranged, land offices were established, and treaties were made with the Cherokees. Hall recommended to the General Assembly, July 8, 1783, that a grant of land be set aside for the support of a state-supported institution of higher learning. The following year, Franklin College was chartered with an endowment of 40,000 acres of land. Franklin College is now the University of Georgia.

In 1818, Gwinnett, Hall, and Walton counties, Georgia were created. Hall County, named in honor of Lyman Hall, was taken from Franklin and Jackson counties and Cherokee lands.

Additional Information

John Adams thought Lyman Hall "intelligent and spirited." He was six feet tall, well educated, had good social habits, and was possessed of a well rounded character. He died on October 19, 1790, at his Shell Bluff Plantation in Burke County, below Augusta, Georgia. In 1848, his remains were moved to the Signers' Monument in Augusta. His original gravestone from his Shell Bluff Plantation was taken to Connecticut and placed in the Wallingford Cemetery.

In 1935, Lyman Hall, Button Gwinnett, and George Walton were admitted to the Georgia Hall of Fame. Their busts were placed in the rotunda of the Georgia Capitol Building.

Genealogy

I. Lyman Hall was born on April 12, 1724, at Wallingford, Connecticut, the son of John Hall and Mary Street. He married first, on May 20, 1752, Abigail Burr, daughter of Thaddeus and Abigail Burr, of Fairfield County, Connecticut. She died on July 8, 1753, without bearing children. Hall married second in October 1753, Mary Osborn, daughter of Samuel and Hannah Osborn, also of Fairfield. They had one son who died in 1791.

His children were: (by first wife) none; (by second wife) John, b. ?, d. 1791.

OSBORN

Mary (Osborn) Hall, Burke County, Georgia, applied for administration of the estate of the Honorable Lyman Hall on February 11, 1792. On May 19, 1792, Mary Hall, relict of the Honorable Lyman Hall, applied for administration with will annexed, on the estate of John Hall, deceased.

Mary Hall was in a list of tax defaulters September 14, 1793. Her executor, Joseph Watts, gave notice to debtors and creditors on January 22, 1794. The estate had not been settled March 13, 1797.

STREET

II. John Hall, 1692–June 18, 1773, married on March 5, 1716, Mary Street, April 16, 1698–October 12, 1778, daughter of Lieutenant Samuel and Hannah (Glover) Street of Wallingford, Connecticut. Lyman Hall was fourth of their eight children. Lieutenant Samuel Street, born at New Haven on July 27, 1667, married first, Madeline Daniels; second, July 14, 1690, Hannah Glover, who died July 3, 1715; third, on December 20, 1716, Elizabeth of unknown ancestry.

Hannah Glover, June 24, 1670–1715, was the daughter of John and Mary (Guppy) Glover who were married January 2, 1660. Mary Guppy was the daughter of John Guppy of Salem, Massachusetts, who was first a Weymouth freeman in 1653, and at Salem in 1672 when his wife was Abigail. He was of Charleston in 1678, and his wife was Elizabeth, with whom he joined the church in 1680. His will was dated April 19, proved May 13, 1695.

John Glover was the son of John Glover, son of Henry. John Glover was at New Haven in 1648, graduated from Harvard College 1651 and died in 1679.

Henry Glover was at New Haven, Connecticut, in 1647 or before. He came in the Elizabeth from Ipswich, England, in 1634, age twenty-four. He died in 1689 and his will was probated in October 1689.

The Reverend Samuel Street, born 1635, son of the Reverend Nicholas Street, graduated from Harvard College in 1664, and became one of the first settlers of Wallingford. He was installed as first pastor there, 1674, and remained until his death on January 17, 1717. He married, on November 3, 1664, Anna, daughter of Richard and Katherine Miles. Lieutenant Samuel Street was the second of their seven children. Anna Miles Street died July 19, 1730. Richard Miles was at Milford in 1639, at New Haven 1643. In 1651, he was a representative. His will dated December 28, 1664, names wife Catherine. She had been married previously, as the will mentions her children of a former husband.

The Reverend Nicholas Street/ Streete, born 1603, came from Taunton, England, but his birthplace is unknown. He was matriculated at Oxford, November 2, 1621, described as eighteen years of age, and from Somersetshire. He received his B.A. degree at Oxford on February 21, 1624/5. About 1638, he was at Taunton in Plymouth Colony and was a colleague of the Reverend William Hooke. He was ordained teacher of the church by Master Hooke, assisted by a Schoolmaster Bishop, and a Mr. Parker, husbandman.

The Reverend Nicholas Street followed the Reverend Hooke to New Haven and took his place as colleague of the Reverend John Davenport, September 26, 1659. He had sole charge of the First Church till his own death on April 22, 1674.

He married first, Ann Pole, daughter of Sir William Pole of Colyton, Devon, England, by whom he had three children; married second, Bethia Farmer after November 18, 1660; and third, Mary Newman (maiden name unknown), widow of Governor Francis Newman of New Haven in 1638, by whom he had five children. The Reverend Samuel Street was the first child of this third marriage.

LYMAN
III. John Hall, December 23, 1670– 1730, married on January 12, 1655, Mary Lyman, b. 1668, daughter of John and Dorcas (Plum/Plumbe) Lyman of Hartford, Connecticut. Dorcas was the daughter of John Plum/Plumbe, 1594– 1648, of Dorchester, who married in England, Dorothy (maiden name unknown) 1623–1725. John Plum/Plumbe came to Wethersfield by 1636, later removed to Branford and died there. His will was probated August 1, 1648.

John Lyman was born in England, September 1623, the son of Richard Lyman the first, who came with Elliott on the *Lion* in November 1631, bringing his wife, Sarah Osborn, and their children. John Lyman married on January 12, 1655, Dorcas Plum/Plumbe.

Richard Lyman of High Onger, England, was baptized October 30, 1580. He was at Roxbury in 1631, freeman June 11, 1633. He removed to Connecticut and was one of the original proprietors of Hartford where he died in 1640, leaving his widow Sarah (Osborn) Lyman. Sarah Osborn was born at High Ongar, baptized February 8, 1621. She was the daughter of Roger Osborn of Halstead, Kent County, England.

WALKER
IV. Samuel Hall, born May 21, 1648, at New Haven, died March 5, 1725, at Wallingford. He was the second son of John Hall and Jane Wallen. He went with the first planters to Wallingford in 1670, and married in May 1668, Hannah Walker, September 27, 1646–December 20, 1728. Samuel Hall was in King Philip's War; deputy to the General Court 1698– 1700; captain of the Train Band in 1704. He, with his brothers John and Thomas, signed the first Plantation Covenant at Wallingford.

Hannah Walker was the daughter of John Walker, who was at New Haven in

1639 and whose inventory was taken April 22, 1652. His widow Grace (maiden name unknown) married Edward Watson on July 1, 1652.

WALLEN

V. John Hall, ca. 1605–1676, the emigrant who came from Coventry, England, to Boston in 1633; removed to Hartford, then to New Haven in 1639. He married Jane Wallen in 1640. He was deputy to the General Court 1653–1661, and was freed from training in 1665, being then in his sixtieth year. He was at Wallingford in 1670, where he and his eldest son John were chosen selectmen. He died early in 1676, leaving a nuncupative will made on his deathbed.

Chapter 15

JOHN HANCOCK

1737–1793

MASSACHUSETTS

JOHN HANCOCK, merchant, patriot, politician, governor of Massachusetts, received his primary education at the Boston School. He attended Harvard College, graduating in 1754. Whether he exhibited great intelligence or held a high rank among his fellow students at Harvard is unknown.

John Adams wrote:

> Nor were his talents or attainments inconsiderable. They were far superior to many who have been much more celebrated. He had a great deal of political sagacity and insight into men. He was by no means a contemptible scholar or orator. Compared with George Washington or Knox, he was learned.

Upon graduation, he entered his uncle's mercantile office as a clerk in his counting house, to be trained as a merchant. In 1760, he was sent to London to learn the English aspects of their business, and to settle accounts for the House of Hancock.

While Hancock was in London, King George II died and he attended the state funeral. He remained there to view the coronation of King George III, and wrote home that it would be "the grandest thing I shall ever meet with."

Hancock was home in Boston in October 1761, and his Uncle Thomas' health was seriously impaired by frequent attacks of gout. He made John a partner on January 1, 1763, and died of apoplexy in 1764. He left his vast mercantile business to John Hancock. At twenty-eight Hancock was the wealthiest man in New England. He was trading in Holland, Spain, and Great Britain, as well as in Nova Scotia and the West Indies. Like most of the "merchant princes," Hancock apparently found illicit dealings profitable.

He joined several local lodges where current events and public concerns were discussed. He was a member of the Merchants' Club, the Long Room Club, the St. Andrews Masonic Lodge, F & A.M., and others. Although grievances were aired, no one was advocating disloyalty to the Crown. Among the members of the Long Room Club, however, were Paul Revere, Thomas Dawes, Samuel Adams, and Dr. Benjamin Church (who would later become a traitor). As British import duties and other taxes were increased by acts of Parliament, the resentment of the colonists was emerging. During 1765, the Stamp Act was enacted, and the merchants were severely affected. He protested the act to his English correspondents and, when the opportunity arose he ran for the office of selectman for the town of Boston and won. His political career had begun. In 1766, he was chosen a representative of Boston in the General Assembly of the province.

In February 1767, fire destroyed more than twenty buildings in Boston, some of which belonged to Hancock. He contributed a large sum to the people made homeless by the fire, as well as giving many gifts to the churches and meeting houses.

In 1768, he was accused of having smuggled cargo ashore from his own sloop *Liberty*, which carried a large cargo of Madeira wine. He engaged John Adams to defend him, but after a while the case was dropped. The *Liberty* was condemned, converted into an armed coast guard vessel and renamed *Gaspée*. The *Gaspée* was attending a British warship which was stationed at Rhode Island to enforce the navigational laws. On June 9, 1772, the *Gaspée* ran aground on Namquit Point, about seven miles from Providence, and was stranded by the receding tide. That night some men from

Providence captured the crew and set fire to the sloop, which later exploded. This was one of the first overt acts of resistance by the American colonists (see chapter 21 for information on Stephen Hopkins). The affair did much to enhance Hancock's local prestige and made him a symbol of the patriotic cause.

During the period between 1772 and 1774, Hancock supplied Boston's first street lamps. He also gave them their first concert hall, but stipulated that no British officers should ever be admitted. On March 5, 1774, Hancock made a speech on the anniversary of the Boston Massacre. He spoke fearlessly in his denunciation of it, and greatly offended Governor Thomas Hutchinson. He had been elected speaker of the Provincial Assembly and was an elected a member of the Executive Council. Samuel Adams' influence was everywhere and he helped Hancock become a favorite so that he won various local offices. In 1774, the General Court became the Provincial Congress and he was chosen its president.

Many events occurred in 1774: John Hancock cut himself off from the Crown; his great friend Samuel Adams and the other delegates from Massachusetts proceeded to Philadelphia to attend the First Continental Congress; the Boston Port Bill came into effect and the British government closed the harbor to all cargoes on May 13, 1774. The Whigs and Tories became increasingly hostile to each other, and threats were being made on Hancock's life. Nevertheless, he accepted the appointment as chairman of the Committee of Safety. When more British troops arrived, he suggested burning the city to get rid of them but this would have gained nothing and most of his own property would have been lost. Hancock

was president of the first and second Provincial Congresses in 1774-75, and he was regarded as a dangerous revolutionary.

Although Hancock did not have the military experience and was not physically strong enough, one of his great disappointments was that he wanted to be commander in chief of the Army. John Adams nominated George Washington and Samuel Adams seconded the motion. John Hancock was unable to hide his disappointment and it affected his friendship with both men.

In April 1775, it was evident that many abuses against the citizens were occurring. The Whigs were sending their families to safer places. Samuel Adams and John Hancock were on their way to Lexington, and were spending the night of April 18-19 in the old Hancock parsonage. General Thomas Gage, intent on arresting them, marched his men to Lexington and Concord on April 18, but Paul Revere warned them and they escaped to safety in Woburn.

In May 1775, Hancock became a delegate to the Second Continental Congress at Philadelphia, and was elected its first president.

On June 7, 1775, Richard Henry Lee, chairman of the Virginia delegation, presented his famous motion for declaring independence. A three week delay was requested in the hope that more time for the colonial assemblies to consider it would achieve a unanimous vote. By July 1, South Carolina and Pennsylvania had been won over, and on the morning of July 2, Caesar Rodney's vote after an all night ride brought Delaware into agreement. New York delegates abstained from the voting as they were bound by their instructions. The vote was unanimous among the twelve colonies voting.

Two days of debate and oratory went on, and about two o'clock in the afternoon of July 4, "The great white paper was reported out of committee to the House with a recommendation for approval, and was immediately ratified." The long wait had ended, and President John Hancock and Secretary Charles Thomson were ordered to sign the declaration. Hancock now made his statement, "I write so that George III may read without his spectacles." As first published the Declaration was sent abroad with only John Hancock's official signature. He signed the engrossed parchment copy of the Declaration of Independence on August 2, 1776.

On August 8, 1776, as president of the Continental Congress, Hancock confirmed the appointment of John Paul (Alias) Jones to a captaincy in the United States Navy. In 1776, Hancock had been commissioned major-general of the Massachusetts Militia. In August 1778, he commanded the Massachusetts troops in the unsuccessful Rhode Island expedition. He resigned as president of the Continental Congress on October 29, 1777, and retired to Quincy, Massachusetts. Hancock had presided over the Continental Congress during the period when independence was voted for, through the signing of the Declaration of Independence. He signed the Articles of Confederation on November 15, 1777, and was one of its ratifying officers on July 9, 1778.

Hancock was appointed Speaker of the Massachusetts House of Representatives in 1779, and was a member and president of the Massachusetts Constitutional Convention in 1780. When the state government began operating, he was the first governor of the Commonwealth, 1780–1785. He was again governor,

1787–1793, and was serving his ninth term at his death.

Additional Information

Hancock lost some of his wealth during the revolution, but he remained socially and financially prominent, and was generous in various public endeavors. He died at the age of fifty-six, while serving in his ninth term as governor of Massachusetts. He was buried in the Old Granary Burying Ground in the ancestral tomb, beside his Uncle Thomas. In 1895, the Commonwealth of Massachusetts placed a granite monument marking Hancock's grave. The Sons of the American Revolution placed a bronze flag holder at his gravesite.

Genealogy

I. John Hancock, January 12, baptized 16, 1737–October 8, 1793, son of the Reverend John and Mary (Hawke) Hancock, Jr., was born at Quincy, Massachusetts. His father died when he was seven and he was adopted by his wealthy uncle Thomas and his wife Lydia (Henchman) Hancock, of Boston. His uncle died August 1, 1764, and John Hancock became the wealthiest merchant in New England. He married, at Fairfield, Connecticut, on August 28, 1775, Dorothy Quincy.

His children were: Lydia, born and died 1776; John George Washington, 1778.

QUINCY

Dorothy Quincy, wife of John Hancock, married second, July 27, 1796, James Scott. She was the youngest daughter of Edmund Quincy V, 1703–1788, who was graduated from Harvard College in 1722. He married, April 25, 1725, Elizabeth Wendall, August 20, 1704–-November 7, 1769, daughter of Abraham Wendall. Edmund Quincy V was judge of the Common Pleas Court, and acting magistrate of Suffolk County, Massachusetts. He wrote a book, *Hemp Husbandry*, which was published in 1765.

Edmund Quincy IV, October 14, 1681–February 23, 1738, was graduated from Harvard College in 1699. He was a representative in 1713; member of the Governor's Council; colonel of a Dorchester regiment 1715 and 1718; a justice of the Supreme Court of the province 1718–1738; sent by the province to the English Court of the sovereign in December 1737. He died at London of smallpox on February 23, 1738, and was buried in Bunhill Field, England, where the General Court of Massachusetts erected a monument to his memory. His will dated December 10, 1737, was probated April 18, 1738. He married, after May 16, 1680, Dorothy Flynt, daughter of the Reverend Josiah Flynt, born August 24, 1645, and Esther (Willett) Flint/Flynt, and died July 26, 1737, age eighty-nine. Esther was the daughter of Captain Thomas Willett. Edmund Quincy IV was the son of Edmund Quincy III, March 15, 1628–January 7, 1698, born in England, the only son among eleven children of Edmond Quincy II, married on July 26, 1648, Joanna Hoar, 1625–May 16, 1680, daughter of the widow Joanna Hoar who died December 21, 1661. Quincy was a freeman in 1665 and a lieutenant and major of a Suffolk regiment. He married second, on December 8, 1680, Elizabeth (Gookin) Eliot, widow of the Reverend John Eliot, Jr.

Edmond Quincy II, baptized 1602 and died 1635, married in England, July 14, 1623, Judith Pares. He arrived in America September 4, 1633, with the Reverend John Cotton of Wigsthorpe, County Northampton, England. He had a land grant at Braintree, Massachusetts, in 1635, and died the same year. His widow married second, Moses Paine, and third, Robert Hall.

Edmond Quincy I, 1559–1627/8, of Wigsthorpe, Northampton, England, married on October 14, 1593, Ann Palmer.

HAWKE

II. The Reverend John Hancock, Jr., was born at Lexington, Massachusetts, June 1, 1702. He graduated from Harvard College in 1719 A.B., A.M. and was librarian at Harvard 1723–1726. He was ordained at Quincy on November 2, 1726, First Church in Braintree; delivered the Artillery Election Sermon in 1730. He married Mary (Hawke) Thaxter, widow of Samuel Thaxter, and lived at Quincy, Massachusetts, 1726–1744. He died May 7, 1744, age 41.

CLARK

III. The Reverend John Hancock, Sr., was born at Cambridge, Massachusetts, March 1, 1671, and died there December 5, 1752. He was graduated from Harvard College 1689 A.B., A.M. and was ordained at Lexington November 2, 1698. He married, November 11, 1700, Elizabeth Clark, lived at Lexington 1697–1752, and died there at the age of eighty-one.

PRENTICE

IV. Deacon Nathaniel Hancock, December 18, 1638/9– April 12, 1719, married first March 8, 1663/4, Mary Prentice. He married second, on December 26, 1699, at Lexington, Sarah Green, daughter of John Green. He was a freeman in 1668.

Mary Prentice, November 25, 1644–1699, was the daughter of Henry and Joanne Prentice who were at Cambridge in 1640; he was an original proprietor and a freeman at Sudbury in 1650. He died June 9, 1654. His first wife was Elizabeth White, whom he married in England November 26, 1638; she died May 13, 1643. He married second, in 1643/4, Joanne (or Jane); she married second, July 24, 1663, John Gibson.

V. Nathaniel Hancock was at Cambridge, Massachusetts, with wife Joan in 1634. He died there before 1652.

Chapter 16

BENJAMIN
HARRISON V

1726–1791

VIRGINIA

BENJAMIN HARRISON, statesman, governor of Virginia, tobacco farmer, attended the College of William and Mary but left without a degree to manage the large Harrison estate when his father was killed by lightning on July 12, 1745.

In 1749, Harrison was elected to the House of Burgesses, sometimes serving as Speaker, until it was dissolved by Royal Governor Dunmore. Harrison was only nineteen when he inherited his father's estate, and he responsibly enlarged it. He grew tobacco, bred horses, built his own ships, and established a large shipyard.

He became a member of the General Assembly in 1752 and served on the Committee of Property and Grievances and the Committee of Trade. In 1761, he was a justice for Charles City County.

Because Harrison was a member of a prominent and influential family, and a man of personal ability, Royal Governor Francis Fauquier offered him a seat on the Executive Council. Harrison declined the governor's offered appointment, and pledged his support to the patriotic burgesses of Virginia in their resistance to the oppressive acts of the British government.

Harrison was a member of a committee in the House of Burgesses which drew up their vigorous protest to the Virginia colonial agent against the Stamp Act of 1764. He assisted in the preparation of correspondence to the House of Commons and the House of Lords which opposed the Stamp Act. Still, in 1765, he was one of the conservatives who were opposed to Patrick Henry's resolutions. He was also opposed to the Townshend Acts of 1767. By 1772, he was urging that the importation of slaves be curbed and heavily taxed.

In 1773, Harrison helped the Virginia Committee of Correspondence plan their program of resistance. When the House of Burgesses was dissolved by Dunmore in May 1774, he joined his fellow members in sending out a call for a general congress of the colonies. He was elected a delegate to the Continental Congress by the convention which met in August 1774 at Philadelphia. He attended the first meeting on September 5, 1774, in Carpenters' Hall. He chaired the early debates on the Articles of Association, and signed them on October 20, 1774.

John Adams wrote, "The gentlemen of Virginia appear the most spirited and consistent of any." Much later, Benjamin Harrison was a victim of Adams' tactless, unkind pen, although Washington and others did not agree. Adams thought him a fat, indolent man, but was deeply impressed when Harrison said he would have come to Philadelphia on foot to attend the Continental Congress, rather than not come at all.

Dr. Benjamin Rush noted that Harrison "had strong state prejudices and was hostile to the leading men from the New England states."

When he first went to Philadelphia, he shared a house with Peyton Randolph and George Washington. Randolph was his brother-in-law; George Washington's wife was Mrs. Harrison's aunt. Harrison was retained in the Virginia delegation until 1778.

Meanwhile, Harrison represented Charles City County in the Virginia Conventions of 1775 and 1776. When the Virginia State government was organized in 1776, he was elected to the new House of Delegates, returning each year until 1781.

Harrison's service in the Continental Congress was notable. His speeches were brief and to the point, and he rarely participated in the debates. When members of the Committee of Secret Correspondence for foreign affairs were chosen in November 1775, he was the first to be selected.

George Washington depended upon his guidance in legislative matters concerning the army. In March 1776, he was on the Marine Committee; in June he was appointed to the newly established Board of War and Ordinance. Though never on a treasury committee, he did serve on several committees dealing with financial problems.

He was Chairman of the Whole from March 1776 to August 1777, and presided over the debates which preceded the vote for independence on July 2, 1776. As Chairman of the Whole, it was Harrison who read Richard Henry Lee's Independence Resolution on July 1, 1776. He voted in favor of independence on July 2 and signed the engrossed copy of the Declaration of Independence on August 2, 1776.

Benjamin Harrison retired from the Continental Congress in October 1777 and was elected to the House of Delegates. He was chosen Speaker in May 1778, and held the office until 1781.

When Governor Thomas Nelson (his second cousin) resigned in November 1781, Harrison was elected to the governorship, then reelected twice. In 1784, he was once more elected to the House of Delegates and remained a member till his death.

At the Virginia Convention of 1788, called to ratify the United States Constitution, Harrison was chairman of the Committee on Privileges and Elections. He was devoted to the Union, but declared opposition to the Constitution as it was presented. He thought a Bill of Rights should precede, not follow, its adoption. When overruled, he fully supported the new United States government and the Constitution.

On April 1, 1791, Harrison was elected to the Virginia Legislature, but passed away on April 24, 1791.

Additional Information

Benjamin Harrison was related to most of the leading pioneer families of Virginia, either by descent or by marriage. In the Continental Congress, Braxton, Nelson, and the Lee brothers were his cousins; Peyton Randolph, its first president, was his brother-in-law. His brother, Carter Henry Harrison, married Susanna Randolph who was a sister of Jane Randolph, mother of Thomas Jefferson.

Benjamin Harrison was a very large man, standing six feet four inches tall and weighing about two hundred and fifty pounds. In Congress, he preferred making short, plainly worded speeches. Thomas Jefferson thought he had made the "readiest and most successful remarks ever heard in Congress." General Washington leaned heavily upon him for legislative matters pertaining to the army. Harrison's bawdy humor was said to have broken the tension in committee rooms. Even John Adams wrote that Harrison had "contributed many pleasantries that steadied rough sessions."

When John Hancock was elected president of the Continental Congress, Benjamin Harrison picked him up bodily and placed him in the presiding officer's chair. At the signing of the Declaration of Independence, there were tense moments. Harrison quipped to Elbridge Gerry who was at the table:

I shall have a great advantage over you, Mr. Gerry, when we are all hung for what we are now doing. From the size and weight of my body I shall die in a few minutes, but from the lightness of your body you will dance in the air an hour or two before you are dead.

Apparently the only time Harrison was angered was when Samuel Adams engineered the cancellation of a ball in Martha Washington's honor.

Benedict Arnold, the traitor and former general in the United States Army, in command of two thousand British troops, landed on the James River late in 1780 and began ravaging the homes there. When they reached Berkeley, Arnold ordered the ancestral portraits of the Harrisons thrown on a bonfire.

Benjamin Harrison died of an attack of gout on April 24, 1791, and was buried in the family cemetery at Berkeley Hundred. The Williamsburg Chapter of the Daughters of American Revolution honored Harrison's memory by erecting a bronze plaque in the Berkeley Plantation Graveyard (1927). In 1972, the Virginia Society of the Daughters of the American Colonists erected a monument honoring Colonel Benjamin Harrison V.

Genealogy

I. Benjamin Harrison V, August 15, 1726–April 24, 1791, was born and died at Berkeley in Charles City County, Virginia. He married Elizabeth Bassett, his second cousin, in 1748, and they had eight children, one of whom was William Henry Harrison, ninth president of the United States.

His children were: Elizabeth, 1751; Anna, 1753; Lucy, ca. 1755; Benjamin, 1755; Carter Bassett, 1757; Nathaniel,

1759; Sarah between 1765 and 1770; William Henry, 1773.

BASSETT

Elizabeth Bassett, December 13, 1730–ca. 1792, wife of Benjamin Harrison, the signer, was the daughter of Col. William Bassett IV, July 8, 1709–before 1752, and Elizabeth Churchill, ca. 1710–April 1779. In 1978, the Virginia Society, Daughters of the American Colonists, erected a monument honoring Elizabeth Bassett, wife of signer Benjamin Harrison.

Elizabeth (Churchill) Bassett married second, William Dawson, president of the College of William and Mary. She was the daughter of William Bassett III, baptized at North Aston, Oxfordshire, England December 2, 1649. He probably came to Bushy Park, Middlesex County, Virginia, before October 5, 1703. He married Elizabeth (Armistead) Wormley, widow of Ralph Wormly, secretary of the Virginia Colony. Elizabeth Armistead Wormly who died November 16, 1716.

William Churchill was the son of John Churchill of North Aston, Oxfordshire, born 1591, who married in 1626, Dorothy (surname unknown). John Churchill was the son of Henry Churchill, 1565–1628, who married in 1589, Bridget, surname unknown, 1565–1625. Henry Churchill's father, Richard Churchill, 1524–1592, was also of North Aston, Oxfordshire, England.

Elizabeth Armistead, died 1716, was the daughter of John and Judith Armistead, probably of Elizabeth City County, Virginia. John Armistead was probably born about 1640 and died at Gloucester County after 1688. He was the son of William Armistead, baptized at All Saints' Church, Kirkdeighton, Yorkshire,

August 3, 1610. He lived in Elizabeth City and Gloucester counties in Virginia and died before 1666. He had married in 1632, Ann Ellis at Giggleswick, Yorkshire, England.

William Armistead was the son of Anthony Armistead of Kirkdeighton, Yorkshire, who was born about 1587 and married by license in 1608, Frances Thompson.

William Bassett III was born at New Kent County, Virginia, about 1676 and died at Eltham October 11, 1723. Probably married at Carter's Creek, Gloucester County, November 23, 1693, Joanna Burwell, born about 1675. She probably died at Eltham October 7, 1727. Joanna Burwell was the daughter of Lewis Burwell II and Abigail Smith, daughter of Anthony and Martha (Bacon) Smith. (To continue the Burwell-Smith ancestry, see the genealogy section in chapter 35 about signer Thomas Nelson.)

William Bassett, Jr., was probably at Newport, Isle of Wight, removed to Blissland in New Kent County, and died between August 28, 1671, and January 4, 1671/2. His wife was Bridget Cary, daughter of Miles Cary.

Miles Cary was baptized January 30, 1622, at All Saints' Church, Bristol, England, the son of John and Alice (Hobson) Cary. He was a draper, lived at Windmill Point, Warwick County, Virginia. He married before 1646, Anne, daughter of Thomas Taylor. Miles Cary was killed during the Dutch Raid at Hampton Roads on June 10, 1667.

Captain Thomas Taylor, mariner of Warwick County, was one of the original patentees in Elizabeth City County in 1662.

William Bassett, Sr., yeoman, was buried at Newport, Isle of Wight, on December 4, 1646. His wife was Ann.

CARTER

II. Benjamin Harrison IV, ca. 1695–July 12, 1745, was born and died at Berkeley. He was married about 1722, to Ann Carter. He was sheriff of Charles City and a burgess from 1736 to 1744. On July 12, 1745, Harrison and his two youngest daughters were killed by lightning at Berkeley. Ann Carter was born about 1702 and died between October 17, 1743, and August 4, 1745. She was the daughter of Robert "King" Carter, 1663/4–August 1732, of Corotoman, who married his second wife about 1701. She was Elizabeth (Landon) Willis, widow of Richard Willis and daughter of Thomas and Mary Landon of Grendenhill, Hereforeshire, England, and at Williamsburg, Virginia, about 1684; Thomas Landon died July 3, 1719. He was the son of Sylvanus and Anne Landon of Grendenhill, Herefordshire, who died in 1681. Robert Carter was a burgess, 1695–1699; treasurer of the Colony, 1694–1732; member of the King's Council, 1699–1732; acting governor 1726–1727. His estate included 300,000 acres of land, one thousand slaves, and £10,100. He was the son of John Carter, ca. 1613–June 10, 1669, and Sarah Ludlow, his fourth of five wives. John Carter was the son of William Carter of Casstown, Hereford County and the Middle Temple, England. He came to Virginia about 1649 and built the ancestral home Corotoman in Lancaster County, Virginia. His will was dated 1669. In another record, John Carter is given as "possibly the son" of John Carter, citizen and vintner of London, 1574–1630, and his wife Bridget Benion who died before 1630 and was buried at Christ Church, Newgate Street, London.

BURWELL

III. Benjamin Harrison III, 1673–April 10, 1710, of Berkeley, Charles City

County, Virginia, married Elizabeth Burwell, daughter of Major Lewis and Abigail (Smith) Burwell. Elizabeth was a sister of Joanna Burwell, mother of Elizabeth Bassett (wife of Benjamin Harrison V, the signer). Honorable Benjamin Harrison III helped revise the laws of the Virginia Colony in 1700. He was treasurer; attorney general; and Speaker of the House of Burgesses.

CHURCHILL

IV. Benjamin Harrison, Jr., September 20, 1645–30 January 1712/3, married Hannah (Churchill?), February 13, 1651–February 16, 1698/9. He was born at Southwark, Surry County, Virginia, and died at Wakefield, Surry County, Virginia.

STRINGER?/SIDWAY

V. Benjamin Harrison, baptized December 1594–ca. 1648/9. He came to America before March 15, 1633, possibly as early as 1631, from the Isle of Wight. He became a tobacco planter, and in 1635 was the first clerk of the Royal Council. He was buried at Jamestown, Virginia. His widow, Mary, married second, Captain Benjamin Sidway. Her will was dated March 1, 1687/8, and was proved May 29, 1688.

Benjamin Harrison may have been the son of Thomas Harrison of Gobion's Manor in Northamptonshire who died before 1616. Thomas Harrison married about 1581, Elizabeth (Bernard?).

Chapter 17

JOHN HART

1708–1779

NEW JERSEY

JOHN HART, farmer, patriot, probably had his education at home. He was brought up on his father's farm and became a successful farmer of considerable means. He acquired land and had interests in fulling mills at Glen Moore and grist and fulling mills at Rocky Hill, New Jersey.

Hart was chosen justice of the peace in 1755; in 1761, he was elected to the twentieth New Jersey Assembly and was reelected to the twenty-first assembly. He continued in his service there until the assembly was dissolved in 1771.

Hart opposed the Stamp Act of 1765. He had also aided in the selection of delegates to the Colonial Congress at Albany, New York, in 1754.

In 1768, Hart favored the address to the king which declared that rights to tax the colonies were vested in the colonies only. He led the opposition against further provisions for royal troops in New Jersey.

Hart was elected, July 8, 1774, to the first Provincial Congress of New Jersey. In 1775, he was serving as judge of the Court of Common Pleas of New Jersey; in January 1775 he was made chairman of the township committees of Hunterdon County, and was also appointed to the Committee of Correspondence, and on August 17, 1775, was placed on the Committee of Safety.

While in the New Jersey legislature, John Hart promoted laws for the founding of schools, improvement of roads, and the administration of justice. He was elected to the Congress in 1774, but resigned the next year to serve as vice president of the Provincial Congress of New Jersey.

On June 22, 1776, the Provincial Congress elected him one of the New Jersey delegates to the Continental Congress to take the places of members who would not vote for independence. Hart was present to give his affirmative vote on July 2, 1776, and signed the Declaration of Independence on August 2, 1776.

John Hart was placed on the Committee of Safety on August 17, 1776. He had become known as a signer of the Declaration of Independence, and when the British invaded New Jersey in the fall of 1776, the Hessians and the British destroyed his mills, ravaged his farm, burned his timber, and butchered his cattle. His family fled to neighboring provinces ahead of the approaching armies, but his wife was on her death bed. Hart could only visit her stealthily at night. To avoid capture by his pursuers, often in need of food, he was forced to seek shelter in caves and outhouses, and on one occasion, to share with its occupant a dog's kennel.

He was elected to the first Assembly under the new state constitution of New Jersey and was unanimously chosen Speaker. He was occupied for the most part by his duties as a member of the Council of Safety, March 18, 1777–October 8, 1778.

Following the battles of Trenton and Princeton, when General Washington had secured the state of New Jersey, Hart summoned the legislature to convene at Trenton in January 1777. They again unanimously elected him Speaker and he held the position until failing health forced him to resign in the autumn of 1778.

John Hart and his children returned to his farm, which had been completely destroyed. His health failed, and he had no hope of rebuilding his fortunes.

In 1865, the state of New Jersey erected a monument in his honor, which was dedicated on July 4, 1865. Governor Joel Parker spoke at the dedication of the monument, saying:

> I am of opinion after a careful examination of the history of New Jersey, during and immediately preceding the Revolutionary War, that John Hart had greater experience in the colonial and state legislation of that day than any of his contemporaries, and that no man exercised greater influence in giving direction to the public opinion which culminated in independence.

Genealogy

I. John Hart, ca. 1712–May 11, 1779, was born at Stonington, Connecticut, and was baptized there on February 21, 1713. He was the son of Edward and Martha (Furman) Hart, who came to New Jersey shortly after his birth. John Hart was baptized a second time at the Presbyterian Church of Lawrence, by the Reverend Jedediah Andrees, pastor of the Presbyterian Church on Washington Square, Philadelphia.

His children were: Sarah, 1742; Jesse, 1744; Martha, 1746; Nathaniel, 1747; John, 1748; Susannah, 1750; Mildred, 1752; Abigail, 1754; Edward, 1755; Scudder, 1757; unnamed daughter, 1761; Daniel, 1762; Deborah, 1765.

SCUDDER

Hart married Deborah Scudder in 1740, and to them were born thirteen children. Deborah died October 26, 1776, age fifty-five. She was the daughter of Richard Scudder, 1671–March 14, 1754, who came from Newtown, Long Island, New York, by May 1709, the date of his deeds which transferred tracts of land to him. His wife was Hannah Reeder, ca. 1671–ca. 1734, by whom he had ten

children. They were the ancestors of the Scudder families at Ewing and Trenton, New Jersey. Richard Scudder was active in the civic affairs of Ewing. He was the son of John Scudder, 1645–1732, who lived at Newtown, Long Island, New York. In 1669, in England, he married Joanna, 1742–1732, the third daughter of Captain Richard Betts, of Newtown, a man prominent in the affairs of the town. John Scudder was the son of the first John Scudder, 1616–1685, who came to Salem, Massachusetts, from England on the James in 1635. With his brothers Thomas and Henry, he moved from Salem to Southold, in 1651, to Huntington in 1657; and by 1660, he was at Newtown, Long Island, and was prominent in the affairs of the town. He married, about 1642, Mary, b. 1623 in England, daughter of William and Dorothy King, who arrived at Salem, Massachusetts, in 1636.

John Scudder's father, Thomas Scudder the emigrant, came from England about 1635, bringing his wife Rachel and a family to Salem, Massachusetts. Thomas was probably a brother of the Reverend Henry Scudder of Colingborne, Wiltshire, England. Scudder was called "Old Goodman Scudders" and he died in 1658. His will dated 1657 named his wife, Elizabeth, who died in 1666.

FURMAN

II. Edward Hart, born in 1687 and died before 1752, married Martha Furman, at the Presbyterian Church of Newtown, Long Island, on May 17, 1712. They were apparently at Stonington, Connecticut, for a few months before moving to Hopewell, New Jersey. Edward Hart at some time raised a corps of volunteers known as the Jersey Blues, although the date and the reason are uncertain. He died before 1752.

HUNT

III. John Hart married Mary Hunt, daughter of Ralph and Mary Hunt, who were at Long Island in 1652. Hunt was a freeman of Connecticut in 1664 and died in 1677. Mary Hunt was a descendant of John and Jane (Coates) Hunt.

IV. John Heart who settled at Newtown, Long Island, New York, early in the seventeenth century. His will was probated in 1671.

Chapter 18

JOSEPH WORTH
HEWES

1730–1779

NORTH CAROLINA

Joseph Hewes

JOSEPH HEWES, merchant, patriot, began his life as a Quaker. Upon completion of his basic education, he was apprenticed to a Philadelphia merchant. He started his own mercantile business and amassed a small fortune. Sometime between 1756 and 1763, he moved to Edenton, North Carolina, and established a thriving mercantile and shipping trade. His chosen town regarded him as "one of the best and most agreeable men in the world," and "the patron and the greatest honor of the town."

In 1766, Hewes began a service as borough member of the Colonial Assembly, in which he continued until the royal government ended in 1775. In 1773, he was a member of the Committee of Correspondence and a delegate to all of the five provincial congresses.

In 1774, Joseph Hewes was elected to the Continental Congress and served until 1777. At the first session he assisted in the preparation of the Statement of Rights of the colonies. He supported the policy of nonimportation, even though it represented losses for his own mercantile business. He spent the entire year of 1776 in Philadelphia. He was a member of the Secret Committee, the Committee on Claims, and the committee to prepare a plan of confederation. In May 1776, though he felt separation from England was premature, he had to present the Halifax Resolves to the Continental Congress, as they had been enacted by the Provincial Assembly. He wrote an English correspondent: "We do not want to be independent; we want no revolution. But every American to a man is determined to die or be free."

Hewes was the most active member and real head of the committee to fit out armed vessels. As Chairman of Marine in 1775, he was the first executive head of the Navy of the United States. His business training and experience as a ship owner made him a wise choice.

On December 27, 1776, Hewes became a Master Mason in the Unanimity Lodge No. 7, F and AM, Edenton, North Carolina.

John Adams maintained that all the captaincies should be New Englanders since they had yielded to the South in selecting George Washington as commander in chief of the Continental Army.

Hewes was a friend and benefactor of John Paul (alias Jones), July 6, 1747–July 18, 1792, born John Paul in Kirkbean Parish, Kirkcudbrightshire, Scotland, who at age twelve was a shipboy on a merchantman, and at twenty-one was master of the *John.* Following two unfortunate shipboard incidents, both occurring at Tobago, Bahama Islands, he arrived in America in 1773, and for the next twenty months probably lived with or near his older brother William Paul at Fredericksburg, Virginia.

Joseph Hewes nominated John Paul Jones for a naval appointment, and he became a first lieutenant in the new U.S. Navy, on December 22, 1775, aboard the *Alfred,* flagship of Commodore Esek Hopkins' squadron.

Gradually Hewes' health became impaired, perhaps as a result of his habit of working from six in the morning until five or six in the evening without food or drink. In March 1776, he became chairman of the Marine Committee. During the July 1, 1776, debate on Richard Henry Lee's independence resolution, Hewes stood up suddenly, lifted both arms to heaven and cried: "It is done, and I will abide by it." He voted for independence on July 2, and signed the engrossed copy of the Declaration of Independence on

August 2. He declined reelection to the Continental Congress for 1777.

Additional Information

Hewes was brought up in the Quaker faith. Prior to the beginning of the Revolutionary War, Hewes had abandoned the Quaker faith completely. He took his nephew, Nathaniel Allen, Jr., son of his older sister Sarah Hewes Allen, with him when he moved to North Carolina. Nathaniel became his partner and inherited much of his fortune.

Hewes became engaged to Isabella Johnson, sister of Samuel Johnson who was president of the provincial assembly and later governor of North Carolina. Isabella died a few days before the date set for their wedding and he never married. He died during the 1779 session of the Continental Congress and was buried in Christ Church Cemetery in Philadelphia.

In 1932, the U.S. Congress provided a monument honoring Joseph Hewes which was erected in front of the court house in Edenton, North Carolina. In 1963, the National Society of the Daughters of the American Revolution of North Carolina erected a bronze plaque marking his grave in Christ Church Cemetery in Philadelphia.

Genealogy

I. Joseph Worth Hewes, January 23, 1730–November 10, 1779, was born at Maybury Hill, on the outskirts of Princeton, New Jersey. He was the son of Aaron and Providence (Worth) Hewes.

WORTH
II. Aaron Hewes married, probably in the mid 1720s, Providence Worth. The will of Giles Worth of Windsor, Middlesex County, New Jersey, dated August 6, 1739, names his mother, Sarah Worth, three brothers and four sisters, one of whom was Providence. His executors were Elizabeth Worth, wife, and his brother-in-law Aaron Hewes.

In 1754, Aaron Hewes was at Burlington, New Jersey, no township given. He paid taxes in 1788 and died in 1789.

An entry from the diary of one Job Whitehall, November 24, 1777:

> Ye English soldiers all moved off this morning and left Woodbury. I walked to where they had their camp and we found our big kettle but not our little pot. Found the brown ox's hide belonging to father that they had killed, and took it to Aaron Hews for him to tan for me. It weighed 50 pounds.

An item from *Notes on Old Gloucester County, New Jersey*, volume II, page 135: September 25, 1819: "Fixed boards to Cousin James Cooper's grave, also new ones to Aaron Hewes' grave, those to the latter having been of red cedar, one decayed, and been standing about thirty years."

On July 10, 1823, executors of Josiah Hewes' estate (son of Aaron) sold at auction the home and was bid off by Dr. Jeremiah Foster at $2,000, but stated its worth at $5,000. On December 5, 1823, an entry states "Aaron Hewes deceased in 1789 now upwards of thirty-four years," refers to a book bought at auction from his personal estate.

III. Edward Hewes was of Oldman's Creek, Salem County, New Jersey. His will, dated December 5, 1739, was proved April 21, 1741. His executors were his wife Hannah and brother James Hewes. He mentions sons James and Aaron Hewes.

The Hewes family is supposed to have fled Indians in Connecticut. They came to New Jersey in 1728.

Chapter 19

THOMAS HEYWARD, JR.

1746–1809

SOUTH CAROLINA

THOMAS HEYWARD, JR., lawyer, statesman, landowner, soldier, received his early education at home and read law in an office at Charleston, South Carolina. He went to London and was admitted to the Middle Temple, Cambridge University, London, on January 20, 1765. On May 25, 1770, he was called to the bar by the Inns of Court.

He was admitted to the bar in South Carolina on January 22, 1771. The following year he was elected to the Commons House of Assembly from St. Helen's Parish, and was a delegate to the provincial convention at Charleston, July 6, 1774, when news of the blockade of Boston Harbor was received.

Heyward attended a Provincial Congress at Charleston on January 11, 1775, which practically took over the functions of government. He was chosen by this congress as one of the thirteen members of the Council of Safety. He was elected to the second Provincial Congress which met November 1, 1775, and was chosen as one of their delegates in their second session beginning February 1, 1776. He served on a committee of eleven to prepare a constitution for South Carolina which was adopted on March 26, 1776.

Heyward was chosen as one of the four delegates from South Carolina to the Second Continental Congress. He voted in favor of independence on July 2, and signed the Declaration of Independence on August 2, 1776.

He was again elected to the Continental Congress on January 10, 1777, and served to the end of 1778. On November 15, 1777, he signed the Articles of Confederation. He returned to South Carolina and on July 9, 1778, became a judge of the Court of Common Pleas, and was one of the ratifying officers of the Articles of Confederation. He was also elected to the South Carolina House of Representatives.

Thomas Heyward, Jr., was a member of the South Carolina militia, and captain of a battalion of artillery in Charleston. His battalion participated in General Moultrie's defeat of the British on February 4, 1779, on Port Royal Island, where he was wounded. He took part in the defense of Charleston and upon the fall of the city on May 12, 1780, he was paroled as a prisoner of war. Soon his parole was recalled. He was sent to St. Augustine, Florida, and was held until exchanged in July 1781.

While Heyward was confined in St. Augustine, the British plundered his White Hall plantation and carried off all his slaves. They were sold to sugar planters in Jamaica. He recovered some, but about one hundred thirty, valued at $50,000, were lost in addition to other property.

Heyward resumed his seat on the bench in 1782, and was actively engaged in judicial duties until 1789. In 1790, he assisted in framing the constitution of the State of South Carolina. He then resigned and turned his attention to agriculture, having been one of the founders of the Agricultural Society of South Carolina in 1785, and became its first president.

Additional Information

The Heyward family was one of only a few to whom a patent for Arms was issued directly to our colonial families. The patent, dated December 1, 1768, from the Herald's College, London, (Grants XI, 326) was issued to Thomas Heyward, Jr., while a student at Middle Temple. The Arms and Crest were granted to his father, Daniel Heyward.

Thomas Heyward, Jr., died on April 17, 1809, and was buried near his father in the family graveyard at "Old House," in St. Luke's Parish, Jasper County, South Carolina. In 1920 the General Assembly of South Carolina appropriated $2500 for a monument, nine feet high, upon which was mounted a bronze bust of the signer. The bust is no longer on the monument.

Genealogy

I. Captain Thomas Heyward, Jr., Esquire, son of Daniel and Mary (Miles) Heyward, was born July 28, 1746, at "Old House" in St. Helen's Parish, now in Jasper County, about twenty-five miles northeast of Savannah, Georgia. He was called Thomas Junior because his father's brother was also Thomas. He married first, April 20, 1773, at Charleston, Elizabeth Matthews; and married second, May 4, 1786, at Charleston, Elizabeth Savage. He had one surviving child by his first wife, three by his second.

His children were: (by first wife) Daniel, 1774; Marie, 1775; Thomas, 1778; John, 1779; Thomas again, 1782; (by second wife) Thomas again, 1789; James, 1792; Eliza, 1794.

MATTHEWS
Elizabeth Matthews died August 16, 1782, in Philadelphia where she had gone to meet her husband upon his release from imprisonment at St. Augustine, Florida. She is buried in St. Peter's Churchyard in Philadelphia. Her brother was South Carolina's governor, John Matthews. She was the daughter of Colonel John Matthews, Esquire, and Sarah Gibbes, born February 17, 1725, who were married on November 10, 1741. Sarah Gibbes was the daughter of John

Gibbes, June 21, 1696–December 18, 1764, who married July 25, 1719, Mary Woodward, born December 18, 1703, daughter of John Woodward, son of Dr. Henry Woodward, the first white settler in South Carolina. Dr. Henry Woodward, 1646–1686, probably born in Barbados, was a surgeon. He surveyed Carolina for settlement in 1665 and planted the first rice fields in 1680. John Gibbes, born 1696, was son of Robert Gibbes, 1644–1715, who was married first in Barbados; married second, Mary (whose surname is unknown).

SAVAGE
Elizabeth Savage, b. post 1765, was the daughter of Colonel Thomas and Mary (Elliott) Savage, of Charleston, South Carolina. Thomas Savage's will was dated February 22, 1786, probated June 10, 1786. He left all his estate to his wife, Mary Elliott. Mary Elliott Savage left a will dated October 31, 1786, probated July 28, 1789. She named Elizabeth, under twenty-one years, wife of Thomas Heyward, Jr. She stated her mother was Elizabeth Butler of Georgia, deceased, who left a will dated November 21, 1775, leaving her children, when of age, land on Great Ogechee River, called Back Plantation.

MILES
II. Daniel Heyward, eldest son of Thomas and Hester (Taylor) Heyward, was born July 20, 1720, on James Island, and died October 4, 1777. He married first, March 8, 1744, Mary Miles, 1727–1761, of St. Andrews Parish, Berkeley County, South Carolina. They had six children, the eldest was Thomas Heyward, Jr., the signer. Heyward married second, Jane Elizabeth Gignilliat, 1743–1771, daughter of John and Mary (DuPre) Gignilliat; and third, on September 8, 1771,

Elizabeth Simons, July 11, 1747–April 1788, daughter of Benjamin Simons of Charleston and his first wife Ann Keating. She died in April 1788 and is interred in St. Phillip's Churchyard. By three wives, Daniel Heyward had eleven children. Mary Miles was the mother of Thomas Heyward, Jr. She was the daughter of William and Mary (Butler) Miles of the Parish of St. Andrew, Berkeley County, South Carolina. Mary Butler was the daughter of Thomas and Elizabeth Butler.

Daniel Heyward was a rice planter. His home plantation was called "Old House" and was near Grahamville. He acquired large tracts of land and cypress swamps, both by grant and purchase, and at the time of his death he owned 25,000 acres of land and many slaves, said to have numbered between nine hundred and one thousand. He died October 4, 1777, and is buried at Old House.

TAYLOR

III. Thomas Heyward, born ca. 1700, was buried March 11, 1736/7. He married on June 4, 1719, Hester Taylor, who died November 25, 1757. Hester (or Esther) Taylor was the daughter of John Taylor, Esquire, and his wife Esther of St. Andrews Parish.

This Thomas Heyward took part in the expedition of Governor Charles Craven to fight the Indians during the Yamassee uprising in 1715. His mother is said to have requested his release as he was an only son and just sixteen years of age. In 1718, he applied for prize money as one of the volunteer crew of the sloop *Revenge*, as the result of the engagement in which the pirate Richard Worly was killed. On March 25, 1724, Heyward was elected a member of the Assembly. On April 10, 1725, the commissioners were directed to be "forthwith prepared for Mr. Thomas

Heyward to be Captain of the James Island Company." His will was dated March 17, 1736, and was probated and recorded January 20, 1743. He and his family are probably buried on his plantation on James Island, bordering on the Stono River.

WRIGHT

IV. Thomas Heyward was born August 19, 1673, and died in the autumn of 1699, probably in the yellow fever epidemic which was said to have killed one hundred-fifty persons. Charlestown records show that in 1698 Thomas Heyward held the position of powder receiver for the colony. His will, dated September 28, 1699, devised all his worldly estate to his widow Margaret and one infant son Thomas.

Heyward married Margaret Wright about 1698. She was of Norfolk and Suffolk, England, perhaps the daughter of John Wright of Virginia, who was an early commissioner for Indians and a member of the assembly of Carolina. John Wright was slain by Indians at Pocotaligo. He was a descendant of Thomas Wright of Kilverstine Manor in the reign of Queen Elizabeth I.

V. Daniel Heyward, 1652–1684, came to South Carolina in 1672 from the County of Derby, England, bringing his wife whose name is unknown, two sons, and one daughter. Heyward brought an old book published in 1532, which he used as a family bible. In America they had Daniel and Thomas born August 19, 1673, and a daughter Elizabeth October 18, 1676; also, son Samuel born September 20, 1679. Heyward's will named only sons Thomas and Samuel, and was probated in November 1700. A copy of his will is in the State Archives Department, Columbia, South Carolina.

Chapter 20

WILLIAM
HOOPER

1742–1790

NORTH CAROLINA

WILLIAM HOOPER, lawyer, patriot, received his preparatory education with Mr. Lovell at the Boston Latin School. He entered Harvard College as a sophomore and graduated in 1760 with an A.B. degree. In 1761, he began to read law under James Otis, 1725–1783, and was admitted to the bar in 1764.

Hooper's family remained loyal to England throughout the Revolutionary War. He, however, had become more liberal, perhaps as a result of his years of study with the patriotic James Otis. He moved to Wilmington, North Carolina, in 1764, and soon was in high favor with the planters and lawyers in the Lower Cape Fear region.

As deputy attorney general, he incurred the hatred of the Regulars and was treated roughly by them. In 1771, he was elected to the assembly from the borough of Campbelltown, and by election from New Hanover County, he remained a member until the royal government was overthrown. He was on the Committee of Correspondence, and when the Boston Port Bill was passed, he led the movement to send relief. He also presided over the meeting which appointed a committee to call the first Provincial Congress and was elected to all five of the congresses. He did not attend the last one. By the first of these congresses, he was elected to the Continental Congress, where he was on many committees and took part in the debates. As an orator, John Adams compared him with Richard Henry Lee and Patrick Henry.

Hooper was the leader of those against new laws by the British party for regulation of the Courts of Justice. He published a series of essays under the name of Hampden which made the people aware of the importance of the issues of the times. His own fortunes suffered because of the resulting suspension of all courts for over a year.

In 1774, 1775, and 1776, he was a delegate to the Continental Congress. He was absent from the vote for independence on July 4, 1776, but returned in time to sign the Declaration of Independence in August. He resigned his seat in the Continental Congress on April 29, 1777.

At the impending capture of Wilmington in 1782, he was driven from his residence nearby. A house belonging to him was fired upon by a British vessel in the Cape Fear River.

In 1782, he went to Hillsborough; two years later he was once again in the House of Commons. He was an advocate of the federal Constitution and although he was defeated in his attempt to be a delegate to the Hillsborough convention, he lived to see the Constitution ratified.

In 1786, Hooper was one of the federal judges who resolved the territorial rights of New York and Massachusetts. He continued to hold a distinguished place at the bar and the Councils of North Carolina until his death.

Additional Information

Hooper was a handsome man, possessed of grace and a charming manner. He had a brilliant mind, as well. He was essentially an aristocrat, cultivated, fearless, and aloof, except to those intimates whom he loved and who loved him. His home on Masonboro Sound near Wilmington, North Carolina, was called Finian. After the Revolution, his family was reunited but much of his property had been destroyed. He was also very ill with malaria. He died October 14, 1790, at Hillsborough, North Carolina, and was buried in Hillsborough Town Cemetery.

On April 24, 1894, Mr. Hooper's remains were reinterred under the Signers' Monument then under construction in the Guilford Courthouse National Military Park near Greensboro, North Carolina. A bronze statue of Hooper was mounted upon the monument which was dedicated on July 3, 1897.

Genealogy

I. William Hooper was born on June 17, 1742, at Boston, Massachusetts, eldest child of the Reverend William Hooper. In 1767, he married Anne Clarke.

His children were: Richard, ca. 1767; William, 1768; Thomas, 1770; Elizabeth,

1772; Aeneas, 1774; a son, 1776; a daughter, 1778.

CLARKE

Anne Clarke was the daughter of Thomas Clarke and Barbara Murray, early settlers of Wilmington, North Carolina, who had come from Boston, Massachusetts. Her brother was General Thomas Clarke of the U.S. Army.

DENNIE

II. The Reverend William Hooper was born in Scotland in 1702; graduated in Edinburgh with an A.B., March 26, 1723. He was ordained at Boston West Church on May 18, 1737, and was settled at Boston, West Church, 1737–1746. The Reverend Hooper married at Boston on October 18, 1739, Mary Dennie. He died at Boston on April 14, 1747.

Chapter 21

STEPHEN HOPKINS

1707–1785

RHODE ISLAND

STEPHEN HOPKINS, colonial governor, educator, judge, merchant, patriot, had little or no formal education. His mother taught him his first lessons. His grandfather and uncle instructed him in elementary mathematics, and he read the English classics in his grandfather's small but well-selected library.

Hopkins grew up on a farm and became a surveyor in that section of Cranston, now Providence, which became Scituate in 1731. He was moderator of their first town meeting. In 1732 he became town clerk, and was president of the Town Council in 1735. He represented Scituate in the General Assembly, 1732–1733, 1735–1738, and again in 1741, and became Speaker in 1742.

In 1736, Hopkins was a justice of the Court of Common Pleas for Providence County; also justice of the peace. In 1741, he was appointed clerk of the Court of Common Pleas. About 1740, he joined his brother Esek Hopkins in commercial ventures and established his permanent residence at Providence in 1742. He served in the General Assembly 1744–1751, was assistant justice of the Rhode Island Superior Court 1747–1749, and became chief justice in 1751.

Hopkins established a subscription library in June 1754. He lost a bid for governor that year, but won the governorship in 1755.

By 1756, the town of Providence was competitive with Newport, and Stephen Hopkins was the leader. Samuel Ward, son of Governor Richard Ward, aristocrat and large landowner in the Narragansett Country, helped defeat Governor Hopkins for reelection. There ensued an eleven year political feud between Ward and Hopkins and their supporters. During this period, Stephen Hopkins was defeated by Ward only three times.

Hopkins was sent to the General Congresses of 1754, 1755, and 1757. At the Albany Congress of 1754, Benjamin Franklin was promoting his plan for uniting the colonies. There our two eldest signers of the Declaration of Independence became friends.

In 1765, after passage of the Stamp Act, Hopkins was chairman of a committee to draft instructions to the Providence General Assembly. He wrote *The Rights of Colonies Examined*, published on December 22, 1764, a pamphlet in which he attacked the Sugar Act and the Stamp Act, stating that direct taxation of an unconsenting people was tyrannous.

In 1768, he chaired the committee to consider the famous circular letter sent by Massachusetts to all the other colonies. From 1769 to 1774, while Hopkins was a member of the Rhode Island General Assembly, and also chief justice of the Superior Court of the Colony, some Rhode Islanders burned John Hancock's merchant ship which had been converted by the British and renamed the schooner *Gaspée*. Governor Joseph Wanton received instructions to arrest those involved and send them to England for trial. Hopkins, as chief justice, stated he would neither apprehend them by his own order, nor suffer any executive officers to do it. For details concerning the *Liberty-Gaspée* incident, refer to Chapter 15 on John Hancock.

At a meeting of the General Assembly of Rhode Island in 1774, Hopkins introduced a bill to prevent further importation of slaves, and freed those which he owned. He signed the Articles of Association on October 20, 1774.

Stephen Hopkins and Samuel Ward, his old political opponent, were Rhode

Island's two delegates to the First Continental Congress. Independence was not
yet openly being discussed, but the delegates were exchanging views. Stephen
Hopkins made the bold prediction to the
members of the Continental Congress
that "powder and ball will decide this
question. The gun and bayonet alone will
finish the contest in which we are engaged, and any of you who cannot bring
your minds to this mode of adjusting
this question had better retire in time."

He signed the Olive Branch Petition
to King George III on July 8, 1775. Hopkins was reelected to the Second Continental Congress where he was placed on
the committee to make plans for a navy;
also on the Committee for preparing the
Articles of Confederation. By May 4,
1776, Rhode Island had renounced its allegiance to King George III. Exactly two
months later, he voted for the Declaration of Independence and signed the engrossed document on August 2, 1776.

In 1777, he served as a member of
the Rhode Island General Assembly, and
between 1776 and 1780 attended some
conventions of the New England states.
He was chosen a delegate to the General
Congress in 1778, and was a member of
the committee which drafted the Articles
of Confederation for the U.S. Government. This was his last contribution to
the Continental Congress, as his health
was failing, and he returned to Rhode Island.

Besides political and civic interests,
Hopkins had interests in education and
science. About 1754, he was influential
in establishing a public library, was the
first chancellor of Rhode Island College
(Brown University) founded at Warren
in 1764, and was instrumental in its
removal to Providence. He helped found
the *Providence Gazette and Country*

Journal in 1762 and wrote several articles
for it.

Hopkins was a member of the
Philosophical Society of Newport,
though admitted as an out-of-town
member. He was involved in erecting a
telescope in Providence for observing the
transit of Venus, which occurred in June
1769.

Additional Information

The story of Stephen and Sarah
(Scott) Hopkins' children was tragic.
One son died at age seven and one
daughter died at age three. Their daughter Lydia died in 1794. The four sons remaining all went to sea. The eldest returned to Rhode Island and died in 1812.
One son died at St. Andre of smallpox,
another (the youngest child) commanded
a vessel sailing from Surinam, stopping
at Charleston, South Carolina, on his return on August 29, 1775; the vessel was
never heard from. Their fifth child, Sylvanus, born 1734, had followed the sea
for about three years. In March 1753, he
went as mate of a small sloop and sailed
to Cape Breton. On his return toward
Louisburg, he was cast away on the Nova
Scotia shore by a strong gale. At the Island of St. Peter's they were surprised by
a great number of Indian canoes. They
were bound, carried ashore one by one,
murdered, and left unburied.

Among Hopkins' many relatives was
General Benedict Arnold, January 14,
1741–June 14, 1801, who was born at Norwich, Connecticut, and died at London,
England.

Stephen Hopkins was for several
years afflicted with "shaking palsy," which
caused his signature on the Declaration
of Independence to appear unsteady. He

stated at the signing, "My hand trembles, but my heart does not."

Stephen Hopkins is buried in the North Burying Ground at Providence. The State of Rhode Island provided a grave monument in his honor.

Genealogy

I. Stephen Hopkins, March 7, 1706/7–July 13, 1785, was born at Providence, Rhode Island, in that part later named Scituate. He was the son of William and Ruth (Wilkinson) Hopkins. He married first, October 9, 1726, Sarah Scott, June 15, 1707–1753, and they had five sons and two daughters. Only one son, Rufus, 1717–1812, and one daughter, Lydia, 1733/4–1793, survived their father. Stephen Hopkins married second, January 2, 1755, Ann (Smith) Smith, October 5, 1717–January 20, 1782, widow of Benjamin Smith. She was the daughter of Benjamin and Mercy (Angell) Smith. Benjamin Smith's will, dated May 25, 1751, named Ann among his heirs. She had four children by Benjamin Smith, none by Stephen Hopkins.

His children were: (by first wife) Rufus, ca. 1728; John, ca. 1730; Ruth, 1731; Lydia, 1733; Sylvanus, 1734; Simon, 1736; George, 1739; (by second wife) none.

SCOTT

Sarah Scott, 1707–1753, first wife of Stephen Hopkins, was the youngest daughter of Major Sylvanus and Joanna (Jenks) Scott. Joanna Jenks, born ca. 1672, died in 1756 in her eighty-fifth year. She was the daughter of Joseph Jenekes (Jenks), one of the earliest settlers at Providence. Sarah (Scott) Hopkins is buried near Stephen Hopkins in the North Burying Ground at Providence. A bronze plaque in her memory has been placed by the Sarah Scott Hopkins Chapter of the Daughters of the American Revolution.

Joseph Jenks, born ca. 1633 in England, died at Providence January 4, 1717. He married Esther Ballard daughter of William Ballard, age thirty-two, and his first wife Elizabeth, age twenty-six, bringing Esther, age two. They came on the *James* in June 1635. William Ballard lived at Lynn, and died July 10, 1689. Grace Berwick, his second wife, died April 27, 1679. Joseph Jenks was the son of Joseph Jenks and his first wife. He lived at Concord, Warwick, and finally at Providence, Rhode Island. His forge was destroyed during King Philip's War.

Joseph Jenks, born about 1589, was a widower, at Lynn, Massachusetts, in 1645, a blacksmith, came from Middlesex or Colnbrook, Bucks County, England. He established the iron works at Lynn; was the first planter in America in 1646. In 1652 he cut the dies for the "Pine Tree Shilling," and in 1654 built the first fire engine. He also invented the grass scythe. He married second, Elizabeth who died 1679. He died in March of 1683, at age eighty-four.

Sylvanus Scott, b. November 10, 1672, was the second son of John and Rebecca Scott. John Scott was the son of Richard Scott, 1605–1680, of Glensford, County Suffolk, England. He was admitted to the church at Boston August 28, 1634. John Scott took the oath of allegiance to King Charles II in 1688.

Richard Scott, 1605–1680, shoemaker at Boston, removed to Providence, Rhode Island. He was an early settler and became the first Quaker preacher at Providence. He was a freeman in 1655. He married Catharine Marbury, daughter of Edward Marbury. Catharine was a niece of Ann Hutchinson, the religious reformer banished from the Massachusetts Colony in 1637. Ann Hutchinson, with her family, was murdered at the Bronx, New York in an August 1643 Indian massacre.

Richard Scott was the son of Edward Scott, ca. 1573 who died after 1640, and his wife Sarah Carter, of Glensford, County Suffolk, England.

Edward Scott was in the fifth generation from Sir John Scott and his wife Anne Pympe, of Scott's Hall, County Kent, England.

SMITH

Ann (Smith) Smith, October 5, 1717–January 20, 1782, twin with Ruth Smith, was a cousin as well as the second wife of Stephen Hopkins. She was the widow of Benjamin Smith, son of Benjamin and Amphilis/Angell Smith of the Christopher Smith line. Ann (Smith) Smith was the daughter of Benjamin and Mercy (Angell) Smith, and a descendant of Christopher (died June 1676) and Alice Smith.

WILKINSON

II. William Hopkins, January 31, 1686–July 8, 1723, of Providence, Rhode Island, was the only child of Major William Hopkins and Abigail (Whipple) Dexter, widow of Stephen, son of Gregory Dexter. He married about 1700, Ruth Wilkinson, eldest daughter of Samuel and Plain (Wickenden) Wilkinson.

Plain Wickenden was the daughter of the Reverend William Wickenden whose wife is unknown, who was probably at Salem in 1639. He signed the Agreement of 1636 and the Compact of 1637. In Rhode Island, he served on the committee to establish a government under the patent of 1648; served as a commissioner at Providence several years; and as a deputy in 1664. He died February 3, 1669/70. His home lot was thirteenth among the earliest settlers, and he was the second minister of the first Baptist church in America.

Samuel Wilkinson, ca. 1650–1727, was the son of Lawrence and Susanna (Smith) Wilkinson.

Lawrence Wilkinson was a lieutenant in the army of Charles I, and was taken prisoner October 22, 1644, by the Scots and parliamentary troops at the surrender of Newcastle-on-Tyne. Deprived of his property, he came to New England sometime between 1645 and 1647, and was at Providence in 1652 with his wife and son; he was a freeman in 1658; chosen deputy to the General Court; was a soldier in the Indian wars and called captain; a member of the Colonial Assembly which met at Portsmouth in 1659. He died May 9, 1692. His wife Susanna, who also died in 1692, was the daughter of Christopher and Alice Smith, also early settlers at Providence.

Lawrence Wilkinson, Sr., 1615–May 9, 1692, was the son of William Wilkinson and Mary Conyers, daughter of Christopher Conyers. He was a great-grandson of Lawrence Wilkinson of Harpsley House, Lancaster, County Durham, England. This Lawrence Wilkinson requested and received Arms, granted on September 18, 1615, by Richard St. George Norrey, King of Arms, as shown on the records of the College of Arms.

WHIPPLE

III. Major William Hopkins, 1647–July 8, 1723, son of Thomas Hopkins, married in 1682, Abigail (Whipple) Dexter, born probably at Dorchester about 1659 and died in 1725. She was the widow of Stephen, son of Gregory Dexter, and the daughter of John and Sarah Whipple (Sarah died age 43 in 1666), of Providence. Major William Hopkins was a freeman April 30, 1672; his will was dated July 1, 1723.

John Whipple, Jr., 1617–1685, was an innkeeper of Providence, a surveyor, carpenter, member of the town council and of the General Assembly. He was also a trader and legal practitioner. In 1632, he was at Dorchester, Massachusetts; a servant of Israel Stoughton; sold his home at Dorchester to George Minot in 1648; and removed to Providence 1658/9. He died May 16, 1685, age 68. His will was made on the day of his death.

ARNOLD

IV. Thomas Hopkins, April 7, 1616–ca. 1676, was at Providence in 1641, having followed Roger Williams from Plymouth. He came to Newport, Rhode Island, with his family on November 19, 1651. He was appointed a member of the town committee in 1661; swore allegiance to Charles I in June 1668; moved to Long Island about 1675 at the outbreak of King Philip's War. He died at Oyster Bay, Long Island, New York. He married an Arnold, probably a daughter of William Arnold.

ARNOLD

V. William Hopkins, of Yeovilton, married before 1613, Joanna Arnold, November 30, 1577, and buried March 10, 1621/2, sister of William and daughter of Thomas Arnold, born 1550. Thomas Arnold lived at Melcombe Horsey Manor

in Dorsetshire in 1598, then went to Cheselbourne Manor. William Arnold, born at Ilchester June 24, 1587, was a brother of the first Thomas. He married before 1610, Christian Peak, baptized February 15, 1583/4, daughter of Thomas Peak of Muchalney, Somerset. She died after 1659 at Patuxent, Rhode Island. William Arnold was at Hingham, Massachusetts, in 1635, and moved to Providence in 1636. He was at Newport, Rhode Island, in 1638, a founder of the first Baptist Church in America.

William Arnold was the son of Thomas Arnold, 1550–January 26, 1622/3, of Yeovilton. Thomas Arnold married Alice Gully, baptized September 29, 1553, and buried April 25, 1596, daughter of John and Alice Gully of Northover in the Parish of Tolpuddle. Thomas Arnold married second, Grace, surname unknown, who survived him. He was the son of Richard Arnold, Jr., wife's name unknown, who was residing at Bagbere Manor, Middleton Parish, Dorsetshire, before 1549. His will dated May 15, 1593, was proved July 9, 1595. He was buried in July 1595, at Milton Church. Richard Arnold was the son of Richard Arnold, Sr., a resident of Street Parish, Somersetshire. He married Emmote, daughter of Pearce Young, of Damerham, Wiltshire. Richard Arnold, Sr., was the son of Thomas Arnold, eldest son of Roger, who succeeded to Llanthony Manor in Monmouthshire. He married Agnes, daughter of Sir Richard Wairnstead, or Warnstead. Roger Arnold was the son of Roger Arnold and Jane Gamage of Llanthony Manor.

Roger Arnold and Jane Gamage were both of royal descent.

Chapter 22

FRANCIS
HOPKINSON

1737–1791

NEW JERSEY

FRANCIS HOPKINSON, lawyer, statesman, author, musician, patriot, received his primary education from his mother. When the College of Philadelphia opened in 1751, his father, Thomas Hopkinson, was one of its first administrators. Francis Hopkinson, at the age of fourteen was its first student, and received the first diploma granted by the College six years later. In 1754, Hopkinson took up the study of the harpsichord, and in January 1757 was proficient enough to perform in a public appearance at the College. His presentation was Thomson and Malet's "Alfred a Masque" which was revised for the occasion. Perhaps Hopkinson helped with the revision; he composed some original music for the program.

In 1763, Francis Hopkinson published *Seven Songs*, a collection of psalm tunes which is thought to be the first book of music to be published by an American composer. He published a translation of the Psalter for the Reformed Protestant Dutch Church of New York City in 1765.

After his graduation from the College of Pennsylvania, he studied law under Benjamin Chew, attorney general of the province. He was admitted to practice before the Pennsylvania Supreme Court in April 1761, and in November 1763 he was appointed collector of customs at Salem, New Jersey. The same year, he acted as secretary at a conference between the government of Pennsylvania and the chiefs of several Indian Nations. He was librarian and secretary of the Philadelphia library in 1764-65.

In the summer of 1766, he traveled to England, hoping that through the influence of relatives there, he might secure a government appointment. Lord Frederick North, a relative by marriage, tried to help him with an appointment but was unable to do so because all the offices in America were being reserved for those who had suffered due to the repeal of the Stamp Act. While in London, he visited Benjamin Franklin, John Penn, and others. He also visited the artist Benjamin West and may have taken training in drawing and painting from him.

Upon his return to Philadelphia, Hopkinson resumed the practice of law, kept a store for a time, and became a member of the two societies which, in 1769, united as the American Philosophical Society.

In 1772, Hopkinson was appointed inspector of customs at New Castle but was soon removed because of his republican beliefs. He lived at Bordentown, New Jersey, for some years and became a member of the Provincial Council, 1774–1776. Having been elected to the Continental Congress on June 28, 1776, he voted in favor of independence on July 2, and signed the Declaration of Independence on August 2, 1776.

On June 14, 1777, Hopkinson's design of the American flag was accepted by General Washington. He designed (in 1769) the seal for the American Philosophical Society in 1770; the great seal of New Jersey; the seal for the University of New Jersey (1787); as well as others. In 1779, his home at Bordentown was plundered by the British. That year he succeeded George Ross as Judge of the Admiralty for Pennsylvania.

Hopkinson had an unusual talent for satirical and humorous writings. His "Battle of the Kegs" ridiculed the British, and is his best known work, although he wrote several pieces during the revolutionary period. After the 1778 alliance between America and France, he wrote "The Temple of Minerva," to celebrate the alliance. In December 1781, Francis Hopkinson composed music for the cantata and directed the performance, which was attended by George Washington and the French Minister.

In 1790, President Washington appointed him U.S. district judge for Pennsylvania.

After his death, *The Miscellaneous Essays and Occasional Writings of Francis Hopkinson* was published in Philadelphia in 1792.

Francis Hopkinson received an honorary degree from the University of Pennsylvania in 1790.

Additional Information

Francis Hopkinson was a man of many talents and abilities. He was a wit and, in his writings, proved himself a master of satire. He was also the inventor of several useful articles: an improved pick for playing the harpsichord, a ship's log, a shaded candlestick, etc.

Hopkinson served as secretary of the convention which organized the Protestant Episcopal Church in 1789. He died suddenly, of a stroke, on May 9, 1791, and was buried in the Christ Church Cemetery at Philadelphia.

Genealogy

I. Francis Hopkinson, October 2, 1737–May 9, 1791, married on September 1, 1768, Ann Borden, of Bordentown, New Jersey. His son Joseph (1770–1842) was a noted lawyer, congressman, and the author of *Hail Columbia*.

His children were: James, 1769; Joseph, 1770; Elizabeth, 1772; Mary, 1773; Thomas, ca. 1775; Anne, 1777; Thomas again, ca. 1779; Francis, c1781; Sarah Johnson, ca. 1783.

BORDEN

Ann Borden, May 9, 1747, died after November 14, 1807. She was the daughter of Colonel Joseph Borden who married, in 1743, Elizabeth Rogers, daughter of Samuel and Mary Rogers of Allentown, New Jersey. Joseph was born on August 1, 1719, and died in 1776.

Elizabeth (Rogers) Borden, July 10, 1725–November 2, 1807, was born and died at New Castle, Delaware. Colonel Joseph was the son of Joseph Borden, May 17, 1687–September 22, 1765, who was the founder of Bordentown, on the Delaware River. His wife was Ann Conover, who died March 11, 1754/5.

Joseph Borden (1687–1750) was the son of Joseph Borden, July 3, 1643, baptized in Rhode Island in 1649. He married in Rhode Island, September 22, 1671, Abigail Glover, baptized July 1652; she died in 1720. Joseph Borden removed to Shrewsbury, New Jersey, where his father had purchased land in 1667. Abigail Glover was the daughter of Henry Glover who was of New Haven, Connecticut, by 1647. Glover came in the Elizabeth from Ipswich, England, in 1634 at age twenty-four. He was a freeman of Connecticut, and lieutenant of Southold, New York, in 1662. His will was proved in October 1689.

Joseph Borden, 1643–1718, was the son of Richard Borden, 1601–May 25, 1671, and Joan Fowle, 1604–1683, of Portsmouth, Rhode Island, who came to New England from Headcorn, County Kent, England, about 1638. The Bordens were Quakers. Richard Borden was an assistant in 1653/4 and was general treasurer of Rhode Island in 1654/5. He belonged to a prosperous family in Kent County, England, of the yeoman class settled there by the fourteenth century. The direct line has been traced to Edmund Borden, Headcorn who died in 1539.

Joan Fowle died July 5, 1683; she was the daughter of Richard Fowle, yeoman, of Frittenden and Headcorn, Kent County, England.

II. Thomas Hopkinson, 1709–1751, came from London, England, to Philadelphia about 1731. He married at Philadelphia, on September 9, 1736, Mary Johnson, born 1718, daughter of Baldwin Johnson. Mary Johnson was a niece of the Bishop of Worcester, England.

Chapter 23

SAMUEL
HUNTINGTON

1731–1796

CONNECTICUT

Sam^n Huntington

SAMUEL HUNTINGTON, lawyer, patriot, received very little formal education. At sixteen he was apprenticed to a cooper and served out the term of the apprenticeship. On his own initiative, he studied Latin and law and was admitted to the bar at Windham and began to practice law. He moved his practice to Norwich, Connecticut, in 1760.

In May 1765, Huntington represented Norwich in the General Assembly, and was active in judicial and legislative affairs of the colony. From 1765 until 1774 he served as King's Attorney for Connecticut.

In 1774, he was appointed associate justice of the Superior Court of Connecticut and served until 1783. He was also a justice of the peace for New London County from 1765 to 1775.

In 1775, he was elected an assistant and accordingly left the General Assembly to take his seat in the upper house of the legislature or senate. He was re-elected as a member of the Governor's Council every year until 1784. In May 1775, the General Assembly appointed him a member of a committee for the defense of the colony.

In 1775, Huntington was elected as a delegate to the Second Continental Congress, where he served on many committees. He signed the engrossed, parchment copy of the Declaration of Independence on August 2, 1776.

In July 1777, he was named by Royal Governor Jonathon Trumbull and the Council as one of a committee to meet at Springfield, Massachusetts, with representatives from Massachusetts, New Hampshire, Rhode Island, and New York concerning the state of the currency.

On July 9, 1778, Connecticut ratified the Articles of Confederation; Huntington was the ratifying officer. He succeeded John Jay as president of the Continental Congress in 1779 when Jay was appointed plenipotentiary to negotiate a treaty between the United States and Spain. Huntington was again elected to the Continental Congress on September 28, 1779. In 1781, he resigned the presidency and requested a leave of absence due to poor health; however, he was once more in attendance in Philadelphia in 1783 and was again president of the Congress for two months.

During 1780–1781, he received honorary degrees from Yale, Dartmouth, and Princeton.

In 1784, he was appointed chief justice of the Supreme Court of Connecticut and in 1785 was appointed lieutenant governor. The following year he became governor of Connecticut and was re-elected concurrently for eleven years until his death.

Huntington strongly supported the Constitution drafted by the Federal Convention in 1787 and ratified in 1788. When the Federal Government was instituted in 1789, he received two of the electoral votes for the first president and vice president of the United States.

Genealogy

I. Samuel Huntington was born July 3, 1731, at Windham, Connecticut, and died January 5, 1796, at Norwich, Connecticut. He was the fourth child, second son, among the ten children of Nathaniel and Mehitable (Thurston) Huntington. He married, in 1761, Martha Devotion; they had no children. They adopted Francis and Samuel Huntington, sons of the Reverend Joseph Huntington, brother of the signer, and his wife,

Hannah Devotion, 1745–1771, sister of Martha (Devotion) Huntington. Samuel Huntington, 1765–1878, was graduated from Yale in 1785 and became Ohio's third governor, 1808–1810.

Samuel Huntington was buried in the Norwichtown Burial Ground, Norwich, Connecticut. His grave monument is a marble slab installed into a brick wall. The monument also honors his wife, Martha Huntington.

DEVOTION

Martha Devotion, March 7, 1738/9–June 4, 1794, was the daughter of the Reverend Ebenezer Devotion and Martha (Lothrop) Devotion, of Windham, Connecticut. The Reverend Ebenezer Devotion, A.B., A.M., Yale 1732, was born at Suffield, Connecticut, May 8, 1714, and died in July 1771. He was ordained October 22, 1735. His widow married second, the Reverend Mr. Cogswell, his successor, and they resided at her home.

Martha (Lothrop) Devotion was the daughter of Colonel Simon Lothrop, 1689–January 25, 1774/5, and Martha Lothrop, born November 15, 1696, and buried October 16, 1775. Colonel Simon was the third son of the second Samuel Lothrop born in March 1650 and his wife Hannah Adgate born in 1653, who were married in November 1675. Martha Lothrop, born 1696, was the daughter of Israel and Rebecca (Bliss) Lothrop, Israel being a brother of Samuel, March 1650–December 9, 1732 (Martha Lothrop and Simon Lothrop were first cousins).

Hannah Adgate was the daughter of Thomas Adgate and Mary (Marvin) Bushnell (widow of Richard Bushnell). Mary Marvin was born ca. 1629 and was living in 1685. She was the daughter of Matthew Marvin, 1603–1687, who came in the *Increase* from London in 1635 with

his wife Elizabeth; they were early settlers at Hartford, Connecticut, in 1638.

Samuel Lothrop, March 1650–January 25, 1774/5, was the son of Samuel and Elizabeth (Scudder) Lothrop.

Israel Lothrop, 1657–March 28, 1730, married Rebecca Bliss, b. 1663, on April 8, 1686. Rebecca was the daughter of Thomas and Elizabeth Bliss of Norwich. Thomas Bliss died April 15, 1688. Israel Lothrop's gravestone is the oldest one in Norwich, Connecticut, giving his death as March 18, 1730, in his seventy-third year. Israel Lothrop was also the son of Samuel Lothrop, 1620–1700/1, and Elizabeth Scudder.

Samuel Lothrop, ca. 1620–February 29, 1700, was brought from England by his father, the Reverend John Lothrop, when he was about fourteen years old. He was a carpenter. He married at Barnstable, Massachusetts, in the home of his father, on November 28, 1644, Elizabeth Scudder, a sister of John Scudder of Boston and Barnstable, who came on the *James* in 1635 from London. Samuel and Elizabeth lived at Boston for a time, moved to New London, Connecticut, in 1648, then to Norwich in 1668.

Samuel Lothrop married second, at Plymouth in 1690, Abigail Doane, daughter of John Doane. Abigail had no children as this was her first marriage when she was sixty years old.

Lothrop's will was made five days before his death and was witnessed by the Reverend John Woodward and Deacon Simon Huntington. It was proved in Prerogative Court in April 1701.

Abigail (Doane) Lothrop lived to the age of 103, dying on January 23, 1734/5. At the time of her death, the descendants of her husband numbered 365.

The Reverend John Lothrop, 1590–November 8, 1653, was educated at

Oxford and preached there for a short time (perhaps also at Egerton, in Kent). He also preached in London where Bishop Laud caused him to be imprisoned for two years (evidently for espousing views considered untenable by the Puritan clergy), during which time his wife died. This wife was Harriet Howse, whom he had married by license October 10, 1610. She was the daughter of the Reverend John Howse. The Reverend Lothrop was released from prison on condition that he leave the country. He embarked for Boston in the *Griffin* with fellow passengers Zachary Symmes and William and Ann Hutchinson, and arrived in Boston September 27, 1634. He married second, about 1635, Ann Hammond, and became the first minister at Scituate. On October 11, 1639, he removed to Barnstable with a large part of his congregation and died November 8, 1653. His will was dated August 10, 1653.

The Reverend Ebenezer Devotion, born at Brookline, Massachusetts, was baptized at Roxbury on October 19, 1684, died April 11, 1741. He graduated with an A.B. degree from Harvard in 1701 and was of Brooklyn, Connecticut. He married in 1710 Hannah Breck who was probably one of the five daughters of John Breck who died February 17, 1691, age forty, and his wife Susanna who died February 8, 1712, age sixty-four. They were of Dorchester, Massachusetts. John Breck was the son of Edward Breck of Dorchester in 1639 who died the first week of November 1662.

The Reverend Ebenezer Devotion was the son of John Devotion, born June 26, 1659, and died before February 1721/3 when his will was probated. He married Hannah Pond, 1660–1732/3, daughter of Daniel and Ann Pond of Dedham, born in England. Daniel Pond was the son of

Robert Pond who was a freeman 1690 and died in February 1698. Daniel Pond had married first, Abigail Shephard, and married second, Ann, who was the mother of Hannah (Pond) Devotion.

Edward Devotion, ca. 1621–September 28, 1685, who lived at Roxbury in that part of Boston called Muddy River, now Brookline. He joined the church at Boston in March 1645, a single man. He married ca. 1648, Mary Curtis, 1621–?1712, baptized on February 25, 1649, the same day her first son Edward, was baptized. Mary was the daughter of William Curtis, 1592–1672. Curtis married at Nazing, England, on August 6, 1618, Sarah Eliot, 1599–1673, daughter of Bennett Elliott (Benit Elyot) who was buried at Nazing, County Essex, on November 21, 1621. William and Sarah Curtis arrived on the *Lion* September 16, 1632, and lived at Roxbury. William Curtis was a freeman in 1633.

Edward Devotion came from France, fleeing persecution there. His will was made on September 28, 1685.

THURSTON

II. Nathaniel Huntington, September 1, 1691–December 1, 1767, married on February 28, 1723, Mehitable Thurston, June 8, 1700–October 4, 1781, of Bristol, Rhode Island. Huntington was a farmer and clothier at Scotland, Windham County, Connecticut. Nathaniel and Mehitable had ten children; three daughters and seven sons. The youngest son died at age seven, the second son Samuel Huntington, the signer, became a lawyer. The five remaining sons were all ministers.

ADGATE

III. Joseph Huntington, born September 1661, at Norwich, died December 29, 1747, at Windham, which had been his home from 1687. He was elected Deacon in Windham Church in 1729. He owned land in Willimantic as well as at Windham. Huntington married, on November 28, Rebecca Adgate, June 1666–March 29, 1713, daughter of Deacon Thomas Adgate and Mary (Marvin) Bushnell, widow of Richard Bushnell. Mary Marvin was the daughter of Matthew Marvin and Elizabeth, his wife, who came in the *Increase*, in 1635, from London, and were early settlers of Hartford in 1638.

CLARK

IV. Simon Huntington, born in England about 1629, and died at Norwich, Connecticut, June 28, 1706. He married in October 1653 at Saybrook, Sarah, daughter of Joseph Clark of Windsor, Connecticut. Sarah died in 1721 at the age of eighty-eight. They had nine children. Simon had a land grant in 1686. He was a deacon of the church until 1696; member of the General Assembly in 1674; townsman 1690–1694; and in 1694 was on a committee to search out and report deficiencies in the public records. In 1697, he was a member of the committee to seat the meeting house. In 1700, he was on a committee to give deeds and fix titles of lands in dispute or with defective titles.

BARRETT

V. Simon Huntington, of England, who married first a wife of unknown name. He married second, in 1627, Margaret Barrett, daughter of Peter Barrett, mayor of Norwich, England. Huntington died of smallpox on the voyage from England to Boston in 1633. Margaret (Barrett) Huntington settled in Roxbury, Massachusetts, in 1633, and married second, early in 1635, Thomas Stoughton of Dorchester, Massachusetts. They removed to Windsor, Connecticut, and she probably died late in 1642 as the distribution of her estate was on March 27, 1643.

Chapter 24

THOMAS
JEFFERSON

1743–1826

VIRGINIA

THOMAS JEFFERSON, architect, lawyer, politician, statesman, vice president, and president of the United States, received his early education at the private school of the Reverend Matthew Maury, then studied French, Latin, and Greek under the Reverend William Douglas. He entered the College of William and Mary in 1760, and graduated in 1762. Five years of study in the law office of George Wythe completed his formal education. He was admitted to the bar in 1767 and established a successful law practice, although he disliked court practice. He soon became involved in civic affairs, closed his law office and never practiced law again. His writings revealed his education and thorough understanding of legal processes.

In May 1769, Thomas Jefferson was elected a member of the House of Burgesses and served, except in 1772, until it was dissolved in 1775. In 1770, he was appointed county lieutenant of Albermarle; in 1773, he was surveyor for the county. By 1774, disputes with England were growing more serious. He was chosen for the Virginia Convention which became the state legislature. He was unable to attend, but sent his "Summary View of the Rights of British America" to the convention. This writing was second in importance only to the Declaration of Independence, and reflects his views of the struggle with Great Britain.

Jefferson worked most successfully in the legislative bodies on committees. He never became an effective orator, but was a very talented writer. His speeches were written out and read.

He was associated early with the aggressive anti–British group. He was a member of the committee which drew up the resolves which created the Virginia Committee of Correspondence and was appointed as a member of the Committee of Eleven. Early in 1775, Jefferson was on the committee appointed to draft the address to Governor Dunmore rejecting Lord North's conciliatory offer.

Thomas Jefferson was elected to the Continental Congress by the Virginia convention, to serve in the event Peyton Randolph (his cousin) was needed at home. He sat in Congress during the summer and autumn of 1775, and drafted several anti–British papers which were too strongly worded to be acceptable to the conservatives.

On September 26, 1775, the Virginia Committee of Safety appointed him county lieutenant and commander of the militia of Albermarle County.

Because of his public duties in Albermarle County, and (probably his mother's illness and death March 31, 1776), he was not in the Continental Congress from December 28, 1775, to May 14, 1776.

Following Richard Henry Lee's introduction of the Virginia Resolutions (June 7, 1776), on July 11, 1776, Thomas Jefferson, John Adams, Benjamin Franklin, Roger Sherman, and Robert R. Livingston (brother of the signer Philip Livingston) were elected to draw up a Declaration of Independence.

Apparently it was more expedient to have one member draft the declaration and then amend it. The tone of his writings of the previous autumn had become more acceptable, and Jefferson's "reputation of a masterly pen" brought him the honor of being asked to author the Declaration of Independence. During the debates and editing, Jefferson was somewhat dismayed by the changes, but he was counseled by Benjamin Franklin.

The document, in its amended form, is a greatly reduced version of his draft but it retains his eloquent writing style.

Jefferson voted in favor of Independence on July 2, was in agreement on the broadside draft of the declaration, and signed the engrossed, parchment copy of the Declaration of Independence on August 2, 1776.

He left Congress in September 1776 and served in the Virginia House of Delegates from October 7, 1776, until June 1, 1779, when he was elected governor of Virginia. Among Jefferson's legislative achievements were disestablishing the Anglican Church; abolishing entail — the inheritance of land through particular lines of descent; abolishing primogeniture — the inheritance of estates only by the eldest son; and reforming the Virginia Criminal Code. The legislature refused to adopt his bill for a public school or library system. He wrote the Statute of Virginia for religious freedom which was finally passed by the legislature in 1786.

Richmond was invaded by Benedict Arnold in January 1781, and some of Jefferson's slaves joined the British. The legislature met at Charlottesville on May 24, 1781. He ended his governorship on June 3, believing his term to be ended. On June 4, Banastre Tarleton raided Monticello. The legislators, who were his guests, all escaped and Jefferson followed. The next day he moved his family to Poplar Forest. In late June he was thrown from his horse Cataracus and injured. His administration ended, and at an assembly meeting in Staunton, Thomas Nelson, Jr., was elected governor.

On June 12, 1781, it was ordered that an investigation of Jefferson's conduct be made with reference to the lack of military precaution and expedition. He was formally vindicated by the House of Delegates.

In 1782, Jefferson was again a delegate in Continental Congress. From 1784 to 1789, he was the U.S. minister to France. Upon his return, he became secretary of state, 1790–1794, in George Washington's administration. It was necessary that he be in constant official association with Alexander Hamilton, the secretary of the treasury. Both were intelligent, patriotic gentlemen, but Hamilton was a Federalist and believed in a powerful, central government by only the wealthy and well-educated "upper class," with restrictions of the right to vote. Thomas Jefferson began his life as a member of a wealthy, aristocratic family, but called himself a "Republican," though there was no such party in his day. He wanted government by the people, particularly property holders. He also advocated complete freedom of speech, religion, and the press, whereas Hamilton favored restriction and control. Years of friction and lack of cooperation caused Jefferson to resign as secretary of state in July 1794, but he remained in office until the end of the year.

In 1796, he was put forward as a candidate for president by the opposition Republican Party. Among four candidates he received the second largest number of electoral votes and became vice president in 1797, under the Federalist President John Adams.

On January 31, 1801, just two months prior to leaving the presidency, John Adams appointed John Marshall, 1755–1835, as chief justice of the Supreme Court, 1801–1835. Although Thomas Jefferson and John Marshall were second cousins, their political views were completely different.

In the election of 1800, Thomas Jefferson and Aaron Burr, both Republicans, received the same number of votes. After thirty-six ballots in the House, Jefferson was declared president and Burr became his vice president. Because of the 1800 presidential election, the twelfth amendment to the Constitution was passed to assure a better method of voting for president and vice president.

Thomas Jefferson was sworn in as president on March 4, 1801. The details of his two eventful terms in office are beyond the scope of the present work but may be found in any American history textbook.

In 1802, James Thomson Callender, an unscrupulous drunkard, a pamphleteer whom Thomas Jefferson had previously supported, launched a character assassination against him. James Callender published in the *Richmond Recorder* a charge of cowardice, dishonesty, and personal immorality against him. Only one charge was admitted by him, and that was an incident during his youth, as a single man, "for which he made restitution."

When President Jefferson left office in 1809, he retired to Monticello, and never ventured more than a few miles from home. His estate had suffered from losses and neglect, and he worked to save Monticello for his one surviving daughter. He was unwilling, or unable for financial reasons, to free his slaves. He disagreed with his abolitionist friends who thought that blacks were equal to whites. His belief in the racial inferiority of blacks seems inconsistent with his wish for human dignity under the laws, and with the revolutionary acts against Great Britain that he participated in.

While still in his twenties, Jefferson had designed and begun building Monticello on top of his "little mountain." He designed many other Virginia houses, wholly or in part, including his own Poplar Forest, Farmington, Bremo, Barboursville, and probably the middle section of Brandon. During his years as minister to France, he designed Virginia's State Capitol Building at Richmond and sent the drawings home to guide the workmen. After retirement from the presidency in 1809, Jefferson designed and supervised construction of the beautiful buildings of the University of Virginia.

During the War of 1812, the British vandalized and burned the Library of Congress. President Jefferson sold the government some ten thousand volumes from his private library which became the nucleus of our present Library of Congress. The sale of these books helped him financially for a few years.

Jefferson owned one of the best private collections of paintings and statuary in the United States, and he has been considered the first American connoisseur and patron of the arts.

Thomas Jefferson was president of the American Philosophical Society from January 6, 1797, and was actively engaged in dissemination of knowledge until 1815. On March 10, 1797, he introduced his megalonyx to his colleagues, and on May 4, 1798, he read to them his description of a mould-board of least resistance for a plow. For this invention, he received a gold medal in 1805. He was elected on December 26, 1801, as Associé Etranger of the Institute of France, probably due to his reputation in France as the most well-known American intellectual.

Jefferson was also a noted scientist

in the fields of geography, botany, pale-ontology, and ethnology. During 1781-1782, his study of a large Indian mound in the vicinity of Monticello brought him recognition as an archaeologist. He was praised for his carefully documented method of entry and the complete records of his findings. He improved or invented several devices, most notably the polygraph and a dumb waiter.

Many honors and memorials have been bestowed upon President Thomas Jefferson; a few notable ones are de-scribed below.

In 1819 the University of Virginia was chartered naming Jefferson rector. The Medical School of Jefferson College of Canonsburg, Pennsylvania, was char-tered in 1825.

The Capitol Square Monument at Richmond was dedicated in 1858. George Washington is the central figure of the statue, encircled by six famous Virgin-ians: Patrick Henry, Thomas Jefferson, Andrew Lewis, George Mason, John Marshall, and General Thomas Nelson, Jr.

In 1874, President Jefferson's statue, by P. J. David D'Angers, was placed in the Capitol Rotunda.

An act of May 16, 1866, brought the nickel into the United States currency system. It began as a shield type, evolved through the liberty head, and the Indian head or buffalo nickel. The newly de-signed nickel by Felix Schlag, honoring President Jefferson, was first struck in 1938 at Philadelphia, Denver, and San Francisco. The profile of Thomas Jefferson appears on the obverse and Monticello on the reverse of the coin.

In 1889, a bust of Thomas Jefferson was installed in the United States Senate Gallery of the Capitol Building, Wash-ington, D.C.

He was elected to the New York University Hall of Fame in 1900, where his bust was placed in the Colonnade on May 13, 1924.

During the 1930s, Jefferson's likeness was sculpted onto Mount Rushmore by Gutzon Borglum, along with George Washington, Abraham Lincoln, and Theodore Roosevelt.

On the two hundredth anniversary of Jefferson's birth, on April 13, 1943, the Jefferson Memorial was dedicated on the rim of the Tidal Basin in Washington, D.C.

Additional Information

Thomas Jefferson was only fourteen when his father died leaving him several thousand acres of land and many slaves. He built Monticello, his best loved estate, which he continued to enlarge and im-prove. He was blessed with good health and few illnesses, and suffered less than most of his fellow signers during the Revolutionary War. His long political ca-reer resulted in financial burdens throughout. His daughter Martha related that the only office he ever held which paid the cost of holding it was the vice presidency.

President Jefferson willed his estate to the government, but his heirs and ex-ecutors contested and broke the will. Many of his possessions were sold to pay his debts. Monticello was sold to James Barkley in 1830; in 1834 Commodore Uriah Phillip Levy purchased it; and in 1875, it was sold to Jefferson Levy. In 1923, the Thomas Jefferson Memorial Foundation by legal title received Monti-cello and it is now a national memorial and shrine.

President Jefferson died at 12:50 P.M.,

July 4, 1826, and is buried at Monticello Cemetery, near Charlottesville, Virginia. His original granite grave monument was being discarded as a new monument was being erected. The University of Missouri requested it and received it from the heirs, July 4, 1883. It was dedicated on the University of Missouri campus at Columbia, Missouri, on July 4, 1885.

Thomas Jefferson's new grave monument in the Monticello Cemetery is a plain six foot obelisk, with the following inscription as desired by him:

Here was Buried
Thomas Jefferson
Author
Of the Declaration of American Independence
of
The Statute of Virginia
for Religious Freedom
and
Father of the University of Virginia
Born April 2nd, 1743 O.S.
Died July 4, 1826

Genealogy

I. Thomas Jefferson, April 2 old style, or April 13, 1743–July 4, 1826, was born at Shadwell Plantation in Goochland, now Albermarle County, Virginia. Shadwell Plantation was a 400 acre tract known as the "Punchbowl Tract" because Thomas' father acquired it in exchange for a bowl of punch.

He was the son of Peter and Jane (Randolph) Jefferson. He married on January 1, 1772, Martha (Wayles) Skelton, October 19, 1748–September 6, 1782. They had six children, only two of which lived to maturity. These daughters, Mary and Martha, were educated in European convents; Mary died in 1804.

His children were: Martha, 1772; Jane Randolph, 1774; unnamed son,

1777; Mary Maria, 1778; Lucy Elizabeth, 1780; Lucy Elizabeth again, 1782.

WAYLES

Martha (Wayles) Skelton, October 19, 1748–September 6, 1782, wife of Thomas Jefferson (her cousin), at nineteen was the widow of Bathurst Skelton, from whom she inherited a considerable estate. Soon after her marriage to Thomas Jefferson, Martha inherited 40,000 acres of land and 135 slaves from her father's estate. Martha Jefferson was a talented and beautiful woman. Her account books reveal a neat handwriting and the ability to keep accurate records. In addition to bearing six children in the ten years of her marriage to President Jefferson, she had much responsibility for the care of the slaves, including their nursing when sick, and giving attention to their clothing and general condition. Gradually her health failed, however, and she died just before her thirty-fourth birthday.

Martha was the daughter of John Wayles, 1715–post 1772, a wealthy lawyer of Charles City County, Virginia. His residence was The Forest and in 1756 he was the King's attorney. John Wayles was born at Lancashire, England, and married about 1747, Martha Eppes, daughter of Colonel Francis Eppes IV (who died in 1655), and his wife Sarah, surname unknown. Martha (Eppes) Wayles may also have been the widow of Colonel Littlebury Eppes who died at Charles City in 1746. Colonel Francis Eppes of Bermuda Hundred was born about 1683, owned land in Henrico County in 1704. He was a burgess from Henrico in 1711-12 and 1712-14, and was sheriff in 1728. His will was dated November 7, 1733, and proved December 1734. His wife, Sarah, left a will dated February 28, 1747/8, proved July 1748, in which she gave her daughter Martha Wayles a mourning ring.

Colonel Francis Eppes IV was the son of Colonel Francis Eppes III, born about 1658, who deposed on August 1, 1691, that he was about thirty-two years of age. However, he administered his father's estate in October 1678, indicating he was probably above twenty-one at that time, and during the same month he administered his stepmother's estate.

When Chesterfield County was formed from Henrico, Colonel Francis Eppes III's home fell into the new county. He was justice of Henrico County on June 1, 1683, and was called captain. He was one of the commissioners for taking subscriptions toward the College of William and Mary which was chartered in 1693. He was a burgess for Henrico County several years between 1691 and 1706. He married Anne Isham, daughter of Colonel Henry Isham and his wife Katherine (Banks) Royal, a widow, who were married sometime between September 23, 1678, and February 20, 1681/2. Anne (Isham) Eppes was a sister of Mary (Isham) Randolph, wife of William Randolph. (To follow the Isham Line, see Jane Randolph Jefferson's ancestry.)

Colonel Francis Eppes III was the son of Captain Francis Eppes II, born about 1628 who died before August 28, 1678. On April 20, 1658, he was a justice of Charles City County. At a militia meeting at Westover on June 12, 1661, it was ordered that a trained band with addition of horse report to Fort Henry upon occasion of alarm and be commanded by Captain Francis Eppes. He soon moved to Henrico County and by February 4, 1664/5, was a Justice, and a burgess from 1670 to 1676.

Captain Francis Eppes II married first about 1658, name unknown, who was the mother of Colonel Francis Eppes III. He married second, about 1661, Elizabeth (?Littlebury) Worsham, widow of William Worsham of Henrico County.

William Randolph, age twenty-eight, stated in a deposition that he was at Colonel Francis Eppes' house one or two days before his death. Eppes was dangerously wounded and had no time to make a will, but he wanted his estate to go to his wife and four children. Elizabeth Eppes left two wills, one dated August 28, 1678, to provide for her Worsham children and the other was dated September 23, 1678, to provide for her Eppes children William, Littlebury, and Mary, and appointed her son-in-law Richard Kennon and her stepson Francis Eppes executors. Both of her wills were proved on October 1, 1678.

Francis Epes I was baptized May 14, 1597, and died before September 30, 1674. Francis Epes I was in Virginia in 1625 with his brothers William and Peter and their first cousin John Fisher. These Epes brothers were three of the fifteen children of John Epes, 1560–1627, of Ashford, Kent, England, and Thomasine Fisher who were married January 16, 1579, at Detling, Kent. Francis Epes was elected in April 1625 from Shirley Hundred to sit in the Assembly at James City on May 10, 1625. He was appointed commissioner for the Upper parts on August 8, 1626, and commander with Captain Thomas Pawlett to attack the Weyanoke and Appomattox Indians on July 4, 1627.

The will of his father, John Epes of Ashford, England, August 10, 1625, proved December 16, 1627, may have been his reason for taking his family to England. On September 8, 1630, a son Thomas was baptized at St. Olave, Hart Street, London, to Francis Eps and Marie. He had returned to Virginia and was a burgess for Shirley Hundred in 1631/2. On August 26, 1635, as Captain Francis Epes, he was granted 1700 acres in Charles City County on the Appomattox River. His wife, Mary or Marie, received money for a ring and the Bible of Captain Thomas Pawlett, by his will dated January 12, 1643/4. Also named in Pawlett's will was his Godson Francis Epes.

Confirmation of the Arms of a John Epes of Old Romney, who died in 1526, from William Segar, Garter-King of Arms, are described in the pedigree of Godfrey of Lydd in the visitation of Kent in 1619–1621.

RANDOLPH

II. Peter Jefferson, February 29, ca. 1707–August 17, 1757, married on October 3, 1731, Jane Randolph, who was baptized February 20, 1720, at St. Paul's Church, Shadwell, London. Jane died at Monticello March 31, 1776. Her sister Susanna married Carter Henry Harrison, brother of signer Benjamin Harrison. Jane Randolph was the daughter of Isham Randolph, January 1685–November 1742, of Turkey Island, Henrico County, Virginia.

Peter Jefferson's will was dated July 13, 1757, and probated October 15, 1757. He named his wife Jane, sons Thomas and Randolph, and daughters Jane, Mary, Elizabeth, Martha, Lucy, and Ann.

Jane (Randolph) Jefferson's will was probated in October 1778; her son Thomas was her executor. Isham Randolph was born at Dungeness, Goochland County. He married at White Chapel, London, about 1718, Jane Rogers, ca. 1695/1700, who died at Dungeness between December 5, 1760, and July 21, 1761. She was the daughter of Charles and Jane (Lilburne) Rogers, married

about 1694, of Newcastle-upon-Tyne, Durham. Charles Rogers died after 1704, and his widow married second, a Linton, and died after 1724.

Isham Randolph was the son of William Randolph, born about 1648 probably at Moreton Morell, Warwickshire, England, and died at Turkey Island, Henrico County, Virginia, April 21, 1711. He married Mary Isham, ca. 1660–post 1713/4, daughter of Henry Isham born 1628 in Northamptonshire and probably died at Bermuda Hundred, Henrico County, Virginia, about 1675.

Henry Isham married about 1659, widow Katherine (Banks) Royall, ca. 1630–1686, of Canterbury, Kent County, England. Henry Isham was the son of William Isham, baptized March 20, 1587/8 at Braunton, Northamptonshire, and died at Toddington, Bedfordshire, August 15, 1625. William Isham married Mary Brett, ca. 1604–before December 22, 1682, daughter of William Brett, 1562–1624, of Bedfordshire, England. William Isham was the son of Sir Euseby Isham, February 26, 1552/3–June 11, 1626, who died at Pytchley, Northamptonshire. He was knighted by King James I on May 11, 1603. He married Ann Borlase of Little Marlow, Buckinghamshire, who died at Pytchley in December 1627.

William Randolph, ca. 1648–1711, was the son of Richard Randolph, baptized at Little Houghton, Northamptonshire, February 24, 1621/2–May 2, 1678, of Moreton Morrell, Warwickshire. Richard Randolph married Elizabeth Ryland, daughter of Richard Ryland, of Warwickshire. Richard Randolph, February 22, 1627–1671, died at Dublin, Ireland. He was the son of William Randolph, perhaps buried at Moreton Morrell in 1657, probably of Courteenhall or Cotton End, Northamptonshire, who married Dorothy Lane, baptized at Courteenhall on September 4, 1589. She was the widow of Thomas West, and daughter of Richard Lane of Courteenhall and his wife Elizabeth Vincent of Harpole, Northamptonshire. William Randolph, 1572–1660, wife unknown, was the son of Robert Randolph, County Sussex, England, who married Rose Roberts, daughter of Thomas Roberts of Hawkhurst, Kent County, England.

FIELD

III. Thomas Jefferson, Jr., born 1679 at Henrico County, Virginia, died at Osbornes, now in Chesterfield County, February 15, 1730/1. He married on November 20, 1697, Mary Field, daughter of Major Peter Field of Charles City, Henrico, February 3, 1679–August 13, 1715, of New Kent County, July 24, 1707. Jefferson married at Chickahominy on October 21, 1678, Judith Soane, ca. 1646–ca. 1703. She was probably born at Litlington, Sussex, and died in Henrico County. She was the widow of Henry Randolph, Jr., and the daughter of Henry Soane, baptized November 17, 1622, at Brighton, Sussex, who died in James City County, Virginia, about 1661/2. Soane married by license, on February 17, 1642/3, Judith Fuller, at Southover Church, Lewes, Sussex, Virginia. She died after 1695.

BRANCH

IV. Thomas Jefferson, Sr., 1651–1697, was in Henrico County, Virginia, and mentioned in the first extant records there. His will was probated December 7, 1687. He married Mary (called Martha) Branch, daughter of William and Jane Branch. Martha married second, Abel Groves.

William Branch, born about 1627, was the son of Christopher Branch, Sr., of Henrico, probably of Charles City County and died about 1665. Christopher Branch, Sr., was born in England in 1602 and died between June 20, 1678, and February 20, 1681/2. He married at St. Peter's Westcheap, London, by license, September 1619, Mary Adde, daughter of Francis Adde of Darton, Yorkshire. Christopher Branch, Sr., was the son of Lionel Branch, baptized at Abingdon, Berkshire, August 18, 1566, who died about 1605. He married at St. Martin, Ludgate, England, on July 8, 1596, Valentia Sparkes. Lionel Branch came from an ancient family of gentlemen of Abingdon, England. Hotten shows their arrival in Virginia as William Branch with his wife and infant son Thomas in 1619, with his transportation being paid by Lieutenant Thomas Osborne.

V. Samuel Jefferson (Jeaffreson) went to St. Kitts with his father and moved to Antigua about 1669. He was baptized at Pettistree, Suffolk, October 11, 1607, married, and died after 1685.

VI. Samuel Jeaffreson, emigrated to the West Indies. He owned the Red House Plantation, St. Kitts. He died there on December 12, 1649, and was buried at St. Thomas' Church, Middle Island.

VII. John Jeaffreson, of Pettistree, married, wife's name unknown, and had four children.

VIII. Samuel Jeaffreson of Pettistree, Suffolk, England, married Elizabeth, surname unknown. He died after October 23, 1590, the date of his will.

Chapter 25

FRANCIS LIGHTFOOT LEE

1734–1797

VIRGINIA

Francis Lightfoot Lee

FRANCIS LIGHTFOOT LEE,
farmer, politician, patriot, was educated
by private tutors. He read widely and was
seriously interested in politics. He was a
member of the House of Burgesses from
Loudon County, Virginia, from 1758 to
1768. Following his marriage in 1769, he
settled in Richmond County and was almost immediately elected a burgess for
Richmond County, 1769–1776.

Lee was a man of considerable political influence. He was at least the equal
of his brother Richard Henry Lee in ability, but he never became a good speaker
as did Richard Henry. He was a more ardent revolutionist, and took part in
every defiant stand against the British
government. Lee signed the Westmoreland Resolves against the Stamp Act on
February 27, 1766. In 1773, Francis Lee
became one of the committee who
formed Virginia's Committee of Correspondence. He became a member of the
Virginia Convention of 1774, and in the
spring of 1775 was chosen as a Virginia
delegate to the First Continental Congress. He was reelected consecutively to
the Continental Congress until 1779.

During his years of service in
Philadelphia, he was active on many
committees. Though he was seldom on
the floor, he was often chairman of the
Committee of the Whole, and a firm
supporter of General Washington.

Lee voted in favor of independence
on July 2, and signed the engrossed copy
of the Declaration of Independence on
August 2, 1776.

After the adoption of the Declaration of Independence, he participated in
framing the Articles of Confederation,
which he signed on November 15, 1777.

Lee was especially interested in establishing free navigation on the Mississippi

River for American citizens, as well as
insisting that peace with Great Britain
should depend on the basis of her con-
cession of American rights in the
fisheries of Newfoundland.

After leaving the Continental Congress, he served in the Virginia senate,
1779–1782. The remainder of his life was
spent at his home, Menokin, in agricultural pursuits and enjoying the life of a
wealthy country gentleman.

Genealogy

I. Francis Lightfoot Lee, October 14,
1734–January 11, 1797, was born at Stratford Hall in Westmoreland County, Virginia, eighth of the eleven children of
Thomas and Hannah (Harrison) (Ludwell) Lee. At his father's death, he inherited an estate in Loudon County where
he resided for several years. Early in
1769, he married his first cousin, Rebecca
Tayloe, and moved to Richmond County
where their plantation on the Rappa-
hanock was called Menokin.

Francis Lightfoot Lee died of
pleurisy at Menokin on January 11, 1797;
his wife had died a few days before him
of the same illness. They were buried in
the Tayloe Family Cemetery, which is
one-half mile behind Mt. Airy the Tayloe
mansion, near Warsaw, Virginia.

In 1950, the Virginia Conservation
Commission provided two small grave-
stones marking their graves. Lee had no
children.

TAYLOE
Rebecca Tayloe, January 17, 1752–
January 7, 1797, was the daughter of the
Honorable John Taylor (alias Tayloe)
and Rebecca (Plater) Tayloe of Mount
Airy, Richmond County, Virginia. John

Taylor/Tayloe was the son of the Honorable William Taylor, the emigrant, of Lancaster and Richmond counties, Virginia. William Taylor married, in 1685, Ann Corbin, February 9, 1664–1694. Ann Corbin's sister, Letitia, 1657–1706, married Colonel Richard Lee of Mount Pleasant and Stratford. Ann and Letitia Corbin were the daughters of Henry Corbin.

LUDWELL

II. Thomas Lee, 1690–November 14, 1650, was baptized on April 29, 1705, married in May 1722, Hannah Ludwell, daughter of Colonel Philip and Hannah (Harrison) Ludwell, Jr., of Greenspring. Thomas and Hannah Lee had nine children and lived at Mount Pleasant, and at Stratford Hall where Francis Lightfoot Lee and Richard Henry Lee were born. Thomas Lee was governor of Virginia, 1740–1745.

Hannah Harrison, December 15, 1678–April 4, 1732, was the daughter of the Honorable Benjamin Harrison II, September 20, 1645–January 30, 1712, of Surry County, and his wife, Hannah Churchill, February 13, 1651–February 16, 1698. Benjamin Harrison was a justice of the peace in 1671; sheriff in 1679; burgess several years between 1698 and 1712; and a member of the King's Council 1698–1712. He was buried at Cabin Point, Wakefield, Surry County. He was the son of Benjamin Harrison I, baptized 1594–1648, who came to America and was at the Isle of Wight before March 15, 1633/4. He took up a patent of land on Warrosquivake Creek, July 7, 1635, and became a tobacco planter. He died in 1648 and his widow, Mary, married Benjamin Sidway. He was perhaps the son of Thomas Harrison of Gobion's Manor, Northamptonshire, who died before 1616,

having married in 1581, Elizabeth Bernard, of Abingdon, of a very prominent family.

Philip Ludwell II was the son of Philip Ludwell I and Lucy Higginson, ca. 1626–November 6, 1675. He married Hannah Harrison, 1678–1731, daughter of the Honorable Benjamin Harrison II and Hannah Churchill. Hannah Harrison Ludwell died April 4, 1731, in her fifty-second year.

Colonel Philip Ludwell, Sr., 1640–ca. 1723, of Greenspring, came to Virginia about 1660 and married, as her third husband, Lucy Higginson (Burwell) (Bernard) in 1667. He was a member of the King's Council; deputy secretary of Virginia; and governor of North Carolina and South Carolina in 1693. Colonel Ludwell married second, Lady Frances Berkeley, the widow of Sir William Berkeley but had no children with her. He returned to England, died about 1723, and is buried at Bow Church, Stratford, Middlesex County.

Lucy Higginson, ca. 1626–November 6, 1675, was born in England, and is buried in Abingdon Parish beside her first husband. She married first ca. 1646 Major Lewis Burwell, married second Colonel William Bernard, and third in 1667 Colonel Philip Ludwell, by whom she had one son and two daughters.

Lucy Higginson was the daughter of Captain Robert and his wife Joanna (Tokesey) Higginson who came to Virginia about 1643. In 1644 he was commander at Middle Plantation, now Williamsburg, and in 1646 he received 100 acres of land as a reward for valiant service. He died in August 1649, leaving an only daughter and heiress, Lucy. According to York County records, he is buried at Carter's Creek, Virginia. Joanna Higginson returned to England in 1650.

Robert Higginson was the son of Thomas and Ann Higginson of Barkeswell, Warwick, and a grandson of John Higginson of Wem, County Salop, England, whose will was dated 1640.

CORBIN

III. Colonel Richard Lee, born 1647–March 12, 1714, was heir to Ditchley and attended Oxford University, England. He married Letitia Corbin, 1657–October 6, 1706, daughter of Henry and Alice (Eltonhead) Corbin. The Honorable Henry Corbin, 1629–January 2, 1676, was born at Hall End in Warwick County, England, and died at Buckingham House in Middlesex County, Virginia. He came to Virginia in 1650 and lived at Stratton Major, King and Queen County. He moved to Buckingham House and was the first registrar of his parish in Middlesex, 1663–1667. He was a member of the King's Council, a burgess from Lancaster County, 1657–1660, from that part which became Middlesex. By his will dated July 25, 1675, he left large estates both in England and Virginia. He married in England on July 25, 1645, Alice Eltonhead, who was a daughter of Richard and Ann (Sutton) Eltonhead of Eltonhead, Lancaster County, England.

Henry Corbin was the third son of Thomas and Winifred (Grosvenor) Corbin of Hall End, Warwick County, England. Thomas Corbin, May 24, 1594–June 1737, was born and died at Hall End; married in 1620, Winifred Grosvenor, daughter of Gawin Grosvenor of Sutton Colfield, Warwick, England. The Grosvenors were descended from Sir Gilbert Grosvenor who came to England with William the Conqueror. Thomas Corbin was descended in the seventeenth generation from Robert Corbion/Corbin, whose son Robert gave lands to the Abbey of Talesworth during the Reign of Henry II of England, 1154–1161.

CONSTABLE

IV. Colonel Richard Lee, ca. 1619–1684, the emigrant ancestor of the Virginia Lees, was called "the Cavalier." He came from Stratford-Langton, Essex, England, and received a 1,000 acre grant of land on August 10, 1642, for bringing settlers into Virginia. He was a burgess of York County, 1647–1657; served as secretary of state under Sir John Harvy. He was the king's counsellor and served as colonial secretary under Sir William Berkeley, and was a member of the council and a justice.

He married Ann Constable of unknown parents. His will, dated 1663, was proved 166(5?).

Chapter 26

RICHARD HENRY LEE

1732–1794

VIRGINIA

Richard Henry Lee

RICHARD HENRY LEE, politician, patriot, plantation owner, statesman, received his primary education from private tutors. He was sent to England to study at the Academy at Wakefield in Yorkshire. After completing his studies and traveling for a few months, he returned home about 1752. He then pursued independent study of the principles of civil law, of history, and particularly that of the colonies and the mother country.

Lee's first public service came in 1757 when he was appointed justice of the peace for Westmoreland County, Virginia. In 1758, he entered the House of Burgesses, where he would serve for the next thirty-three years. Richard Henry Lee, like his brother Francis, was shy as a young man but, unlike his brother, he became skilled in the art of public speaking. About 1759, Lee made an important speech on his opposing views on slavery. He proposed that a heavy duty be imposed on the importation of slaves, so heavy that it would "put an end to that iniquitous and disgraceful traffic within the Colony of Virginia." He advised the House to give serious attention to debate concerning slavery. He could not have imagined that a cousin would be born at Stratford Hall thirteen years after his death, who would become the great Confederate general, Robert Edward Lee, 1807–1870.

Lee, together with Patrick Henry, who was not yet a member of the House, worked to have the offices of the Speaker of the House and the treasurer separated. He instigated an investigation of the treasury, which lost him some political supporters for a time.

When Parliament's plan to tax the colonies became known in March 1764, Lee at once was one of the first champions of colonial rights. He wrote to a friend in England that "free possession of property, the right to be governed by laws made by our representatives, and the illegality of taxation without consent" were principles of the British constitution. When the House of Burgesses registered a protest against the Stamp Act, Lee was the committeeman chosen to draft an address to the king, another to the House of Lords, and a remonstrance to the House of Commons.

He was in agreement with, but not in the House on May 30, 1765, when Patrick Henry proposed his five resolutions denouncing the Act. In February 1766, Lee formed an association of men from Westmoreland County to prevent the sale of stamped paper. He led these people to the house of one collector and forced the surrender of all stamps in his possession, and extracted an oath that the collector would refrain from the distribution of stamps. He also drafted the petition to the king recounting the grievances of the colonists with regard to the quartering of the military, as well as to the unjust levying of taxes.

In a July 25, 1768, letter to John Dickinson, Lee suggested the idea of a correspondence society as an efficient means of achieving united opposition as well as diffusing intelligence. This was first put in practice in 1773, between the Virginia and Massachusetts colonies.

Between 1768 and 1773, Lee was engaged in shipping tobacco to his brother William, who was a London merchant. This was a relatively quiet pre–Revolutionary period. In 1769, his resolutions against the assumed right of England to bind the colonies caused dissolution of the Virginia Assembly. He immediately became active in forming nonimportation societies, and their restrictions were to be strictly adhered to.

In 1772, he protested against the establishment of admiralty courts, which took away the right of trial by jury. When the Boston Port Bill was passed, he proposed that a general congress take place. Thomas Jefferson came into the House of Burgesses in 1769, and with Richard Henry Lee and Patrick Henry and a few others they began to share their ideas and efforts. In March 1773, they originated the intercolonial Committees of Correspondence which Lee declared ought to have been fixed from the beginning "as leading to that union, and perfect understanding of each other, on which the political salvation of America so eminently depends." In May 1774, this same group, as expressed by Thomas Jefferson, "cooked up" a resolution to make May 13, 1774, the day the Port of Boston was to be closed, a day of "fasting, humiliation, and prayer."

Richard Henry Lee had prepared resolutions which declared that the closing of the Port of Boston was a "most violent and dangerous attempt to destroy the constitutional liberty and rights of British America." Notable also, was a call for a general congress of the colonies to adopt means for securing these rights.

The fast-day resolution brought about dissolution of the Virginia Assembly, but the burgesses met and summoned a convention. Before the Virginia Convention could assemble, Massachusetts had already called for the general congress and named Philadelphia and September 1, as the place and time. Virginia's delegates were Peyton Randolph (a conservative), Speaker of the House of Burgesses, who was the first named; Richard Henry Lee was named second. The other five delegates to the First Continental Congress were George Washington, Patrick Henry, Benjamin Harrison, Richard Bland, and Edmund Pendleton. During this first congress, Lee formed a lifelong friendship with Samuel Adams.

Benjamin Rush, an avid note-taker observed, "I never knew so great an orator whose speeches were so short." Rush continued, "He conceived his subject so clearly, and presented it so immediately to his hearers, that there appeared nothing more to be said about it."

During this First Continental Congress which met in Carpenters' Hall on September 5, 1774, he served on all the important committees, and among others, made a motion "to apprise the public of danger, and of the necessity of putting the colonies in a state of defense. This was overruled as premature. In the Assembly of Virginia, Patrick Henry proposed arming their militia and Lee seconded the proposal. He was also on the Committee of Congress which drafted the commission of George Washington as commander in chief of the army. He signed the Articles of Association on October 20, 1774.

On October 3, 1775, Lee was appointed to the Marine Committee. In November 1775, he agreed with John Adams that it was time the colonies became self-governing.

Lee wrote the second address to the people of Great Britain, and on June 7, 1776, moved

> that these united colonies are, and of right ought to be, free and independent states, that they are absolved from all allegiance to the British Crown, and that all political connection between them and the state of Great Britain is and ought to be, totally dissolved.

Illness in his family caused him to leave Philadelphia, and he was not present when his resolution was voted upon or at the drafting of the Declaration of

Independence. He had been appointed to the committee for its drafting on June 10, 1776, but was replaced by Thomas Jefferson. He was not present to sign the engrossed copy of the Declaration with the greater number of members on August 2, 1776. His signature was affixed to the document on September 4, 1776.

While at his home, he narrowly escaped capture by the British. He remained in the Continental Congress until 1779.

Lee played an important role in the preparation of plans for treaties with foreign nations. For a while, he commanded the militia of Westmoreland County, Virginia, against enemy attacks along the coast. He returned to Congress in 1784, where he was unanimously chosen president for a year.

Under the Constitution, he was the first Senator from Virginia, and retired from public life on October 22, 1792.

Genealogy

I. Richard Henry Lee, January 20, 1732–June 19, 1794, was the seventh of eleven children of Thomas Lee and Hannah Ludwell. Hannah was the daughter of Philip Ludwell, Jr., and his wife Hannah Harrison of Greenspring, who were married in 1722. (See the genealogy section of Francis Lightfoot Lee in chapter 25 for continuation of Lee, Ludwell, Harrison, Corbin, and Constable lines.)

Richard Henry Lee married first, on December 3, 1757, Ann Aylett, who died in December 1768, by whom he had four children. He married second, in 1769, Mrs. Anne Gaskins Pinckard, by whom he had two children. About 1766, Lee lost the four fingers from his left hand when he was shooting fowl on the Potomac River. He wore a black silk scarf to cover it.

He died at his home Chantilly and was buried in the Burnt House Field where his parents, his wives, and other ancestors and relatives are buried. Burnt House Field is a part of the gardens of Machotick which was the plantation house of Richard Lee, which burned down in 1729.

An historical highway marker was erected by the Society of the Lees of Virginia in 1966, guiding visitors to Burnt House Field, near Hague, in Westmoreland County, Virginia.

His children were: (by first wife) unnamed child, 1756; unnamed child, 1758; Thomas, 1758; Anne, ca. 1759; Ludwell, 1760; Mary, 1764; Hannah, 1766; (by second wife) Child, ca. 1772; Sarah, 1775.

AYLETT

Ann Aylett, died December 1768, wife of Richard Henry Lee, was the daughter of William Aylett and his second wife, Elizabeth Eskridge. Elizabeth Eskridge was a daughter of George Eskridge of Sandy Point. William Aylett had married first, Ann Ashton, daughter of Colonel Henry Ashton, by whom he had a daughter also named Ann who married Augustine Washington, elder half-brother of George Washington. Colonel William Aylett was born in 1700 and died March 29, 1744. His will was proved August 28, 1744. He was the son of Captain William Aylett, born 1662, and his wife Sibylla who was living in 1749. Sibylla Aylett had been the widow of Matthew Hubbard.

Captain William Aylett bore the same arms as his ancestors of Braxted Magna, England. He was clerk of King William County, Virginia, 1702–1714;

member of the House of Burgesses 1723–1726; and vestryman of St. John's Parish in 1731. His land patents were in Essex, 1704 and 1717. Captain William Aylett was the son of Philip and Martha (Dandridge) Aylett, daughter of William Dandridge. Philip Aylett lived at Fairfield in King William County in 1686.

Captain John Aylett emigrated to America and his wife was Ann (possibly a daughter of Col. Richard Lee). Once a captain of horse at the Battle of Worcester, he was pardoned by Cromwell, but continued in acts against him in 1655. John Aylett fled to Virginia in 1656 and settled in King William County. He was the fourth son of Sir Benjamin Ayloffe who died in 1662/3, by his second wife Margaret Fanshawe, daughter of Thomas and Joan (Smith) Fanshawe, Esquire. Sir Benjamin Ayloffe was the son of Sir William Ayloffe, who was knighted by King James I, then advanced by King James I to Baronet in 1612. He was the fourth William Ayloffe in a family of Saxon origin, which was anciently seated at Bocton Aloph, near Wye in Kent County, England.

GASKINS

Ann Gaskins Pinckard, second wife of Richard Henry Lee, was the daughter of Colonel Thomas Gaskins, and the widow of Thomas Pinckard.

FRANCIS LEWIS

1713–1802

NEW YORK

FRANCIS LEWIS, merchant, patriot, attended Westminster School in London, England, and was then apprenticed to a London merchant where he worked in the counting house to prepare for a career in the mercantile business.

In 1738, Lewis emigrated to New York, bringing a cargo purchased with an inheritance. He took some of the cargo to Philadelphia where he remained for a year. Returning to New York, he formed a partnership with a Mr. Annesley and established his permanent home. He carried on the business for a while in New York and Philadelphia and returned to England for two years. His business was successful and he made numerous trips between America, England, and the northern ports of Europe including two trips to Russia. He was twice shipwrecked off the coast of Ireland.

During the French and Indian War, Lewis served as clothing contractor for the British troops under General Hugh Mercer. He was at Oswego, New York, during Montcalm's attack and upon surrender of the fort in 1754; its sixteen hundred men became prisoners of war. He was one of the thirty prisoners who were deported to Canada in August 1757, and thence to France and was there exchanged in 1763. The British government granted him 5,000 acres of wild land for his military service.

By 1765, Lewis had become influential in New York and had amassed sufficient wealth to retire to his Whiteside estate on Long Island. He became a member of the Stamp Act Congress in 1765, and was an early and most generous supporter of the Sons of Liberty. Now he became entirely occupied in the public service.

In 1771, he returned to the city to assist his el[...] They went t[...] trade conne[...] supply of d[...] pany, Franci[...] carried on s[...]

In 1774 [...] Provincial C[...] the Commit[...] actually a co[...] Lewis was o[...] in July 1774 [...] cessive cauti[...] Britain's par[...] ing 1775-76 [...] tion of a stat[...] He signed th[...] July 8, 1775.

In May [...] tion chose hi[...] delegates to [...] gress, only fi[...] any one time [...] were to be m[...] five who wer[...] Richard Hen[...] independenc[...] tions did not [...] against it. Th[...] draw and this [...] fore, New Yo[...] 1776. When t[...] sented in Co[...] the New York [...] their authoriz[...] on that day. [...] Lewis' home i[...] the British ar[...] tured.

Lewis wa[...] nental Congre[...] 1779, and serv[...] sioners of the [...] July 1781. He [...] not participat[...]

FRANCIS LEWIS

1713–1802

NEW YORK

FRANCIS LEWIS, merchant, patriot, attended Westminster School in London, England, and was then apprenticed to a London merchant where he worked in the counting house to prepare for a career in the mercantile business.

In 1738, Lewis emigrated to New York, bringing a cargo purchased with an inheritance. He took some of the cargo to Philadelphia where he remained for a year. Returning to New York, he formed a partnership with a Mr. Annesley and established his permanent home. He carried on the business for a while in New York and Philadelphia and returned to England for two years. His business was successful and he made numerous trips between America, England, and the northern ports of Europe including two trips to Russia. He was twice shipwrecked off the coast of Ireland.

During the French and Indian War, Lewis served as clothing contractor for the British troops under General Hugh Mercer. He was at Oswego, New York, during Montcalm's attack and upon surrender of the fort in 1754; its sixteen hundred men became prisoners of war. He was one of the thirty prisoners who were deported to Canada in August 1757, and thence to France and was there exchanged in 1763. The British government granted him 5,000 acres of wild land for his military service.

By 1765, Lewis had become influential in New York and had amassed sufficient wealth to retire to his Whiteside estate on Long Island. He became a member of the Stamp Act Congress in 1765, and was an early and most generous supporter of the Sons of Liberty. Now he became entirely occupied in the public service.

In 1771, he returned to the city to assist his eldest son, Francis, in business. They went to England to establish his trade connections, and returned with a supply of dry goods and formed a company, Francis Lewis and Son. The son carried on successfully and Lewis retired.

In 1774, he was a delegate to the Provincial Convention and a member of the Committee of Fifty-One, which was actually a committee of correspondence. Lewis was one of the eleven who resigned in July 1774 to protest against their "excessive caution" in opposing Great Britain's parliamentary legislation. During 1775-76 he participated in the formation of a state government for New York. He signed the Olive Branch Petition on July 8, 1775.

In May 1775, the Provincial Convention chose him to be one of their twelve delegates to the second Continental Congress, only five of whom could attend at any one time; attendance arrangements were to be made among themselves. The five who were in attendance favored Richard Henry Lee's resolution declaring independence, but believed their instructions did not allow them to vote for or against it. They requested leave to withdraw and this Congress granted it. Therefore, New York did not vote on July 2, 1776. When the engrossed copy was presented in Congress on August 2, 1776, the New York delegation had received their authorization and probably signed on that day. On September 19, 1776, Lewis' home in Whiteside was burned by the British army and his wife was captured.

Lewis was a member of the Continental Congress, May 1775–November 1779, and served as one of the commissioners of the Board of Admiralty until July 1781. He was not a speaker, and did not participate in the debates. However, he was a valuable member of the committees of marine, secret, and commercial, and of course, the Admiralty Board. He often was charged with duties connected with supplies for the army, and was a strong supporter of George Washington during the Conway Cabal Plot to remove him from the supreme command because he would not promote Thomas Conway to major-general in the U. S. Army.

Lewis signed the Articles of Confederation on November 15, 1778. He retired from the Continental Congress in September 1779.

Dr. Benjamin Rush called Mr. Lewis "a very honest man, and very useful in executive business."

Genealogy

1. Francis Lewis was born March 21, 1713, at Llandaff, Glamorganshire, Wales, the only child of the Reverend Francis Lewis and his wife Amy Pettingal. He married, on June 15, 1745, Elizabeth Annesley, sister of his business partner. They had seven children; only two sons and one daughter survived infancy. His daughter married a loyalist and went to England. Lewis was a vestryman of Trinity Church in New York City, 1784–1786. The Revolutionary War cost him his home and most of his wealth, and his last years were spent with the families of his sons. He died December 31, 1802, in his ninetieth year and was buried somewhere in the Trinity Church graveyard.

In 1947, a bronze plaque in Lewis's honor was erected by the Descendants of the Signers of the Declaration of Independence.

His children were: Morgan, 1745; Ann, 1748; Francis, 1750; and four unnamed infants who died in 1752, 1754, 1756, 1758.

ANNESLEY

Elizabeth Annesley was of New York; her parents are unknown. Her brother was Edward Annesley. When the Lewis's home at Whiteside, Long Island was burned, Mrs. Lewis was imprisoned in New York. George Washington, at the order of Congress, procured her release about two months later by placing two Tory ladies under house arrest in their Philadelphia homes until they could be exchanged for her. She died in 1779. In England, the Annesley/Anglesey family is an ancient one.

PETTINGAL

II. The Reverend Francis Lewis was Rector of Llandaff, Glamorganshire, Wales. He married, 1712 or before, Amy Pettingal of Caernarvon, North Wales. The Reverend Lewis may have been the male child christened February 8, 1691, at Carmarthen, Laugharne, Wales, whose parents were Jones and Jane Lewis.

Chapter 28

PHILIP
LIVINGSTON

1716–1778

NEW YORK

PHILIP LIVINGSTON, merchant, philanthropist, statesman, was graduated from Yale in 1737. In 1754, he was appointed alderman of the East Ward of New York City, then having a population of 10,881, a position he held for nine years. He became a successful importer in New York City. Sir Charles Hardy, governor of the Province of New York, wrote of him in 1755 that, "among the considerable merchants in this city, no one is more esteemed for energy, promptness, and public spirit than Philip Livingston."

He was one of the first to advocate the founding of Kings, now Columbia, College. In 1746, he provided for the establishment of a Professorship of Divinity at Yale which was named for him, and he was one of the builders of the meeting house on John Street for the first Methodist Society in America. Following the example of Benjamin Franklin and his associates, in 1754 Livingston helped organize the New York Public Library.

In 1758, he was a member of the Colonial House of Assembly of New York City. In 1764, he assisted in the preparation of the address to Lieutenant-Governor Colden, requesting his help to secure that "great badge of English liberty" the right of His Majesty's subjects everywhere to be taxed only with their own consent.

Livingston attended the Stamp Act Congress of 1765 and spent much of the time with the committee drafting a protest to the House of Lords. He objected to the methods of the Sons of Liberty, but worked with the lawyers and merchants in a more "dignified" way.

In 1768, he was elected to the Assembly for the third time and on October 27 was chosen speaker. However, in 1769

the assembly refused to allow him to represent Livingston Manor because he did not live there. The Assembly was dissolved in 1769.

Livingston founded the first Chamber of Commerce in 1770. In 1771, he was the first governor of New York Hospital.

In 1774, he was a member of the Committee of Fifty-One, which chose the New York delegates to the First Continental Congress, and was one of the five selected. He signed the Articles of Association on October 20, 1774. Philip Livingston was a member of the Committee of Sixty to enforce the terms of the "Association" and was placed on the Committee of One Hundred to carry forward provincial affairs until the first Provincial Congress in 1775. On July 8, 1775, he was president of the Provincial Congress of New York, and signed the Olive Branch Petition. In September 1775, Livingston was on a committee with Thomas McKean and Benjamin Franklin to obtain gunpowder and ordnance.

He and his cousin, Robert R. Livingston, were members of both the New York Congress and the Second Continental Congress. They had probably agreed that one of them would attend the New York Congress, the other the Continental Congress.

On July 19, 1776, his Brooklyn residence was the site of General George Washington's council of war. Philip Livingston was not present for the vote for independence as he was attending a session of the New York Congress. He signed the engrossed copy of the Declaration of Independence on August 2, 1776.

In the Continental Congress he served on many committees; on the Treasury Board, Commerce, a board to inspect Washington's army, Indian Affairs, and the Marine. In 1777, he was chosen by the New York State Convention as senator for the Southern District in the Upper House of their new legislature.

As a New York state senator, he was recognized as one of the purest and most devoted of the patriots. He attended their first meetings, and though in ill health, he once again joined the Continental Congress in York, Pennsylvania, took his seat in May 1778, and served until his death on June 12, 1778.

In 1948, a Pennsylvania historical highway marker was erected in Livingston's honor at the entrance to Prospect Hill Cemetery at York Pennsylvania.

Additional Information

John Adams' characterization of Livingston was, "Philip Livingston is a great, rough, rapid, mortal. There is no holding any conversation with him. He blusters away, says if England should turn us adrift, we should instantly go to civil wars among ourselves."

Livingston's home was on Duke Street in Brooklyn Heights, overlooking the harbor, where his ships brought ever increasing wealth. Livingston appeared to have a forbidding manner, except to his intimate friends who found an affectionate disposition and kindliness. He died at York, Pennsylvania, while serving in the Continental Congress. His funeral was attended in a body by Congress, and mourning was worn for him for one month.

Livingston was buried in the Prospect Hill Cemetery, where a monument was erected by his grandson, Stephen Van Rensselaer. Near the monument is a

Daughters of the American Revolution flagholder.

Genealogy

I. Philip Livingston, January 15, 1716–June 12, 1778, was the fifth son of Philip Livingston and his wife Catharine Van Brugh. He married, on April 14, 1740, Christina Ten Broeck; they had nine children.

His children were: Phillip, 1741; Dirck (Richard), 1743; Catharine, 1745; Margaret, ca. 1747; Peter VanBrugh, 1751; Sarah, 1752; Abraham, ca. 1754; Alida, 1757.

TEN BROECK
Christina Ten Broeck, wife of Philip Livingston, was the daughter of Colonel Dirck Wesselse Ten Broeck, 1638–1717, son of Wessel Ten Broeck who possibly came from Holland with Peter Minuit in 1626. Derck Ten Broeck appeared at Albany about 1662. He was magistrate, commissary, alderman and recorder, mayor of Albany, 1696–1698, a member of the first to the fifth Provincial Assemblies, commissioner of Indian Affairs for many years, and political agent to Canada four times. He married, in 1663, Christyna Van Buren, 1644–1729.

VAN BRUGH
II. Philip (Philippus) Livingston, christened July 25, 1686, at the Albany First Reformed Dutch Church, died in 1749. He was the Second Lord of the Manor of Livingston, and married, on September 19, 1707, Catharine Van Brugh, baptized November 10, 1689. She was the daughter of Captain Peter Van Brugh, mayor of Albany, whose father-in-law was Hendrick Cuyler, buried July 20, 1740.

SCHUYLER

III. Robert Livingston, the emigrant, first lord of Livingston Manor, arrived in America in 1673. He was born December 13, 1654, and died October 1, 1728. He married, July 9, 1679, Alida (Schuyler) Van Rensselaer, widow of Domine Nicholas Van Rensselaer. Alida was born in 1656 and died in 1729. She was the daughter of Philip Pieterse Schuyler, a citizen of Albany, who died in 1683. Schuyler married in 1650, Margarita Van Slickenhorst, 1628–1711, daughter of resident director of Rensselaerwyck. Robert Livingston, first lord of the manor, was the son of the Reverend John Livingston who emigrated to Rotterdam in 1663, due to the religious persecution in Scotland. He became one of the commissioners in negotiations for the peace which caused the transfer of New York to England. His son Robert emigrated to America in 1678, and the Reverend John Livingston obtained a patent for Livingston Manor on the Hudson River in Columbia County, New York.

V. Reverend William Livingston, 1576–1641, minister of Lanark, Scotland. His daughter married Donald, King of the Hebrides.

VI. The Reverend Alexander Livingston, who died ca. 1598, was rector of Monyabroch VII.

VII. James Livingston, died before October 13, 1547. In the mid–sixteenth century he was appointed Regent of Scotland during the minority of King James the First.

VIII. William Livingston, Fourth Lord of Callandar, died about 1514.

Chapter 29

THOMAS LYNCH, JR.

1749–1779

SOUTH CAROLINA

THOMAS LYNCH, JR., patriot, farmer, was educated at the Indigo Society School, Georgetown, South Carolina. His father sent him to England in 1764 to complete his education at Eton and Cambridge. He studied law at the Middle Temple, 1764–1772. On March 6, 1767, he was admitted to the Middle Temple Law School in London. On May 18, 1767, he began studies in Conville and Caimus College, Cambridge. By the time he returned to South Carolina in 1772, he had decided not to pursue a career of law. His father presented him with Peach Tree plantation, and he thus became a planter.

Being the only son of the prominent and wealthy Thomas Lynch, Sr., he was easily introduced into public service. He was a member of the first and second Provincial Congresses, 1774–1776; of the constitutional committee for South Carolina in 1776; the first state General Assembly in 1776; and the Second Continental Congress in 1776; the first state General Assembly in 1776; and the Second Continental Congress in 1776-77.

On June 12, 1775, the Provincial Assembly elected him one of the captains of the first South Carolina Regiment. He accepted, and in July went into North Carolina to recruit his company. During this service he contracted malaria which made him a partial invalid for the rest of his life.

On March 23, 1776, the General Assembly of South Carolina, organized under the constitution which he had co-operated in drafting, elected him to the Continental Congress so that he might care for his father who was in Philadelphia and had suffered a stroke.

Thomas Lynch, Jr., was now also too incapacitated to continue in public service, but was present at the vote for adoption of the Declaration of Independence on July 2. He signed the engrossed document on August 2, 1776, three days before his twenty-seventh birthday.

Genealogy

I. Thomas Lynch, Jr. was born on August 5, 1749, at Hopsewee Plantation, St. George's Parish, Winyaw, South Carolina. He was the only child of Thomas Lynch, Sr., 1727–1776, by his wife Elizabeth Allston, 1728–1749. Lynch had no children.

SHUBRICK
Lynch married on May 13, 1772, Elizabeth Shubrick, d. 1779; they had no children. Elizabeth Shubrick was the daughter of Thomas and Mary (Baker) Shubrick of Charleston, South Carolina. (See chapter 43 on Edward Rutledge for details about her family.) On May 11, 1779, Thomas Lynch of Santee made his will in which he mentions his wife "Elizabeth, sisters Sabina, Esther, and Elizabeth Lynch; also Mrs. Lynch widow of my late honored father, and others.... Sister Sabina Lynch during her life, then to her eldest son when of age. If failing to have a son, then to sisters Esther and Elizabeth in like manner. Person who shall be entitled to take the said Plantation under and by virtue of this Will shall take and use the Surname 'Lynch' and no other ... it having been my Father's Intention and it being my meaning to limit a part of his estate as far as the Law will Permit to such of his Family as shall use the Surname of 'Lynch.' Executors to move body of my father from Annapolis and to be interred in the Parish Church Yard at Santee with a plain marble monument erected...."

In the hope of improving his health, Mr. and Mrs. Thomas Lynch, Jr., took passage for the West Indies in the late autumn of 1779, expecting to board a vessel there to travel to the south of France. The ship on which they sailed was never heard of again and it is supposed that all its passengers were lost.

Thomas Lynch, Jr.'s nephew John Lynch Bowman changed his name to John Bowman Lynch. He was the only son of John and Sabina (Lynch) Bowman. John Bowman Lynch had three sons and four daughters. All three of the sons were killed in the Confederate service during the Civil War. They left no descendants.

ALLSTON

II. Thomas Lynch, 1727–December 1776, was born in St. James Parish, Berkeley County, South Carolina. He married first, on September 5, 1745, Elizabeth Allston who was the mother of Thomas Lynch, Jr.; married second, on March 6, 1755, at Georgetown, Hannah Motte, by whom he had three daughters. Lynch was a delegate to the Second Continental Congress, but because he suffered a stroke was unable to continue his service and South Carolina sent his son to serve in his place. En route from Philadelphia to South Carolina Lynch died of a second stroke and was buried in St. Anne's Churchyard in Annapolis, Maryland.

Elizabeth Allston was the daughter of William Allston, Collector of Customs for Georgetown. She was born in 1728 and died sometime between August 5, 1749, and March 6, 1755. William Allston died in 1733 or 1734. His wife was Esther LaBruce, 1704–1781, whom he married June 1721, daughter of Dr. Joseph La-Bruce de Marboeuf alias La Brosse, son of Julien Marboeuf of Bretagne, France, and his wife Esther Robins. William Allston was a son of William Allston, Sr., of Prince George Parish, Craven County, South Carolina, whose will was dated January 29, 1743. The Alston/Allston line traces to William Alston of Stisted in Essex, in the reign of Edward I, 1273–1307.

Hannah Motte was the fourth daughter of Jacob Motte, the Huguenot ancestor of the family, who was treasurer of South Carolina. Hannah Motte Lynch married second, General William Moultrie.

VANDERHORST

III. Thomas Lynch was the youngest son of Jonack (or Jonah) Lynch, the emigrant. He discovered a method of cultivating rice on their lands which were periodically flooded. He was granted large tracts of tidal areas on the North and South Santee Rivers and built a fortune which he bequeathed to his son. Lynch married first, Mary Fenwick; married second, Sabrina Vanderhorst daughter of John Vanderhorst. Sabina Vanderhorst Lynch married second on March 10, 1767, William Cattell.

IV. Jonack Lynch came from Dublin, Ireland, to South Carolina at the fall of Limerick, probably 1690/l. This family had its origin in Austria, and were natives of the town of Lintz. A branch of the family moved to England and settled in Kent County. They had migrated to Connaught in Ireland, and from there Jonack Lynch came to America.

Chapter 30

THOMAS
McKEAN

1734–1817

DELAWARE

THOMAS MCKEAN, lawyer, chief justice, governor of Pennsylvania, received his elementary education at home, and at nine years of age was sent to the Reverend Francis Allison's Academy at New London, Pennsylvania, where he studied for seven years. He then went to New Castle, Delaware, to study law under his cousin, David Finney.

He first became junior clerk in the office of the prothonotary at New Castle, and was then appointed deputy prothonotary and recorder for probate of wills in the county. Admitted to the bar in the lower counties of Delaware in 1754, he soon became deputy attorney general and clerk of the Delaware Assembly. At twenty-four, he was admitted to practice before the Supreme Court of Pennsylvania. About 1756, the attorney general of the Province appointed McKean as his deputy to prosecute all claims for the Crown in Sussex County. In 1757, at the age of twenty-three, he was allowed to practice in the Supreme Court of Pennsylvania. At the same time, he was elected clerk in the Delaware House of Assembly. He declined reelection in 1758 in order to go to London for further legal studies at the Middle Temple, where he was admitted on May 9, 1758. After his return, he practiced law for ten years in New Jersey, Pennsylvania, and Delaware. In 1762, he and Caesar Rodney were appointed to revise and codify laws passed after 1752 for the three Lower Counties.

In 1763, he received an honorary M.A. degree from the College of Pennsylvania. In October 1762, he was elected to the House of Assembly from New Castle and served there until 1780, seven years of which, 1772–1779, were as Speaker. He had become a resident of Philadelphia in 1774, though he still had a home in New Castle. He declined reelection to the House of Assembly on October 1, 1779.

McKean and Caesar Rodney were delegates to the Stamp Act Congress of October 7–26, 1765. McKean served on a committee with James Otis of Massachusetts and Thomas Lynch, Sr., of South Carolina, to prepare an address to the British House of Commons. He denounced the chairman of the Congress, who refused to sign the address, and ordered officers of his court to use unstamped paper. Also in 1765, he was appointed sole notary public for the lower counties on the Delaware, and he subsequently held the offices of justice of the peace, judge of the Court of Common Pleas and Quarter Sessions, and the Orphans' Court. In 1766, he was a member of the Committee of Correspondence for the three lower counties.

In 1766, Governor William Franklin of New Jersey, upon the recommendation of the New Jersey Supreme Court, admitted him to practice law in any of its courts. In 1771, he was appointed collector of the customs for the Port of New Castle.

On September 10, 1772, he became Speaker of the Provincial Assembly of the lower counties. In March 1768, McKean became a member of the American Philosophical Society. In 1769, he was a trustee of the original Academy of Newark, which was a continuation of Francis Allison's school at New London. In 1773, McKean was speaker pro tem of the Pennsylvania Assembly, justice of the peace for the Province of Pennsylvania, trustee of the Wilmington Academy, while continuing a member of the Committee of Correspondence for the lower counties.

McKean strongly supported the

movement for the General Congress which had been suggested in the Massachusetts circular letter. He was elected a delegate to the First Continental Congress and was present at its opening September 5, 1774. On October 20, 1774, he signed the Articles of Association. From that date, he was to remain an active member of the Continental Congress until the signing of the Treaty of Paris on September 3, 1783. He signed the Olive Branch Petition to King George III on July 8, 1775. On September 19, 1775, he was clerk of the Secret Committee appointed to procure gunpowder and ordnance. On November 4, 1775, he was appointed by the Continental Congress to a committee to help resolve the boundary dispute between Pennsylvania and Connecticut.

Prior to July 4, 1776, he was on five standing committees: secret, qualifications, prisoners, claims, treasury, and on many other committees. Having supported the patriot causes early, by 1776 he was a zealous supporter of the movement for separation. When Richard Henry Lee's resolution for independence was presented for a vote on July 1, he sent for Caesar Rodney because conservative George Read was opposed to it. Rodney arrived in time on July 2 to vote in favor of the resolution which gave Delaware the affirmative majority.

Immediately following the vote for independence on July 4, Colonel Thomas McKean hastened to the command of a group of Pennsylvania "associators" at Perth Amboy, New Jersey. He was therefore not present at the August 2, 1776, signing of the Declaration of Independence. He probably signed the document on or soon after January 18, 1777.

McKean helped frame Delaware's first constitution in the fall of 1776. Because of

loyalist opposition, McKean was not reelected to Congress from Delaware. In 1777, he became chief justice of Pennsylvania, but retained some offices in Delaware for about six years. His activities made him a target for persecution and pursuit. His family was forced to move five times within a few months. He settled them in a little log house on the Susquehanna River, but they were driven away from it by the Indians.

On Christmas 1780, McKean wrote to the Delaware legislature requesting to be excused for health and financial reasons. His request was denied, and he stayed on until 1783. From July 10 to November 5, 1781, he was president of the Continental Congress. He was chosen chief justice of the Supreme Court of Pennsylvania and served twenty-two years, 1777–1799.

McKean was a Federalist, and actively supported ratification of the federal Constitution in the 1787 convention. In 1799, he was nominated for governor, and as governor he removed his political enemies from office, giving their posts to his Republican allies. He was reelected in 1802 by more than a 30,000 vote majority, and again in 1805.

At the session of 1807-1808 of the Pennsylvania legislature, his opponents presented articles of impeachment against him for maladministration, which closed with a resolution that "Thomas McKean, the Governor of the Commonwealth, be impeached of high crimes and misdemeanors." The charges were brought fully before the House, but by the summary measure of indefinitely postponing their consideration, they were never acted upon.

McKean was a member of the Philadelphia conventions which ratified the U.S. Constitution in 1788, and framed that of Pennsylvania in 1790. He received the degree of LL.D. from Princeton in 1781, and honorary degrees from Dartmouth in 1782 and the University of Pennsylvania in 1785.

On March 26, 1804, Governor Thomas McKean signed the act of legislature which ended the Yankee-Pennamite War. On August 30, 1806, he purchased 299 acres of the unsurveyed land in the area of the Pennsylvania-Connecticut land controversy. In 1814, he was chairman of the Committee of Defense for Philadelphia.

In 1946, a historical highway marker at Port Allegheny, McKean County, Pennsylvania, was erected to honor McKean.

Additional Information

John Adams described Thomas McKean as one of the three men in the Continental Congress who "appeared to me to see more clearly to the end of the business than any others of the whole body." McKean was regarded as somewhat "harsh and domineering" by some, but friends admired him.

He was survived by four of his eight children, and his wife. His will disposed of a large estate including large tracts of land in Pennsylvania and stocks and bonds. McKean died at the age of eighty-three, and was survived by only five of the other signers of the Declaration of Independence.

Thomas McKean was buried in the McKean Family Plot at Laurel Hill Cemetery in Philadelphia.

Genealogy

I. Thomas McKean, March 19, 1734–June 24, 1817, was born in New London Township, Chester County, Pennsylvania, and died at Philadelphia. He married first, on July 21, 1763, Mary Borden, July 21, 1744–March 13, 1773, and they had six children. He married second, September 3, 1774, Sarah Armitage, December 19, 1746–May 6, 1820, and they had two children.

His children were: (by first wife) Joseph, 1764; Robert, 1766; Elizabeth, 1767; Letitia, 1769; Mary, 1771; Ann, 1773; (by second wife) unnamed son, 1775; Sarah, 1777; Thomas, 1779–1783; Sophia, 1783; Maria Louisa, 1785–1788; and six infants born and died in the years 1787, 1789, 1791, 1793, 1795, 1797.

BORDEN

Mary Borden, daughter of Colonel Joseph and Elizabeth Rogers Borden, of Burlington, Bordentown, New Jersey. She and her sister, Ann, wife of signer Francis Hopkinson, were said to be two of the most beautiful women in America. (To continue Mary Borden's ancestry, please see the genealogy section of Francis Hopkinson in Chapter 22.)

ARMITAGE

Sarah Armitage, December 19, 1746–May 6, 1820, second wife of Thomas McKean, was the daughter of James Armitage of New Castle County, and his second wife, Frances Land. James Armitage probably was born ca. 1688, at Kirkburton Parish, Yorkshire. He died before July 15, 1755, at White Clay Creek, New Castle County, Delaware. He was a justice of the peace and judge of Courts of New Castle. Sarah Armitage was the granddaughter of Benjamin Armitage, 1660/1–November 28, 1735, and his wife Mary, 1670–February 16, 1730. They came from Holefreth, Yorkshire, England, about 1700, and settled at Cheltham,

Philadelphia County, Pennsylvania. They both are buried in the old Presbyterian Graveyard at Abingdon Church, of which Benjamin Armitage was a founder. He was the son of James Armitage, who was baptized at Lyddgate, Yorkshire, in February 1633/4, and his wife, Martha Hatfield, who were married in 1660, and grandson of Godfrey and Anna Armitage of Yorkshire. Another James Armitage married first name unknown, married second, Mary Land, daughter of Francis and Christian Land. He had, by his first wife, a daughter Hannah born November 6, 1715, who married the Reverend Francis Allison, D.D., whose academy at New London several of the signers attended, including Thomas McKean and his brother Robert McKean.

FINNEY

II. William McKean, ca. 1705–1769, married about 1731, Letitia Finney, daughter of Robert and Dorothea Finney of New London. William McKean became an innkeeper in New London. Letitia died in 1742, and in 1745, William married Ann Logan, a widow of Londonderry township, New London. He removed to the Logan plantation where he kept a tavern until his death, November 18, 1769. Ann (Logan) McKean died in 1751. Robert Finney was born in Ireland in 1668, brought his wife Dorothea and their

children to Pennsylvania, and settled in New London Township, Chester County, before 1720. In 1722, he purchased a 900-acre tract and named his plantation Thunder Hill. He died there in March 1755, at the age of eighty-seven. Dorothea Finney died in 1752, age eighty-two years.

CREIGHTON (Susannah, maiden name unknown)

III. William McKean was the son of John McKean of Londonderry and Ballymony, Ireland. In 1725, he came with his wife Susannah, her son John Creighton of a former marriage, and their sons William and Thomas McKean and two daughters, Barbara and Margaret. They settled on a 300-acre plantation in Chester County, where he died. His widow Susannah McKean, continued to reside on the plantation until her death in 1731. Her will dated December 29, 1730 was proved in February 1730/1.

IV. John McKean, son of John McKean of Londonderry, Ireland, removed to Ballymoney, where he died.

V. John McKean, a loyal defender of Londonderry in 1668–1669, died at Ballymony, Ireland. He was the son of William McKean of Argyleshire, Scotland.

VI. William McKean, of Argyleshire, Scotland, in the late 1600s, sought asylum in Ireland because of religious and political persecution.

Chapter 31

ARTHUR
MIDDLETON

1742–1787

SOUTH CAROLINA

ARTHUR MIDDLETON, patriot, plantation owner, received his early education in South Carolina, and at the age of twelve was sent to study at Harrow School; in 1757 he attended Westminster School; and in 1760 was admitted to Trinity College, London. He toured Europe for two years before returning to South Carolina on the ship *Nancy*, arriving December 24, 1763.

In 1764, Middleton became a justice of the peace. In October 1764, he was elected to the colonial House of Assembly, in which he became a member of a Committee of Correspondence with the colonial agent in England until 1768. In May 1768, he went to Europe and did not return until September 1770. While in Rome Middleton studied music and painting. Upon his return to America, he took up residence at Middleton Place which he had inherited from his mother.

At home he found Americans were in political turmoil. His conservative father had allied himself with the patriots. Taking up the cause, Arthur began writing political papers which he signed Andrew Marvel.

In 1772, Middleton was elected to the House of Assembly; a few months later, to the first Provincial Congress representing Charleston. On June 14, 1775, he was one of three chosen for a council of safety. On February 11, 1776, he was appointed to the Committee of Eleven to prepare a constitution for South Carolina.

When the South Carolina constitution was adopted in February 1776, Middleton was appointed with Henry Drayton and others to prepare a seal for the state of South Carolina. Middleton drew the obverse side of the design that was adopted and is still the official seal. He served on a secret committee of five which arranged and directed the actions of three parties of citizens which seized powder and weapons from public storehouses on the night of April 21, 1776, two days after the battle at Lexington.

His father, Henry Middleton, who had represented the state at the First Continental Congress, resigned to let his more radical son succeed him as one of South Carolina's delegates in the Second Continental Congress. Being duly elected, Middleton left for Philadelphia.

In Philadelphia Middleton shared a house with John Hancock, with whom he was compatible in wealth, position, and taste. This compatibility seems to have outweighed the regional jealousies which were prevalent among the delegates. Together, Middleton and Hancock hosted important visitors to Philadelphia.

Arthur Middleton was present in Congress on May 20; also, to vote for independence on July 2, 1776. He signed the engrossed copy of the Declaration of Independence on August 2, 1776.

He served until the end of 1777 but declined reelection and did not attend in 1779 or 1780, due to his service in the South Carolina militia. His plantation was ravaged by the British in 1779.

At the fall of Charleston on May 12, 1780, he was serving in the militia and became a prisoner of war. His parole was revoked by Sir Henry Clinton and he was sent to St. Augustine, Florida, and served time on the *Jersey*, a British prison ship. He was exchanged in July 1781, presented his credentials to the Continental Congress on September 24, and was reelected by the Jacksonborough Assembly, and sat in the session of 1782.

Middleton served in the House of Representatives of South Carolina in 1785, and was on the board of trustees of Charleston College.

Genealogy

I. Arthur Middleton was born June 26, 1742, died January 1, 1787, at The Oaks, his home on the Ashley River. He was the eldest child of Henry Middleton and his wife Mary Williams. Middleton married on August 19, 1764, Mary Izard. His sisters married well, Sarah to Charles Pinckney, and Henrietta to signer Edward Rutledge. Middleton inherited Middleton Place from his mother.

Federal troops set fire to Middleton Place in February 1865. In 1975, it was designated a national historic landmark.

Arthur Middleton is buried with his mother in the Middleton Mausoleum located on the grounds of Middleton Place. Charles Pinckney, and other family members, are also buried here.

His children were: Henry, 1770; Maria Henrietta, 1772; Eliza Caroline, 1774; Emma Philadelphia, 1776; Anna Louisa, 1778; Isabella Johannes, 1780; Septima Sexta, 1783; John Izard, 1785; unnamed son, 1787. Biographers say he had twelve children.

IZARD

Mary Izard, July 31, 1747–June 1814, was the daughter of Walter Izard, born May 15, 1692, and died February 17, 1750. He was a justice of the peace at Cedar Grove, Berkeley County, and was captain of a Berkeley regiment in 1712 and served in the Yemassee War. He married on May 19, 1713, Mary Turgis, daughter of Francis and Elizabeth (Axtell) Turgis of Berkeley County. Elizabeth Axtell was the daughter of Landgrave Daniel Axtell, a member of the King's Council in 1681.

Walter Izard was the son of the the Honorable Ralph Izard, born in England, who came to South Carolina in 1682, and was of Charleston by October 3, 1682. He settled at St. James Parish and married first, in 1687, Mary (Smyth) Middleton, widow of Arthur Middleton. Her will was proved on July 26, 1700. Izard married second, Dorothy Smith who was the widow of Christopher Smith of Stock Prior, Berkeley County, Virginia.

Ralph Izard, citizen and grocer of London, married Elizabeth (Prive?). His will was proved there November 8, 1699.

WILLIAMS

II. Henry Middleton, 1717–1784, was probably educated in England. He married first, Mary Williams, who was the mother of his twelve children. He married second, after January 9, 1761, Maria Henrietta Bull, daughter of Lieutenant Governor William Bull. She died on March 1, 1771, and Mr. Middleton married third, Lady Mary Mackenzie, widow of John Ainslie and daughter of George Mackenzie, Third Earl of Cromerlie.

Mary Williams, August 7, 1721–January 9, 1761, was the only child of John and Mary (Baker) Williams who were married June 16, 1720, at Berkeley, St. Andrews. Williams was a member of the House of Commons from St. George's.

Henry Middleton owned approximately twenty plantations and about eight hundred slaves. He was the second president of the Continental Congress, October 22, 1774–May 10, 1775. In 1780, when Charleston fell to the British, he was one of those who accepted defeat and took protection under the British flag.

AMORY

III. Arthur Middleton, acting colonial governor of South Carolina, was born at The Oaks in 1681, and died September 7, 1737. He was the son of Edward Middleton and was probably educated in England. He inherited estates in England, Barbados, and South Carolina. Middleton married first, in 1707, Sarah Amory, who died in 1722. He married second, August 3, 1723, Sarah (Wilkinson) Morton, widow of Joseph Morton, a landgrave (a county nobleman) of South Carolina. By her he had no children. She died in 1765 at Goose Creek.

Sarah Amory, 1685–1722, was the daughter of Jonathon and Martha Amory of Charleston. Jonathon Amory, merchant, was born March 14, 1653/4 at Bristol, England, and died at Charleston in 1699 of the plague (yellow fever). He was a merchant and came from England via Jamaica to South Carolina August 29, 1682. He was appointed by the Crown as advocate general in South Carolina Admiralty Courts in 1697; Speaker of the House of Commons; was a large land holder; and was receiver for the public treasury in 1699. He had married first about 1679, Rebecca Houston, widow of David Houston of Lazyhill, near Dublin, Ireland. Amory married second, Martha,

surname unknown, who died in 1699, at Goose Creek, South Carolina, after October 30 but before November 13. Jonathon Amory was the son of Thomas Amory, born 1608–died 1657 in Ireland, and Ann (Elliott) married in 1631, of Bristol, England. Jonathon was also the grandson of Hugh Amory who died December 29, 1626, who was of Somerset, England, in 1605.

Hugh Amory married Agnes Young, daughter of Nicholas and Joanne Young who died 1640. Their son Thomas Amory of Bristol, England, was born 1608 and died 1657 in Ireland. Thomas Amory married, in 1631, Anne Elliott.

FOWLE/FOWELL

IV. Edward Middleton, born 1620, at age fifteen came with his brother Arthur on the *Dorset*, embarked September 30, 1635, to Barbados, then to South Carolina in 1678. He was Lord Proprietor's deputy and assistant justice and a member of the Grand Council 1678–1684. He married second, in 1680, Sarah Fowle/Fowell, widow of Richard Fowell of Barbados. Middleton died at Charleston in 1685.

Chapter 32

LEWIS
MORRIS

1726–1798

NEW YORK

Lewis Morris

LEWIS MORRIS, lord of the manor of Morrisania, major-general of the militia, patriot, received a carefully supervised elementary education. He attended Yale College, graduating in 1746 with an A.B. degree.

He returned to Morrisania, in Westchester County, New York, to assist with management of the large estates of his father. His father died in 1762, and as the eldest son, he became the third and last lord of the manor.

In 1760, he was appointed by the Crown to be judge of the Court of Admiralty. He resigned his admiralty judge post in 1774.

At this time he became quite interested in politics. Morris served one term in the Provincial Assembly of Westchester County, New York, in 1769 but was expelled because he resided for a time outside of Westchester County.

He was named chairman of a delegation of eight deputies who were chosen to attend a provincial convention meeting in New York City on April 20, 1775. They were instructed to support a resolution to send delegates from New York to the Second Continental Congress.

Lewis Morris was chosen as one of the delegates to the Continental Congress and took his seat on May 15, 1775. His services in the Continental Congress were mainly on committees to select posts to be defended in New York and to provide the colonies with ammunition and other military supplies such as cloth for tents, and the manufacture of sulfur and saltpeter. On July 8, 1775, he signed the Olive Branch Petition which King George III rejected.

In September 1775, Morris traveled to Pittsburgh as commissioner for Indian Affairs, to discuss establishing trade relations with the western tribes. He became a member of the Permanent Commission on Indian Affairs.

On June 6, 1776, Morris was appointed brigadier-general of the militia in Westchester County, New York. He took a leave from Congress and assumed his post, and was therefore not in Philadelphia to vote for adoption of the Declaration of Independence on July 2. He was present in the Provincial Congress in White Plains, New York, on July 9, 1776, when the action of the Continental Congress was endorsed. He returned to Congress and signed the Declaration of Independence on August 2, 1776. He withdrew from the Continental Congress in June 1777, recommending his half-brother, Gouverneur Morris, be elected in his place.

Morris served as county judge of Westchester County from May 8, 1777, until February 17, 1778, and between 1777 and 1790 was several times a member of the upper house of the state legislature. On June 25, 1778, he was again brigadier-general of the Westchester County Militia.

After the Revolutionary War ended, Morris retired to Morrisania with the rank of major-general of militia, and turned his attention to rebuilding his estates which had been burned and plundered by the British.

In 1784, he supported the reopening of King's College under the name of Columbia College. From 1784 to 1798 he was a member of the first Board of Regents of the University of the State of New York. Two years later he was named a member of the Council of Appointments. In 1788, he attended the convention at Poughkeepsie as a member of the Hamiltonian forces in favor of ratification of the United States Constitution.

Lewis Morris sold Morrisania to his half-brother Gouverneur Morris in 1786, who completed its restoration about 1790. Morris shares some memorials with this brother; however, one monument at Morrisania reads:

IN THE CRYPT OF ST. ANN'S CHURCH IN THIS CHURCHYARD LIES THE BODY OF LEWIS MORRIS, ONLY SIGNER OF THE DECLARATION OF INDEPENDENCE FROM THE CITY OF NEW YORK.

THIS MONUMENT WAS ERECTED BY THE CHILDREN OF THE PUBLIC SCHOOLS OF THE BRONX AD 1929.

St. Ann's Church of Morrisania is a landmark of New York.

Additional Information

In 1776, Morris's family was driven from their home which was devastated by the British. They returned to Morrisania in 1783 after the British had left New York, and Morris declared he had restored the manor to its prewar magnificence. He was a tall, handsome man, and continued a member of the "landed aristocracy" of New York. He died in 1798, and was buried under the Chancel of St. Ann's Church of Morrisania, also known as the Church of the Patriots.

Morris's half-brother Gouverneur Morris became known as the "Penman of the U.S. Constitution"; he was a Pennsylvania delegate to the federal Constitution Convention, and signed the Constitution for Pennsylvania. He was also the author of the Preamble to the U.S. Constitution.

Lewis Morris's grave is identified by a large bronze plaque which was erected on February 28, 1932, by the Washington Heights Chapter of the Daughters of the American Revolution.

Genealogy

I. Lewis Morris, April 8, 1726–January 22, 1798, A.B. Yale, 1746, married on September 24, 1749, at New York, New York, Trinity Church, Mary Walton, daughter of Jacob and Mary (Beekman) Walton. They had ten children.

His children were: Catherine, 1750; Mary, 1752; Lewis, 1754; Jacob, 1755; William Walton, 1757; Sarah, 1759; Helena Magdalena, 1762; James, 1764; Staats, 1765; Richard Valentine, 1768.

WALTON

Mary Walton, February 1727–March 11, 1794, was the daughter of Jacob and Maria (Beekman) Walton of New York City. Jacob Walton and his brother William, sons of Jacob and Mary (Cruger) Walton, deceased, were brought up by their father's sister who was a Beekman.

Mary Cruger was the daughter of Henry Cruger, Elder of the City of New York. At the time of his death, Henry Cruger was living at Bristol, England. His will was dated June 11, 1779, and was proved March 2, 1780. Among his bequests were two entries to his daughter Mary Walton wife of Jacob Walton of the City of New York, merchant, £1,000. Also, from residue of estate, one fourth to daughter Mary Walton.

Gerardus Beekman, born 1653, was named in honor of his great grandfather, Gerardus Beekman. He married on October 25, 1677. Magdalen Abeel, 1661–1730, daughter of Stoffel Janse Abeel, a master carpenter who died in 1684, and who served as commissary for the West Indies Company. Gerardus Beekman was a physician and councilor, and acting governor of New York, and a deacon at Flatbush. He was the son of William

Beekman, the emigrant, 1623–1707, who came to America at Christmastime 1646. He arrived in the expedition of Peter Stuyvesant, on the Princess, May 11, 1647.

STAATS

II. Judge Lewis Morris, Second Lord of the Manor of Morrisania, was born September 1698, died in 1762. He married, in 1723, Katrintja Staats, who died after August 15, 1730. He married second, Sarah Gouverneur, daughter of Nicholas Gouverneur who died January 14, 1726. The Gouverneurs were Huguenots who came to New York after the revocation of the Edict of Nantes.

GRAHAM

III. Lewis Morris, October 15, 1671–May 21, 1746, was the first royal governor of New Jersey, 1738–1746. Both of his parents died in 1672, and he was reared by his uncle, Lewis Morris. He married, on November 3, 1691, Isabella Graham, 1672–March 30, 1752, daughter of James and Dorothy (Howard) Graham of Westchester County, New York. In 1791, he inherited from his uncle the Bronck's land estate of about 2,000 acres, as well as 3,500 acres at Monmouth County, New Jersey. He established a home called Tintern in New Jersey, which was named for the Morrises ancestral home in Monmouthshire. Governor Fletcher issued royal letters patent in May 1697, erecting

the Morris estate into the manor of Morrisania. James Graham, born 1650 at Edinburgh, Scotland, was the son of Patrick and Agnes (Smythe) Graham. He arrived in New York, August 7, 1678, and was attorney general for New York State; New York assemblyman 1691–1699; colonel of a Westchester regiment. He married first, Dorothy Howard who died in 1682. He married second, in New York City on July 18, 1684, Elizabeth Windebank. Graham died March 1, 1700/1 in Westchester County. His will dated January 12, 1700/1 was proved April 3, 1701.

POLE

IV. Richard Morris, 1616–1672, served in Cromwell's army, was captain, British office of Parliament. He married at Barbados, Sarah Pole (?Poole) who possessed a considerable fortune. She was the daughter of Sir William and Sarah (Vignor) Pole of Kent County, Virginia. Richard Morris and his brother Lewis were both merchants of Barbados in 1670 when they purchased a tract of 500 acres known as Bronck's land, located north of the Harlem River in New York. There Richard Morris and his wife both died in 1672.

WALTERS

V. William Morris was of Tintern, Parva, Monmouth, Wales. His wife was Lucy Walters.

Chapter 33

ROBERT
MORRIS

1734–1806

PENNSYLVANIA

ROBERT MORRIS, merchant, financier, patriot, statesman, came from Liverpool, England, to Oxford, Maryland, at the age of thirteen. He completed his primary education in England. For a short time, he was tutored by the Reverend William Gordon. His father sent him to Philadelphia's leading schoolmaster, but he disliked schoolwork and after a year of study his formal education ended.

In 1748, Robert Morris, Jr., left Oxford, Maryland, to live with Robert Greenway, a merchant friend of his father. Although Greenway arranged a tutor for Morris, he soon deserted his studies, and was apprenticed to Charles Willing, a shipping merchant and prominent citizen of Philadelphia.

In 1754, at the age of twenty, Robert Morris was made a member of the firm of Willing, Morris, and Company. For nearly forty years he was to be actively involved in this company or its successors under different names. The Willing Company had its own ships and its own banking business, and were importing British and exporting American goods.

The British colony in the West Indies, then known as the Sugar Islands, was one of their ports. Charles Willing died of typhus. After his death on or soon after November 29, 1754, his son Thomas Willing returned from being educated in England and headed the firm.

Morris asked permission to go to the Sugar Islands on one of their ships and was charged with selling the ship and cargo at Jamaica, which task he performed successfully. On a second voyage to the West Indies, a Jamaican merchant had corresponded with Thomas Willing who had written of his "great esteem" and his hope to see Morris "advantageously

engaged anywhere." Though the offered partnership was tempting Morris decided to remain in Philadelphia with his friend and partner.

On the return voyage, the brig on which Morris was traveling was captured by French privateers. The passengers were robbed of everything, but Morris, their captain, and the American crew escaped and managed to reach Cuba. Half starved, they arrived in Havana, which had been destroyed by the French three years earlier. They had lost their money and baggage and were stranded. One day Morris repaired a man's watch, for which he was paid, and the man sent him other customers who needed repairs done. He was then able to buy food and other essentials. Then an American ship arrived and brought him home.

Morris was now twenty-two and Thomas Willing offered him a partnership. This young man who had been orphaned at fifteen, without a relative in the colonies, had in ten years become a thriving businessman. As a partner in a successful mercantile business in the largest city in America with a busy port, he became wealthy.

After the French and Indian War, 1754–1763, Great Britain needed money and began to enact laws to regulate trade, which was a lucrative source of income to them but seriously affected the merchants. One law required ships returning home from Europe and Africa to stop at an English port, thereby lengthening the voyages and costing time and money. To avoid the English import tax or duties, smuggling was often attempted and this, in turn, prompted the British to begin inspections of merchants and shipping. Their naval vessels were used to enforce their revenue acts.

Willing and Morris remained above

reproach in their foreign trade, but the government's practices became increasingly restrictive. This weighed heavily on Thomas Willing and he became gloomy and discouraged, and greater responsibilities were shifted to Morris. Then in 1763, Willing was elected mayor of Philadelphia and Robert Morris took over the management of the business.

Parliament passed the Stamp Act in March 1764, and at a meeting at Davenport's Tavern, some four hundred Philadelphia merchants signed the Nonimportation Resolutions. It seemed to be a patriotic duty to resist the British acts. In October 1764, Morris served on a committee of citizens appointed to force the collector of the stamp taxes in Philadelphia to desist from performing his duties. Morris was opposed to the Stamp Act, but refused to sign the nonimportation agreement in 1765 because it affected his business.

In March 1768, Bostonians revived the nonimportation of British goods. New Yorkers agreed to join their movement if the Philadelphia merchants would also participate; however, it was nearly a year before the conservative Philadelphians would take part in it.

Morris was attending a dinner of the Society of the Sons of St. George when a courier arrived, April 23, 1775, bearing the news of the Battle of Lexington. This was the event which caused him to become a fully committed patriot. On June 30, 1775, the assembly appointed him a member of the Council of Safety. On October 20, he was reappointed on the new council to serve during the next year. In September, a secret committee of the Continental Congress contracted with Willing and Morris for the importation of arms and ammunition. In October, Morris was elected to the last Pennsylvania Assembly held under the colonial charter, and was a member of the Committee of Correspondence.

In November 1775, Morris was sent by the Assembly as a delegate to the Continental Congress, where his commercial experience was extremely useful. He was a member of the committee charged with procuring munitions, frequently acting as its banker. Within two weeks after taking his seat in the Congress, he was appointed to provide two swift vessels to carry dispatches. On November 29, he succeeded Thomas Willing on the secret committee for procuring munitions and then was placed on the committee for providing naval armaments.

He was appointed to the Committee of Secret Correspondence on January 30, 1776, which drew up instructions to Silas Deane, envoy to France. In March he was on a committee to consider fortifying one or more seaports. Through his firm of Willing and Morris, he continued to import supplies for the army and occasionally was charged with the banking business of the Continental Congress.

Apparently in response to a query from Horatio Gates, John Adams wrote in his reply:

> You ask me what you are to think of Robert Morris? ... I think he has a masterly understanding, an open temper and an honest heart.... He has vast designs in the mercantile way. And no doubt pursues mercantile ends, which are always gain, but he is an excellent member of the body.

Being a Pennsylvania "moderate" he was not sure it was yet time for separation from England, and on July 1, 1776, he voted against independence. He did not attend Congress on July 2, when the "radicals" or "violents" voted for independence. He did, however, sign the engrossed parchment copy of the Declaration of Independence on August 2, 1776, saying that it was "the duty of every individual to act his part in whatever station his country may call him to in hours of difficulty, danger, and distress."

During the winter of 1777, the desperate struggle went on. Congress was slow in procuring food and money for the army, and General Washington appealed to Robert Morris for help.

On Christmas night, Washington crossed the Delaware, capturing more than a thousand Hessian soldiers, bringing the British their first important defeat.

Behind the scenes, Robert Morris worked night and day to pay the soldiers and supply their food, clothing, and ammunition. On one occasion, Washington's soldiers were without lead to make bullets for cartridges, when even the house drains and piping of the city of Philadelphia had gone into bullets, and lead was fifty cents a pound. Morris stripped one of his privateers of its ballast of ninety tons and turned it over to General Washington, who never forgot how much he had relied upon Robert Morris.

In March 1778, Robert Morris signed the Articles of Confederation on behalf of the state of Pennsylvania. In August he was made chairman of the Congressional Committee on Finance, and served until he retired from Congress on November 1, 1778, at the end of his term. Just five days later he was elected to the Pennsylvania state assembly. He took his seat on November 6, swore allegiance to the new Pennsylvania Constitution, but reserved the right to agitate toward its amendment.

Thomas Paine, in January 1779,

attacked Morris through the press for conducting private commercial business while holding a public office, and on January 9, Henry Laurens made charges of fraudulent transactions against Willing and Morris. Morris requested that a congressional committee examine his books. They reported their opinion "that the said Robert Morris ... has acted with fidelity and integrity and an honorable zeal for the happiness of his country." These controversies affected the opinions of his political opponents. He did not hold another office until November 1780, when he was again elected to the Pennsylvania Assembly, and he served until June 1781.

During the winter of 1780-81, paper currency had become worthless. The states had not responded with their quotas. The treasury was empty and credit was unavailable. In September 1779, Alexander Hamilton had mentioned Morris for a post as financier instead of the service committees. In February 1780, Peletiah Webster advocated the same. The Continental Congress recognized that a "financial dictator" was needed and on February 20, 1781, without a single dissenting vote, chose Morris as superintendent of finance. After several weeks he took the office with a definite program which included federal taxes laid in specie, to be used in paying interest on the debt; requisitions from the states to be used for carrying on the war; a possible loan from France; and vigilant economy.

On September 8, 1781, Morris personally accepted the Agency of Marine to save expenses, and on September 12, 1781, he was authorized to fit out and employ the ships of the United States. Some of his measures were unpopular.

He established the Bank of North

America with a loan of $200,000 in specie, brought by the French fleet. Its doors were opened in January 1782 and Robert Morris was one of its heaviest subscribers, strengthening the bank by his own credit. He wrote John Jay, "that the bank shall be well supported, until it can support itself." From it he could borrow heavily on behalf of Congress. The states did not respond to their obligations, and he failed to secure the revenue expected. In January 1783, there was no way to pay the debts he had contracted after taking office as there had been two years earlier. Disgusted with the states and the Congress, he tendered his resignation on January 24, but was persuaded to stay in office until the army was paid and disbanded.

The bank was dissolved on August 23, 1784. John Adams obtained a loan in The Netherlands which carried him through. In September 1784, he left the office with his personal fortunes unimpaired, and with the public credit as high as it could be placed under the circumstances. He sat in the convention at Philadelphia in 1787, which framed the constitution of the United States, but took little part in debates or committee work. He signed the United States Constitution on September 17, 1787.

Morris was offered, but declined, the position of secretary of the treasury in President Washington's first cabinet. He was one of the two Pennsylvania men to be sent on October 1, 1788, to the United States senate upon the organization of the new government. He served in the senate from 1789 to 1795. During 1793, he was in a partnership in East Indian and China trade with Gouverneur Morris.

While still a senator, he began to speculate in undeveloped land. He bought a huge tract of land in western New York in 1796. He sold several portions lying on the Genessee River and mortgaged the rest to the Holland Company. Because Morris was unable to pay the taxes on it and the interest charges on his loans to the Holland Company, they foreclosed and received full title to the land. Among those who lost large sums as investors in his venture were Thomas Willing, Alexander Hamilton, John Jay, and his wife's brother, Bishop William White.

One small but insistent creditor aroused and organized other creditors and refused to wait for payment. In February 1798, Morris was taken to Prune Street debtors' prison, where he remained for three years, six months, and ten days. He was released on August 26, 1801, after the federal bankruptcy law was passed. By then he was broken in body and in spirit.

After his release from prison, Gouverneur Morris invited him to spend some time at Morrisania. He provided Robert Morris with an annuity for the rest of his life.

The United States Census of 1790 lists Robert Morris, Esquire, merchant and counting house. His household shows seven males above age sixteen; two males under sixteen; five females; and four other free persons.

Summerseat, once the home of Robert Morris, later was the home of George Clymer. It later became a part of Robert Morris High School.

The Pittsburgh School of Accounting which was founded in 1921, became the Robert Morris Junior College in 1969.

Genealogy

I. Robert Morris, January 31, 1734– May 8, 1806, was born at or near Liverpool,

England, the son of Robert and Elizabeth (Murphet) Morris. In 1747, he came to Oxford, Maryland, to join his father. He stayed in his father's house only a short time, possibly due to conflicts with his father and his "friend" Mrs. Sarah Wise. Eventually, he became a wealthy merchant of Philadelphia.

Morris married, on March 2, 1769, Mary White, and to them were born seven children. In 1770, he bought an eighty acre farm on the eastern bank of the Schuykill River, where he built a home he named The Hills in an area that is now Fairmount Park. This beautiful estate had a greenhouse where he grew oranges and pineapples, two farmhouses, barns, and various other buildings. He later began to build a mansion which was known as "Morris' Folly," and was never completed. The Hills was sold at auction in 1799.

Morris was 6 feet tall, well built, and had blue eyes and sandy hair. His disposition was pleasant and he was a good conversationalist. He died of asthma on May 8, 1806, and was buried in the family vault of William White and Robert Morris behind Christ Church, Philadelphia.

Near the burial vault is a 12" × 15" bronze plaque, erected by the Pennsylvania Constitutional Commemoration Committee in 1937.

His children were: Robert, 1769; Thomas, 1771; William White, 1772; William White, again, 1773; Hetty, 1774; Charles, 1777; Martha, christened 1779; Mary, christened 1779; Henry, 1784.

WHITE

Mary White, ca. 1749–1827, was the daughter of Colonel Thomas and Esther White. She was a sister of William White, bishop for fifty years in the American Episcopal Church. Colonel White married after 1738, Esther (Hewlings) Newman, ca. 1719–December 21, 1790, whose first marriage was recorded as "Hester Heulings, Burlington, New Jersey, married September 12, 1738, John Newman of Philadelphia."

MURPHET

II. Robert Morris, Sr., April 7, 1700–July 12, 1750, was also born at Liverpool, England, where he was an ironworker. Following the death of his wife, Elizabeth Murphet, he came to Maryland about 1738 as agent for Foster, Cunliffe and Sons, of Liverpool, for whom he purchased and shipped baled leaf tobacco to England. He was the originator of the tobacco inspection law, and had it passed over powerful opposition. He was considered a mercantile genius, and was the first to keep his accounts in money rather than in gallons, pounds, yards, etc.

Morris gave a dinner party for friends aboard one of the Foster, Cunliffe and Sons ships which had just arrived with cargo. As the small boat taking him to shore was about halfway across the water, a farewell salute was fired from the ship. Wadding from one of the shots passed through the backboard of the boat and penetrated his arm above the elbow, breaking the bone. As a result, he died of blood poisoning on July 12, 1750. Soon after his death, Mrs. Sarah Wise gave birth to his son Thomas.

Robert Morris, Sr.'s will dated April 17, 1749, bequeathed legacies to his sisters Ellen (Eleanor) and Margaret, and to the two daughters of a sister Easter, late of Liverpool. He also mentioned Robert Morris, Jr., employed by Robert Greenway, merchant of Philadelphia. He further provided £250 to Mrs. Sarah Wise.

SIMPSON

III. Andrew Morris, mariner, of Liverpool, Lancashire, England. Andrew married Magdalene Simpson on January 26, 1703, at Childwall, Lancashire. Andrew and Magdalene also had a daughter Eleanor christened on November 3, 1704, at St. Peter's Church in Liverpool. They were both deceased when Robert Morris, Sr., made his will in April 1749.

Magdalene Simpson was baptized June 27, 1677, at Cartmel, Priory Church, County Lancashire, England. She appears in some records as Mauslin or Maudlin. Her baptismal record names her father as Robert Simpson, but no mother is identified.

Chapter 34

JOHN
MORTON

ca. 1724–1777

PENNSYLVANIA

John Morton

JOHN MORTON, surveyor, farmer, judge, patriot, received only three months of formal schooling. He was tutored at home by his well-educated stepfather, John Sketchley, an Englishman who was by profession a surveyor and farmer.

Morton took an early interest in public welfare and affairs. In 1756, he was elected to the Provincial Assembly from Chester County, and subsequently elected for ten years. He served as justice of the peace in 1757 and was high sheriff of Chester County from 1766 to 1769. In 1775, he was appointed speaker of the Provincial Assembly.

In 1765, Morton was one of the four Pennsylvania delegates to the Stamp Act Congress. Though he had no formal legal training, Morton was appointed president judge of the Court of General Sessions and Common Pleas. In 1774, he became an associate judge of the Supreme Court of Pennsylvania.

Morton was a delegate to the Continental Congress from 1774 to April 1777. In the session of July 1776, his vote, with James Wilson and Benjamin Franklin put Pennsylvania on the side of independence by a majority vote of one. He served on several important committees and was chairman of the Committee of the Whole on the adoption of the Articles of Confederation, which were finally ratified after his death. Following the battle of Lexington, he was offered the colonelcy of a volunteer corps in Pennsylvania, but declined the honor due to his other duties.

Morton is not noted for any outstanding contributions in the Continental Congress, but he was recognized as a man of good judgment and pleasant social manner. He took an early, unrelenting stand in favor of independence at a date when opinions were very seriously divided.

Two Pennsylvania historical highway markers have been placed to honor Morton, one in Chester County, the other at Ridley Park. A museum of Swedish-American interests erected in Philadelphia was later named the John Morton Memorial Building. There is also a tablet to his memory in the Independence Chamber of the state house in Philadelphia.

Genealogy

I. John Morton was born late in the year 1724 or early in 1725, at Ridley, Chester County, Pennsylvania. He was the only child of John and Mary (Archer) Morton; his father died before he was born. His widowed mother married John Sketchley, a well-educated Englishman who efficiently trained him in the common branches of study. Morton's early employment was with his stepfather as a surveyor and farmer of their lands. He married, in 1754, Ann Justis (or Justice) also of Swedish descent, and they had three sons and five daughters who survived their father. He died in April 1777, and was buried in the Old St. Paul's Churchyard in Chester County, Pennsylvania. On October 9, 1845, members of his family provided his gravestone. The Morton homestead in Prospect Park has been restored and is maintained by the Pennsylvania Historical and Museum Commission.

His children were: Aaron, ca. 1751; Sketchley, ca. 1753; Jacob, before 1753; Mary, 1754; John, ca. 1755; Sarah, 1759; Elizabeth, 1760; Lydia, ca. 1761; Ann, 1763.

JUSTIS

Ann Justis's genealogy cannot be

identified with certainty. The surname had been Gustafson, later changed to Justis/Justice. Among the Swedish records of Mr. Rudman in 1697-98 of the Gloria Dei Church of Philadelphia, there were listed four Justis men: John Justis, widower, living in the family of Peter; Peter Justis (had three sons); Gustavus (had seven sons); Mouns Justis (had two sons). It is probable that Ann Justis was the daughter of one of these twelve sons, possibly of Andrew Justis, 1690–June 1756, son of Gustavus Justis. John Justis appears to be the emigrant; his daughter Anna married Mathias Morton, son of Morton Mortonson, before 1690.

ARCHER

II. John Morton (Martonson, Mortonson), June 1, 1683–1724 was the fourth son of Marton Martonson and Margaret, ca. 1679–February 1755 (whose surname was not found), of Calcon Hook, Chester County. Morton married in 1723/4, Mary Archer of Ridley, Pennsylvania. On August 7, 1708, Marton Martonson of Calcon Hook, deeded to his son John, three hundred acres of land on Schuylkill (part of the 1200 acre patent). He is later "of Ridley" in Chester County, yeoman. His will was dated February 6, 1724, and proved 20 of 12 month 1724/5. Due to old style dating this may mean March 20, 1725.

Mary Archer was the daughter of John and Gertrude (maiden name unknown)

Archer of Ridley. The sons of Arian Johnson, at Tinnicum, took the name of Aretzon and this surname was afterwards changed to Archer.

III. Marton Martonson (Morton Mortonson, or Morton) of Calcon Hook, County Chester, eldest son, was born ca. 1655, and died after May 24, 1703. He had a deed March 12, 1694/5, Andrew Jansen to Marton Martonson, for a tract of land at Amosland (variously called Amsland, Amosland, Ammesland, and Millkill, in Ridley). He married, before 1675, Margaret whose surname is unknown; she died in February 1755, age seventy-six years. They had eight children. Martonson's land grant was as follows: "Patent, 1701, 20 October. William Penn by his commissioners, to Marton Martonson, for land on the east side of Schuylkill, adjacent lands of Andrew Peterson Longacre and Otto Erick Cock, being 1200 acres." The will of Marton Martonson (otherwise Morton) dated November 1, 1718, was proved at West Chester January 1, 1718.

IV. Marton Martonson, b. ca. 1625, wife Helene, sailed from Gothenburg, Sweden, in 1654 and was of full age in 1655 and living on the Delaware. He settled between the Christiana and Wickeeoe suburbs of Philadelphia. He appears in the townships of Springfield and Ridley, Pennsylvania.

V. Marton Martonson, probably born between 1595 and 1600, of Sweden.

Chapter 35

THOMAS NELSON, JR.

1738–1789

VIRGINIA

THOMAS NELSON, merchant, soldier, general governor of Virginia, patriot, received his primary education from the Reverend Yates of Gloucester County, Virginia. He was sent to England in 1753, to attend private school at Hackney. He entered Christ's College, Cambridge in May 1758, and was graduated in 1761.

While Nelson was still on board the ship bringing him home from England in 1763, he was chosen by the voters of York County, Virginia, to be their representative in the House of Burgesses. He was a justice of the peace in 1764.

He was a member of the House of Burgesses in 1774, when it was dissolved by Lord Dunmore because of its resolutions censuring and condemning the Boston Port Bill. The following day he was one of the eighty-nine delegates who assembled at the Raleigh Tavern and formed the association which resolved, at all hazards, to defend their rights and maintain their liberties.

Nelson was elected to represent York County at the first Virginia Convention which met at Williamsburg, August 1, 1774. In March 1775, he was again a representative and was prominent in the debate on the advisability of a military force. In July 1775, he was appointed colonel in the second Virginia Infantry Regiment.

On August 11, 1775, Nelson was appointed a delegate to the Continental Congress. He resigned his military command and took his seat in Congress on September 13, 1775. He was one of the first to advocate separation of the colonies from the Crown. In May 1776, he was a member of the Virginia Convention which met to frame a constitution for Virginia.

Throughout the Congressional sessions of 1776 he maintained his stand, and on July 2, he voted in favor of independence. He signed the engrossed copy of the Declaration of Independence on August 2, 1776.

Nelson was a delegate from York County to the third Virginia Convention held at Richmond July 17, 1776. Colonial troops were now being raised. Patrick Henry was made colonel of the first regiment raised; Thomas Nelson was made colonel of the second regiment raised.

During the latter months of his term in the Continental Congress and the beginning of 1777, Nelson served on several important committees and was active in matters which advanced the general welfare of the new states. On May 2, 1777, while in his seat in Congress, he was seized of "a recurring trouble of the head." He returned home and allowed his term to be completed by another delegate.

In August 1778, the British fleet appeared off the coast of Virginia a second time. Nelson was appointed brigadier-general and commander in chief of the forces in the Commonwealth. He raised a company, using a large amount of personal funds, and marched to Philadelphia. These troops were disbanded when Congress felt unable to support them.

Nelson returned to Congress in February 1779, but after several months became ill again and returned to Virginia. During the remainder of the war he served as governor, financier, and commander of the militia of Virginia.

In 1781, he became the first elected conservative governor of Virginia. In September, with over three thousand Virginia militia, he joined George Washington at the siege of Yorktown. Nelson directed American fire upon his own home during the final siege because it was occupied by Cornwallis. Nelson House has been preserved and still bears cannon scars from that attack.

In his orders of the day for October 20, 1781, General Washington expressed his deep appreciation to Mr. Nelson to whom he said, "The highest Praises are due" for activity and bravery.

Thomas Nelson's personal fortune was ruined by the Revolutionary War. When, in 1780, the Virginia Assembly requested $2,000,000 to help the Continental Treasury pay for the French fleet, Nelson tried to raise the money. On his own personal security, he raised a large part of the loan. He was forced to redeem the security at a great sacrifice. The government never compensated him for the loss. He had also advanced huge sums of money for other purposes, including the fitting and provisioning of troops.

Before the end of 1781, illness had forced Nelson to resign the governorship. He moved to a small estate named Offley in Hanover County, where he died in 1789. He was buried in an unmarked grave in the churchyard at Yorktown to keep creditors from holding his body for collateral.

In 1858, the state of Virginia honored his memory with a life-size bronze statue on the George Washington equestrian statue in Capital Park at Richmond.

Genealogy

I. Thomas Nelson, Jr., December 26, 1738–January 4, 1789, was born at Yorktown, Virginia, the son of William and Elizabeth (Burwell) Nelson. He married, on July 29, 1762, Lucy Grymes, with whom he had eleven children. He was called "Jr." because his uncle Thomas Nelson was also of Yorktown. Among Thomas Nelson's cousins in the Continental Congress were Benjamin Harrison, Carter Braxton, the Lee brothers, Peyton Randolph, and Thomas Jefferson.

His children were: William, 1763; Thomas, 1764; Philip, 1766; Francis, 1767; Hugh, 1768; Elizabeth, 1770; Lucy, 1770; Mary, 1774; Robert, 1778; Susanna, 1780; Judith, 1782.

GRYMES

Lucy Grymes, ca. 1745–ca. 1834, wife of Thomas Nelson, Jr., was the daughter of Philip Grymes who married in 1743, Mary Randolph, of Brandon, Middlesex County, Virginia. Mary was a sister of Peyton Randolph, 1722–1775, president of the First Continental Congress, who married Elizabeth Harrison, sister of Benjamin Harrison, the signer.

Mary (Randolph) Grymes was the daughter of Sir John Randolph, knight, born at Turkey Island in April 1689. He married, in 1718, Susanna Beverly, daughter of Peter Beverly of Gloucester County, Virginia, and lived at Williamsburg. Sir John Randolph was a brother of Isham Randolph, the father of Jane (Randolph) Jefferson (mother of Thomas Jefferson). Sir John Randolph was the son of Colonel William Randolph, born 1651, the emigrant from Yorkshire, England, in 1674, who married in 1680, Mary Isham, daughter of Henry and Catherine Isham. (See the genealogy of Thomas Jefferson in Chapter 24 for details on the Randolph and Isham lines.)

BURWELL

II. William Nelson, 1711–November 19, 1772, of Yorktown, Virginia, married, in February 1738, Elizabeth Burwell, born 1719, daughter of the Honorable

Nathaniel Burwell, baptized October 14, 1680–1721, of Fairfield, Gloucester County, Virginia. Nathaniel Burwell married in 1709, Elizabeth Carter, 1680–1721, daughter of Colonel Robert "King" Carter, 1663–August 4, 1732, and his first wife, Judith Armistead who died in 1699. Judith was the daughter of Colonel John and Judith (Bowles) Armistead of Hesse, Gloucester County, Virginia.

Colonel Robert Carter was the son of Colonel John Carter the emigrant, who came to lower Norfolk County, Virginia, in 1649, where he was a burgess. He removed to Lancaster County and built Corotoman, served as a burgess for Lancaster 1653–1658; was a member of the King's Council, 1658–1659; and held other important posts. John Carter married five times; Robert Carter was a son of his fourth wife, Sarah Ludlow, who was born before 1639 and died about 1668. She was the daughter of Gabriel Ludlow, baptized February 10, 1587, at Dinton, England. Gabriel Ludlow was called to the bar in 1620. His wife was Phillis of surname unknown; he died in 1639.

John Carter, 1620–1669, the emigrant, was the son of the Honorable William Carter of Casstown, Hereford County and the Middle Temple, England. Gabriel Ludlow was the son of Thomas Ludlow of Dinton, who died in 1607, and Jane Pyle, daughter of Thomas Pyle of Bopton, Wilts. Thomas Ludlow was the son of George Ludlow of Hill Deverill and was high sheriff of Wiltshire in 1567; he married Lady Edith Wyndsore who died in 1580. The ancestry of this family traces to King Henry III of England, 1206–1272, who married in 1236, Eleanor of Provence who died in 1291.

Honorable Nathaniel Burwell, 1680–1721, was the son of the Honorable Lewis and Abigail (Smith) Burwell II, of Kings Creek. Abigail Smith, 1656–1692, was the daughter of Anthony and Martha (Bacon) Smith of Colchester, England. Martha Bacon was of Burgate, Suffolk County, England. Anthony Smith died about 1665.

The Honorable Lewis Burwell II was the son of Lewis Burwell I who built Fairfield, the Burwell ancestral home. Lewis Burwell I, born March 5, 1621, married in 1646, Lucy Higginson daughter of Captain Robert Higginson, and died November 18, 1653. He was the son of Edward and Dorothy (Bedel) Burwell of Harlington, Bedford County, England.

Edward Burwell was baptized at Toddington, Bedfordshire, August 24, 1579, and died between October 18 and November 9, 1626. He resided at Houghton Park, Ampthill and Harlington, Bedfordshire, England.

READE/REID

III. Thomas Nelson, February 20, 1677–October 7, 1745, was the emigrant called "Scotch Tom" who came from Scotland about 1690. He founded and laid out the town of York in 1705. He was a merchant, and built the first custom house in the colonies. He built Nelson House, which was rebuilt by his son, Governor William Nelson in 1740.

Thomas Nelson was foreman of the Grand Jury for the General Court in October 1716, the jurors of which included Dandridge, Lightfoot, Miles Cary, John Armistead. Thomas Nelson married, about 1710, Margaret Reade, daughter of Robert Reade, a justice of Yorktown, who married Mary Lilly, daughter of John Lilly and (first name unknown) Mallson, heiress of Edward Mallson of York County. Robert Reade's will was proved March 16, 1712; his wife's will was proved November 20, 1722.

Robert Reade was the son of Colonel George Reade, who married Elizabeth Martian, daughter of Nicholas Martian, a French Walloon, who patented the first site at Yorktown. He represented Kent Island, York and Chiskiack in the House of Burgesses in 1632. Elizabeth Reade's will was proved January 24, 1687. Nicholas Martian's will, dated March 1, 1656, was proved in 1657. George Washington was also a direct descendant of George and Elizabeth Reade. Colonel George Reade was the son of Robert Reade who married on July 31, 1600, Mildred Windebank, daughter of Sir Thomas Windebank who was buried November 25, 1607.

Sir Thomas Windebank, of Haine's Hill, in the Parish of Hurst, Berkshire, was clerk of the signet to Queen Elizabeth and King James I. His wife was Frances Dymoke, daughter of Sir Edward Dymoke of Schriveley, Lincolnshire, England.

In the Domesday Survey, the Manor of Linkenholt belonged to Ernalf de Hording, who gave it to the Abby of St. Peter, Gloucester County, England. The manor was sold to Richard Reade, Esquire, afterward knighted. In 1585 the Manor of Linkenholt, County Southampton, England, was conveyed to Andrew Reade. This ancestry traces to King Edward I, of England, and Princess Eleanor of Castile.

Chapter 36

WILLIAM PACA

1740–1799

MARYLAND

WILLIAM PACA, jurist, patriot, governor of Maryland, received his early training, including classical languages, probably from tutors. He was sent to Philadelphia College at fifteen and graduated with a master of arts in 1759. He then studied law in the office of Hammond and Hall in Annapolis. He was admitted to practice before the Mayor's Court in 1761, where Samuel Chase was a fellow student. He completed his legal training at the Middle Temple in London. Paca was admitted to the bar of the Provincial Court in 1764.

In 1765, when the Stamp Act alerted the people of the colonies to their common and ever-increasing danger, Paca and others opposed its operation. He condemned every British act which asserted their right to tax the colonists without their consent, and soon became a favorite of the people because of his patriotic stands. Paca was first elected to the Provincial Legislature in 1768. He, with Samuel Chase and others, urged that Royal Governor Eden's proclamation regulating the fees of civil officers be rescinded. It was later recalled. Similar proclamations were becoming more frequent, and when a poll tax took effect for the support of the clergy of the Church of England only, Paca led the opposition.

During this controversy concerning the poll tax in 1774, Chase, Paca, and the lawyer Thomas Johnson wrote an article in rebuttal to one signed by the Tories Daniel Dulaney and James Holliday in defense of the tax. The article was reprinted in London, which brought the names of Paca and the others into considerable prominence.

While in the Assembly, Paca was on the committee which directed the construction of the State House at Annapolis.

He was appointed a member of the Committee of Correspondence in 1774, and in June 1774, was elected as a delegate to the First Continental Congress. On October 20, 1774, he signed the Articles of Association and returned to Annapolis. He was one of the representatives of Annapolis in the Provincial Convention which met November 21–24, 1774. He signed the Olive Branch Petition on July 8, 1775. He was a member of the Second Continental Congress 1775–1779, serving on many important committees, including the special Committee of Thirteen for Foreign Affairs.

When Maryland removed the restrictions on her delegates in June 1776, Paca and his colleagues voted for independence on July 2 and signed the Declaration of Independence on August 2, 1776. Soon the conflict began and Paca served in the militia and spent several thousand dollars of his own money outfitting troops. In August 1776, he was also a delegate to the convention that framed a constitution for Maryland. He was a member of Maryland's first senate.

Paca was appointed chief judge of the Maryland General Court, 1778–1784. Two years later, he was appointed by Congress as the chief justice of the Court of Appeals in Admiralty and prize cases.

Paca was elected governor of Maryland in November 1782, and served three terms, the last term expiring November 26, 1785. As governor, he was interested in the welfare of the returning soldiers. He was on the board of directors when Washington College was chartered at Chestertown, Maryland, and in 1783 laid the cornerstone of the first building.

In 1784, Governor Paca was an honorary delegate to the council which organized the Order of the Cincinnati, and was elected vice president of the Maryland Society, though the order was exclusively for those who served as army officers.

He was a delegate of the Maryland Convention which adopted the United States Constitution in 1788. He proposed twenty-eight amendments, but voted for adoption when the convention decided it had to accept or reject the Constitution as it had been submitted. President Washington appointed Paca a federal district judge, and he held the position until his death.

John Adams identified Paca as a "deliberator." In Congress he was considered one of the quiet ones. Benjamin Rush wrote that he was "a good-tempered, worthy man, with a sound understanding which he was too indolent to exercise, and hence his reputation in public life was less than his talents." Rush adds that Paca "was beloved and respected by all who knew him, and considered at all times as a sincere patriot and honest man."

An historical highway marker has been placed near Paca's Wye Plantation by the State Road Commission of Maryland.

Genealogy

I. William Paca, October 31, 1740–October 13, 1799, was born at Chilbury Hall on the north shore of Bush River, near Abingdon, now in Harford County, Maryland. He was the son of John and Elizabeth (Smith) Paca. He married first, on May 26, 1763, Ann Mary Chew, and by her had five children of which only one, a son, lived to adulthood. Paca married second, on February 28, 1777, Ann Harrison by whom there were no children.

He also had two illegitimate daughters, Hester and Henrietta Maria.

In the 1790 United States census, Paca's household in Queen Anns County, consisted of: Two males above age sixteen and ninety-two slaves. He died October 13, 1699, in Talbot County, and was buried in a private graveyard on Wye Plantation a few miles north of Easton, Maryland.

In 1910, a gravestone was provided by the Maryland Society of the Sons of the American Revolution.

His children were: (by first wife) Henrietta Maria, ca. 1766 died; unnamed daughter, 1767; John Philemon, 1771; (by second wife) William, ca. 1776; Henry, 1778. Two daughters: Hester, 1775, by Levina Hester; Henrietta Maria, ca. 1777, by Sarah Joice.

CHEW
Ann Mary Chew, 1736–1774, was the daughter of Samuel Chew, ca. 1704–1736/7, and Henrietta Maria Lloyd, 1765, of Annapolis, who were married on September 28, 1735.

HARRISON
Ann Harrison, ca. 1758–1780, was the daughter of Henry Harrison, Esquire, ca. 1713–1766, a Philadelphia merchant, and Mary Aspden. Ann was a granddaughter of Mathias Aspden, another Philadelphia merchant, who died in 1765.

SMITH
II. John Paca, ca. 1712–1785, of Baltimore County, married on November 2, 1732, Elizabeth Smith, who died in 1766. Elizabeth was the daughter of William Smith who died in 1731/2, also of Baltimore County, and his wife Elizabeth (Martin) Dallam, widow of Richard

Dallam who died in 1714. John Paca was the son of Aquila Paca, ca. 1676–1721.

PHILLIPS

III. Aquila Paca, ca. 1676–1721, lived in Ann Arundel County, Maryland. He married Martha Phillips, who died in 1746. She was the daughter of James Phillips, who died in 1689, and his wife Cessionee, who died in 1708. Aquila Paca was of the Anglican religion until about 1708/9. By 1814, he was of the Quaker faith.

PARKER

IV. Robert Paca, died in 1681. He came to Maryland before 1660. He married, after 1660, Mary (Parker) Hall, 1632–1699, widow of John Hall, who died in 1660. She was the daughter of William Parker, who emigrated in 1651 and lived in Ann Arundel County, Maryland. Robert Paca was in Calvert County in 1654.

Chapter 37

ROBERT TREAT
PAINE
1731–1814
MASSACHUSETTS

ROBERT TREAT PAINE, Puritan, jurist, patriot, began preparation for the ministry at the Latin School in Boston, taking the highest rank. He entered Harvard College at age fourteen and was domiciled with the Reverend Nathaniel Appleton, the college chaplain. After graduating in 1749, he taught for a time. During his short career in the ministry he served as chaplain on the Crown Point Expedition of 1755. For reasons of health he went to sea: to Carolina, the Azores, Spain, England, and finally a whaling voyage to Greenland.

Though still pursuing theological studies, he began to read law and supported himself by teaching. He took a law course with Benjamin Pratt and was admitted to the bar in 1757. Paine was a Master Mason in the Roxbury Lodge, F & AM in 1759. He first hung out his shingle at Portland, Maine, but moved to Taunton, Bristol County, Massachusetts, in 1761. In 1763, he was a justice of the peace at Taunton and in 1764 became barrister.

In 1768, Paine was a member of the convention which met upon Governor Thomas Hutchinson's dissolution of the General Court, for its refusal to rescind a circular letter which had been sent to the other colonies calling for concerted action against infringement of their chartered rights. Following the Boston Massacre on March 5, 1770, he was appointed associate prosecuting attorney in the trial.

His view that the underlying issue was whether Parliament had the right to quarter a standing army in a town without its consent, brought his name to people's attention throughout the colonies. Paine represented Taunton in the Provincial Assembly, 1773–1778, except

1776; in 1773 he chaired a large committee for resistance to threatened tyranny. Also in 1773, as a member of the General Assembly, he assisted in the impeachment of Chief Justice Peter Oliver for receiving his stipend from the king instead of a grant from the Assembly.

In 1774, Paine was appointed a delegate to the First Continental Congress, and from 1774 to 1779 he served on its important committees, but remained active in the legislature of Massachusetts. He signed the Articles of Association on October 20, 1774. Also in October 1774, Paine was the patriot of the forum when Taunton raised the Liberty and Union Flag in defiance of the military governor, General Thomas Gage.

During the Second Continental Congress, after the Battle of Bunker Hill, he was a member of a committee to reorganize the militia. At first he favored his college mate Artemus Ward for commander in chief; however, John Adams persuaded him to vote for George Washington.

On July 8, 1775, he was a signer of the Olive Branch Petition to King George III. In the same year, he became active in promoting the manufacture of saltpeter and cannons, and visited the northern army under command of Philip Schuyler. On January 18, 1776, he was elected to the Second Continental Congress but did not return in 1777 due to poor health.

On July 2, 1776, Paine voted in favor of independence. During this session, he, with Edward Rutledge and Thomas Jefferson, reported rules of conduct of Congress in debate and for fasting and prayer. He signed the engrossed copy of the Declaration of Independence on August 2, 1776.

In 1777-78 he was for a time Speaker

of the Massachusetts House of Representatives, and was appointed state attorney general. In 1778, he was on a committee to regulate the price of labor, provisions, and manufactures on account of the depreciation of the continental currency. He was appointed in 1778 to be a member of the committee to draft a new constitution for Massachusetts. In 1779, he was a member of the Executive Council of Massachusetts. He declined the office of associate justice of the Supreme Court in 1783 when offered by John Adams, but accepted the appointment by Governor John Hancock in 1790.

When Paine accepted the office of associate justice of the Supreme Court, Maine was still part of Massachusetts. As Justice-in-Eyre, his travels to the more remote areas were difficult. On one occasion, Paine was arrested for traveling on the Sabbath. He was fined by a crossroads court for violating a law which he himself had been instrumental in framing. After fourteen years' service, increasing deafness hastened his retirement from the bench in 1804. He then became Counselor of the Commonwealth. Paine was one of the founders of the American Academy of Arts and Sciences, 1780.

On November 15, 1904, a statue of Paine by sculptor Richard Brooks was dedicated on Taunton Green.

Genealogy

I. Robert Treat Paine was born March 11, 1731, in School Street on Beacon Hill at the foot of which stood the Old South Church where he was christened. He died on May 11, 1814, and was buried in the Old Granary Burial Ground only a few feet from the place of his birth. He married on March 15, 1770,

Sally Cobb, 1744–1816, and to them were born eight children. In 1780, Paine moved his family from Taunton to Boston in the spot that later became Post Office Square. His last public appearance was at the installation of Edward Everett as minister to the Brattle Street Church.

In 1798, Robert Treat Paine, Jr., a Federalist editor, wrote "Adams and Liberty." It was sung to the tune which was later used for the "Star Spangled Banner."

Paine was descended from *Mayflower* passenger Stephen Hopkins. Through his Winslow ancestry, he was descended from William the Conqueror, Alfred the Great, several Magna Carta barons, and other royal and noble lines. John Adams characterized Paine as "fitful, witty, learned, and conceited."

His children were: Robert Treat, 1770; Sally, 1772; Thomas, 1773; Charles, 1775; Henry, 1777; Mary, 1780; Maria Antoinette, 1782; Lucretia, 1785.

COBB
Paine's wife, Sally Cobb 1744–June 16, 1816, was the daughter of General David Cobb who crushed Shay's Rebellion in southeast Massachusetts. Her brother was Colonel David Cobb, an aide to General George Washington. They were descendants of Augustine and Bethia Cobb of Taunton through one of their two sons, Morgan or Samuel.

TREAT
II. The Reverend Thomas Paine, Esquire was baptized April 8, 1694. He left the ministry to engage in mercantile trade at Boston and Nova Scotia. He married Eunice Treat, daughter of the Reverend Samuel Treat.

The Reverend Samuel Treat, baptized September 3, 1648, died March 18, 1717. He graduated from Harvard College in 1669. He married first in 1674, Elizabeth Mayo, daughter of Samuel and granddaughter of the Reverend John Mayo. She was born in 1652 and died December 4, 1696, age forty-four. The Reverend Treat married second on August 29, 1700, Abigail Willard (Widow Esterbrook), daughter of the Reverend Samuel Willard of Groton and Boston.

The Reverend Samuel Treat was the son of Governor Robert Treat of Milford, Connecticut, born about 1622, died July 12, 1710, at the age of eighty-eight. Governor Treat married first Jane Tapp born 1628, died April 8, 1703. She was the only daughter of Edmund Tapp who died 1653; his will was dated April 1, 1653. Edmund Tapp was at Milford 1639, and was one of the pillars at the founding of the church at New Haven August 22, 1639. His inventory was taken April 26, 1653.

Governor Robert Treat married second at the age of 83, widow Elizabeth Bryan on October 22, 1705, and she died in January 1706. Governor Robert Treat was the son of Richard Treat baptized August 28, 1584, at Pitminster, England. His second wife, Alice Gaylord, was baptized May 10, 1591, and died after 1670. She was the daughter of Hugh Gaylord and Joan, surname unknown. Hugh Gaylord was born 1553, Somersetshire, England. Richard Treat/Trott, was born about 1500 at Somerset, England, and married Joanna (surname unknown) who was buried at Otterford, Somerset, on August 14, 1577.

The Reverend Samuel Willard of Groton and Boston, second son of Major Simon Willard, was ordained July 13, 1662. He was born January 31, 1640; became a freeman in 1670 and was installed on March 31, 1678, as successor to the Reverend Thacher, the first minister of the Old South Church.

The Reverend Willard was instrumental in recovering the public judgment in the witchcraft madness and in forcing the resignation of Increase Mather as president of Harvard. He was made Mather's successor on September 6, 1701. He resigned August 14, 1707, and died September 12, 1707. He married first, August 8, 1664, Abigail Sherman, daughter of the Reverend John Sherman; and married second Eunice Tyng, daughter of Edward Tyng.

Major Simon Willard of Cambridge and Concord was baptized April 7, 1605; came to America in May 1634; was a major in 1655. He was the son of Richard Willard of Horsemonden, County Kent, England. He married three times: first, Mary Sharpe, daughter of Henry Sharpe, baptized October 16, 1614, at Horsemonden; second, Elizabeth Dunster, sister of the first president of Harvard; third, Mary Dunster, niece of the president of Harvard College. Henry Dunster came from Lancashire, England.

Abigail Sherman, born February 3, 1648, daughter of the Reverend John Sherman, born about 1614 (age 24 in 1638) who married first probably after 1638, Mary (surname unknown) who died September 8, 1644. He married second, late in 1645, Mary Launce, who was a maiden in the home of Governor Theopolis Eaton. The Reverend John Sherman arrived in America in the *Elizabeth* in June 1634, He was a cousin of Captain John Sherman, and an ancestor of Paine's fellow signer Roger Sherman. These Shermans were from Dedham, Essex, England.

THACHER

III. James Paine, born July 6, 1665, died July 13, 1711. He was a son of Thomas Paine, Sr., Esquire, of Eastham,

Massachusetts. He married first on April 9, 1691, Bethia Thacher of Yarmouth, born July 10, baptized July 16, 1671, died 1734. She was the daughter of Colonel John Thacher.

James Paine's second wife, whom he married January 11, 1684, was Lydia Gorham, daughter of John and granddaughter of Ralph Gorham. She was born June 6, 1661, and died August 2, 1744, age eighty-four. Colonel John Thacher was born at Marblehead, March 17, 1639, married first November 6, 1644, Rebecca Winslow, daughter of Josiah and niece of Governor Edward Winslow. Colonel John Thacher was the youngest son of Anthony Thacher from Salisbury in Wilts, England, of Sarum. He was born at Marblehead and died at Yarmouth age seventy-five, May 8, 1718.

Anthony Thacher, curator of Sarum in 1631 and 1634 for the Rector of St. Edmunds, had lived in Holland for twenty years. He embarked on the *James* on April 6, 1635, at Southampton and arrived Boston on June 3. He was called a "taylor" (tailor) for deception. He brought his second wife, four children, and his nephew Thomas Thacher, age fifteen, as well as his cousin the Reverend Joseph Avery and his six children.

On August 15, 1635, all their families except the nephew Thomas, embarked in a pinnace belonging to Isaac Allerton to travel from Ipswich to Marblehead. The next day they were wrecked on a ledge off Cape Ann. Of twenty-three persons aboard, only Anthony Thacher and his wife survived. They settled before 1643 at Yarmouth, Massachusetts. He had married Elizabeth Jones in England a few weeks before sailing. Anthony died at Yarmouth, age eighty, and his inventory was dated August 22, 1667. Elizabeth (Jones) Thacher died in 1670.

By his two wives, James Paine had twenty children.

SNOW
IV. Thomas Paine, Sr., Esquire, an early settler at Eastham in 1655, was born January 18, 1613, in England and died in 1706. He became a freeman June 2, 1641, and married about 1650 Mary Snow, daughter of Nicholas Snow and Constance Hopkins. Mary (Snow) Paine died in 1704. Paine's will was dated May 12, 1705, and was probated October 20, 1706.

Nicholas Snow came on the *Ann* in 1623; died November 15, 1676. He married Constance Hopkins, a *Mayflower* passenger with her father in 1620. Nicholas and Constance Snow had twelve children, all born before 1650.

Stephen Hopkins signed the Mayflower Compact, lived at Plymouth, and died in 1644. He was an assistant in 1633 and 1634. An abstract of his will is in *Genealogical Register IV, 281*.

Rebecca Winslow, born 1642, died 1683. Her father, Josiah Winslow came in the *White Angel* with Isaac Allerton, arriving at Saco June 27, 1631. Josiah Winslow was born February 11, baptized February 16, 1606, at Droitwich, England, one of the five sons of Edward Winslow, Sr. He married before 1637, Margaret Bourne, daughter of Thomas Bourne of Marshfield, Massachusetts.

Edward Winslow, Sr., was born in 1560, in Worcester County, England, and married in 1594, Magdalene Ollyver. He was the son of Kenelm Winslow who married Katharine; Kenelm was a son of John Winslow born about 1410 who married Agnes Throckmorton, daughter of John Throckmorton, treasurer of England, born about 1380 and his wife Eleanor Spiney. Sir John Throckmorton was fourth in line from Robert de Throckmorton, born about 1275, and his wife Alice Mortimer, daughter of Hugh Mortimer who married Agatha, daughter of William de Ferrers, Earl of Derby.

From this de Ferrers marriage, Robert Treat Paine was descended from the Magna Carta Baron Saire de Quincy who married Margaret Bellemont. Ancestry from this marriage includes Charlemagne, Alfred the Great, William the Conqueror, and many more royal and noble families. John Winslow was a son of William Winslowe born about 1375, son of Thomas Winslowe, born about 1355, who married Cecilia Thinly; William Wankel born about 1300 in County Essex, England, died in 1391.

Thomas Bourne, 1581–1664, came from Kent County, England. He was at Plymouth in 1637 and became a freeman January 2, 1638. His wife Elizabeth (surname unknown) was born 1590 and buried July 18, 1660. He died about 1664 leaving a widow Martha.

?TUTHILL

V. Thomas Paine/Payne was born December 11, 1586, son of Thomas and Catharine Paine of Cookie near Halesworth, County Suffolk. He married in England, Elizabeth (possibly Tuthill), 1583–1657, in 1610. Thomas Paine age fifty, with wife age fifty-three, and six children were transported to New England in the *Mary Ann of Yarmouth* in April 1637, as found in admiralty records.

Chapter 38

JOHN PENN

1741–1788

NORTH CAROLINA

JOHN PENN, lawyer, patriot, received only a meager elementary education at a local school in Caroline County, Virginia. Penn was eighteen years old when his father died in 1759, leaving him a comfortable fortune. His uncle Edmund Pendleton, who was licensed to practice law at age twenty, allowed him the use of his excellent library. There he studied law books, and at twenty-one was licensed to practice law. He practiced successfully in Virginia for about twelve years.

Many of Penn's relatives had moved to Granville County, North Carolina, and in 1774 he moved his family to the area of Williamsboro, in Granville County. He quickly became a community leader, and in 1775 was sent to the Provincial Congress where he served on important committees and won a reputation for tireless attention to his duties. He was a persuasive orator and won agreement among the local voters. Within a month, he was elected to the First Continental Congress and took his seat October 12, 1775.

Penn wrote a letter from Philadelphia in February 1776 which read, "My first wish is that America may be free; and second, that she may be restored to Great Britain in peace and harmony and upon just terms." Hearing reports from the other colonies, he soon abandoned all hope of working with the royal government. He wrote to his friend Thomas Person, "For God's sake, my Good Sir, encourage our people, animate them to dare even to die for their country." As a member of the Provincial Congress at Halifax in April 1776, he favored the instruction to vote for independence. He returned to Philadelphia for the July 2 vote and to sign the Declaration of Independence on August 2, 1776.

He was a member of the Continental Congress until 1777, was reelected in 1778, and served until 1780. On November 15, 1777, he signed the Articles of Confederation. He had declined a judgeship in 1777. In 1780, Penn became a member of the North Carolina Board of War. He did a major part of the work on this board, although it was opposed both by the army and by Governor Thomas Burke. It was abolished in 1781. In July 1781, he refused to serve on the Council of State, due to illness, and resumed his law practice.

Penn was one of the sixteen signers who also signed the Articles of Confederation. In 1784, Robert Morris appointed him receiver of taxes for the Confederation in North Carolina. He resigned in a few weeks. He was, with Thornton Yancey, appointed in August 1783 tax collector for Granville County; in 1784 and 1785, he was a bondsman.

Despite Penn's "attractive and congenial" personality, there is a traditional story that while he was in Philadelphia, Henry Laurens (1724–1792), who was at that date president of the Continental Congress (1777–1778), challenged him to a duel for unknown reasons. The two men were living at the same boarding house and had eaten breakfast together on the appointed day set for the duel. Although only fifty-four years of age, Laurens is described as "elderly" and required assistance from Penn in crossing the street. En route to the proposed site, Penn convinced Laurens that they should settle their differences, and the duel never took place.

Genealogy

I. John Penn was born on May 27, 1741, at Port Royal, Caroline County,

Virginia, the only child of Moses and Catherine (Taylor) Penn. He married, on July 28, 1763, Susanna Lyne, daughter of Henry Lyne of Caroline County, Virginia, and Granville County, North Carolina. They had two surviving children, William the eldest, and Lucy who married the Honorable John Taylor, son of James and Ann (Pollard) Taylor of Orange County, Virginia.

John Penn's will, in his own handwriting, made March 1, 1784, in *Abstracts of Granville County Wills*, names his two children but does not mention his wife Susanna, apparently deceased. In the state census of North Carolina in 1786, Penn's household in Island Creek District shows: white males 21–60, three; under 21, none; no females; blacks 12–50, thirty-nine; under 12 and over 50, thirty-one.

Penn died September 14, 1788, and was buried at his own home place a few miles northeast of Stovall in Granville County, North Carolina. On April 25, 1894, his remains were reinterred under the Signers Monument then under construction in State Park, Guilford Courthouse, Guilford County, Greensboro, North Carolina. The monument was dedicated on July 3, 1897.

His children were: William, ca. 1764; Lucy, ca. 1766; and an unnamed child who died, ca. 1768.

LYNE

Susanna (Lyne) Penn was the daughter of Henry Lyne, and was probably born in Caroline County, Virginia, as her father was still living there in 1747. Henry Lyne was probably born about 1720 in King and Queen County, Virginia. Possibly he was a grandson or great-grandson of William Lyne who sailed from Liverpool, England, and came to Virginia prior to 1635, with three sisters, viz. Lucy who married John Taylor of Caroline County, Virginia; Ann who married Mr. Shackelford of Dragon Swamp, King and Queen County; and Susanna who married a Mr. Starling.

Henry Lyne's household in the Nutbush District in the 1784–1787 census of North Carolina was: white males twenty-one to sixty, none; above sixty, one; white females, three; blacks forty-seven. His will was dated October 1797, and proved in May Court 1798, Granville County, North Carolina. He left his grandson William Penn a mulatto boy and $1800. Further, he states: "the land whereon I formerly lived in King and Queen County, Virginia"; also, "to my grand son Edmund Lyne, 52½ acres whereon my water grist mill is in King and Queen County, Virginia, and my still which is now in possession of his father ...."

The Lyne family in England dates back to the Norman Conquest; they came from Lille in Flanders and were linen makers. Their coat of arms was bestowed during the reign of Bloody Queen Mary.

Oliver Cromwell's mother was a Lyne. These Lynes all emanated from Oxford, England, from nearby Swal Cliff. Henry Lyne was probably a brother of William Lyne II. George and John Lyne, were all of King and Queen County, Virginia, and all were officers in the Revolutionary War.

Ship records show they were in the West Indies before coming to Virginia by 1665. During the reign of Charles II, Richard Lee, secretary of the King's Council, mentioned his friend Mr. Lyne.

TAYLOR

II. Moses Penn, 1712–November 4,

1759, of Caroline County, Virginia, married at St. Marks, on July 4, 1739, Catherine Taylor, December 30, 1719–November 4, 1774. They had an only child, John Penn; both apparently died in Caroline County, Virginia.

Catherine Taylor was the daughter of John Taylor, November 10, 1696–March 22, 1728, and his wife Catherine Pendleton, December 8, 1699–July 26, 1774, who were married February 14, 1716. John Taylor moved to Granville County, North Carolina and died there. His will gave his grandson, John Penn, £100. He was the youngest child of James Taylor, the emigrant.

James Taylor, the emigrant, was born in 1615 at his ancestral home, Pennington Castle, about twenty miles from Carlisle, England. He died September 22, 1698. He was a descendant of Baron Taillefer of the Battle of Hastings, known as the Earl of Pennington. The name Taillefer was Anglicized to Taylor.

James Taylor arrived in Virginia in 1635 and settled on Chesapeake Bay between the York (now James) and North Rivers and established Hare Forest. He married first about 1666, Frances Walker, who died in 1680. He married second, on August 10, 1682, Mary Gregory, 1665–1747, daughter of John and Elizabeth Gregory of Sittenbourne Parish, Rappahannock County, Virginia.

James and Frances (Walker) Taylor were ancestors of U. S. presidents James Madison and Zachary Taylor. With his wife Mary Gregory, James Taylor was great-grandfather of John Penn, the signer.

Catherine (Pendleton) Taylor, wife of John Taylor, 1696–1728, was the daughter of Philip Pendleton, March 26, 1650–November 9, 1721, who came to Virginia in 1674. Philip was born in Norwich, England. He married in 1682, Isabella Hurt of Virginia, and they had seven children, among them Philip and Catherine.

Philip Pendleton was the son of Henry Pendleton, ca. 1615–1680, who married Elizabeth, parents unknown, and was of Norwich England. Henry Pendleton, 1575–July 12, 1635, married at St. Simon's and St. Jude's, Norwich, on September 30, 1605, Susan Camden, daughter of Humphrey and Cicily (Pettus) Camden. Henry was the son of George Pendleton, Jr., gentleman, born ca. 1532, died 1603, who married at St. Peter's, Norwich, on July 21, 1568, Elizabeth Pettingale, daughter of John Pettingale, gentleman, of that city.

George Pendleton Sr., Esquire, of County Lancashire, England, town of Pendleton, was born about 1500. His wife's name is unknown. This family's name was well known in public life during the reign of Henry VIII, 1491–1547.

III. John Penn born ca. 1690 and died before May 8, 1741, at which time his last will and testament was presented in Court by Elizabeth Penn and Moses Penn, executrix and executor therein named, and proved by John Taylor, gentleman, and Edmond Taylor, witnesses thereto. They entered into bond with George Penn, their security. On February 11, 1742/3, John Pendleton and Phebe his wife acknowledged their deed of lease and receipt to Moses Penn.

During the 1730s, in Caroline County, Virginia, were the above George Penn, Joseph Penn (he married Mary Taylor in 1735, sister to Catherine Taylor Penn), and John Penn, Jr., all adult. In 1747, John Penn, Jr., was constable.

Chapter 39

GEORGE READ

1733–1798

DELAWARE

GEORGE READ, lawyer, statesman, received his primary education at Chester, Pennsylvania, and later at the Reverend Francis Allison's Academy at New London. At fifteen he began the study of law under a Philadelphia lawyer, John Moland.

In 1753, Read was admitted to the bar at Philadelphia and began to practice law there. He moved to New Castle in 1754 where his "profound legal learning, clear reasoning, and calm deliberation soon won him the title of the honest lawyer."

His first political appointment, on April 3, 1763, was that of attorney general for the lower counties. Newcastle elected him to the Provincial Assembly in October 1765, where he remained for twelve years. In this capacity, he protested the Stamp Act. In July 1765, he declared that if this or any similar law imposed an internal tax for revenue were enforced, the colonists "will entertain an opinion that they are to become the slaves of Great Britain and will endeavor to live as independent of Great Britain as possible." He wanted to support colonial rights but wished to avoid extreme measures. During the early Revolutionary period, Read was a moderate Whig. He shared many views with his Quaker friend John Dickinson.

On June 5, 1766, with Thomas McKean and Caesar Rodney, Read was appointed to a Committee of Correspondence. He participated in the adoption of a nonimportation agreement in his home county in 1769. He also helped secure relief for Boston in 1774 when the harbor was closed, and in proceedings leading to the First Continental Congress of which he became a member. He resigned his post in the Provincial Assembly

on October 15, 1774. He signed the Articles of Association on October 20, 1774, before the First Continental Congress adjourned.

He was chairman of the first Naval Committee, 1775–1777. On July 8, 1775, he signed the Olive Branch Petition. He was a private in the Delaware militia.

He also served in the Second Continental Congress until 1777, and although he often was in agreement with the radicals, he refused to vote for Independence on July 2, 1776. However, after the Declaration of Independence was adopted, he did sign it on August 2, 1776.

In 1776, Read was presiding officer of the Delaware Constitutional Convention. As a member of the drafting committee, his opinions were highly valued. Also in 1776, also, he was elected to the legislative council, became its Speaker, and was vice president of Delaware.

When the British attacked Wilmington during September 1777, they took President (governor) John McKinly prisoner. Read took his family across the Susquehanna River to safety. En route from Philadelphia, he narrowly escaped capture in crossing the Delaware River.

Read took charge of the Delaware state affairs in November 1777 and worked to raise troops, clothing, and provisions, and gradually aroused patriotic spirit in the state. Though he continued his membership in the council, he requested to be relieved of the presidential duties on March 31, 1778.

On December 5, 1782, Congress elected him a judge of the Court of Appeals in admiralty cases. From 1782 to 1788, he was in Delaware's legislative council, where his influence was useful in improving commerce and the state's finances.

Read was a commissioner in the

boundary dispute between Massachusetts and New York in 1785. He was a representative at the Annapolis Convention and endorsed the movement for a general convention at Philadelphia in 1787. In the 1787 convention, he was an outspoken advocate for the rights of the smaller states. His fear was that the larger states would get too much power, and "will probably combine to swallow up the smaller ones by addition, division, or impoverishment." Largely through his efforts, Delaware was the first state to ratify the U.S. Constitution. At the request of John Dickinson, he signed the Constitution of the United States on September 17, 1787.

In March 1789, George Read was one of the first senators from Delaware elected for a term of two years, and was reelected in 1790. He resigned on September 18, 1793, to become chief justice of Delaware, and held that post until his death in 1798.

Additional Information

Read earned only a moderate income and did not become one of the wealthy signers. Fortunately his home and related property was spared during the revolution. His home was destroyed by fire in 1834.

Read was tall, slender, and had fine features. He was a man of the highest character and was dignified, and had a pleasant disposition. His message to the British was: "I am a poor man, but, poor as I am, the King of England is not rich enough to purchase me." He died suddenly at New Castle, Delaware, on September 21, 1798, three days after his sixty-fifth birthday, and was interred in Immanuel Church cemetery at New Castle.

A white marble monument marks his grave.

Genealogy

I. George Read, September 18, 1733–September 21, 1798, was born in northeast Cecil County, Maryland, the son of Colonel John Read and Mary (Howell) Read. On January 11, 1763, he married Gertruce (Ross) Till, the widowed sister of signer George Ross. To them were born one daughter and four sons.

His children were: John 1763/4 died; George, 1765; William, 1767; John Again, 1769; Mary Howell, ca. 1770.

ROSS
Gertrude Ross Till, born ca. 1734, was the daughter of the Reverend George Ross and his second wife Catherine VanGezel. Gertrude married first, on June 18, 1752, Thomas Till (son of William). On January 11, 1763, she married George Read. Though her birth and death dates are not given, she is buried with her husband. Her inscription on their monument states: "and of Gertrude, wife of George Read, and Daughter of the Reverend George Ross." (See Chapter 41 on George Ross for her Ross and VanGezel ancestry.)

HOWELL
II. Colonel John Read, the emigrant, was born about 1688 in Dublin, Ireland. He was sixth in descent from Sir Thomas Read of Berkshire. He purchased his manorial tract in Maryland from Lord Baltimore, but soon moved to New Castle, Delaware. He married Mary Howell, 1711–1734, daughter of a Welsh planter. Mary was the aunt of Colonel Richard Howell, governor of New Jersey,

who was the son of Ebenezer Howell of Delaware.

MOLINES

III. Henry Read, baptized June 11, 1662, at St. Bride's, Dublin, Ireland, married Mary Molines (?Mullins).

RUSSELL

IV. Sir Charles Read, baptized at Dunster, April 22, 1622, married Catherine Russell. He was of Whitefriars, London, and Dublin, Ireland. He belonged to a branch of the family of Reade of Barton, Oxfordshire, and went to Ireland "in the King's Cause." Sir Charles Reade was descended from Sir Thomas Reade of Barton Court, Berkshire, England, and ninth from Edward Read, lord of the manor, of Beedon, Berkshire, the last named, being high sheriff of Berkshire, and in 1451 was a member of Parliament.

Chapter 40

CAESAR
RODNEY

1728–1784

DELAWARE

CAESAR RODNEY, patriot, statesman, major-general and colonel of the
Delaware militia, was privately educated,
perhaps by his parents. Upon the death
of his father in 1745 he was placed under
the guardianship of Nicholas Ridgeley,
prothonotary and clerk of the peace of
Kent County, Delaware.

Rodney's public service began in
1755 when he was commissioned high
sheriff. Subsequently, he was registrar of
wills, recorder of deeds, clerk of Orphans' Court, and justice of the peace.

In 1758, he was justice of the Superior Court of the lower counties of Kent,
New Castle, and Sussex on the Delaware
River. In the same year, he was elected as
a delegate from Kent County to the
Colonial Legislature at New Castle. Rodney's plantation, Byfield, was a tract of
nearly 1,000 acres, and he owned two
hundred slaves. In 1762, he opposed the
bill to reimburse masters for their militia
service. In 1766, as a member of the
Delaware Assembly, he favored a bill to
ban the importation of slaves.

In 1762, he was appointed assistant
to Thomas McKean to revise and print
the provincial laws of the three lower
counties. On October 7, 1765, he was
elected by the House of Assembly as representative of Kent County to the Stamp
Act Congress, and attended its sessions
in New York. He signed the Declaration
of Rights which condemned the Stamp
Act.

In 1769, Rodney was appointed
cotrustee with John Vining of the Kent
County Loan Office, and served as sole
trustee from 1775 until his death. Also in
1769, Rodney was appointed third justice
of the Supreme Court for the three lower
counties; and was commissioned second
justice of the Supreme Court in 1773.

Following Parliament's passage of
the Boston Port Bill in the spring of 1774,
Rodney was speaker of the assembly and
at the request of meetings of the three
counties he called the assembly for a special session at New Castle on August 1,
1774. He signed the Articles of Association on October 20, 1774. This body appointed Rodney, McKean, and Read to be
their representatives at the First Continental Congress scheduled to convene in
May 1775. He signed the Olive Branch
Petition on July 8, 1775.

Rodney had also been elected
colonel of the upper regiment of Kent
County militia. In September following,
he was elected brigadier-general of Kent
County militia and of the western battalion of Sussex County. As speaker he
presided over the regular session in October 1775. Once again he was returned
to the Continental Congress. In June
1776 he presided over the Colonial Assembly's session at New Castle. They
passed a resolution supplanting the authority of the Crown in the three lower
counties. They also issued new instructions to Rodney and his fellow delegates
to the Continental Congress, authorizing
them to cooperate with the other
colonies.

On June 22, 1776, Rodney went to
Sussex County to investigate a threatened Loyalist uprising and had just returned home when he received an "express" from Thomas McKean, urging
him to return to Philadelphia to vote on
Richard Henry Lee's resolution for independence. He rode the eighty miles from
Dover to Philadelphia on horseback in a
torrential rainstorm, arriving late in the
afternoon of July 2, 1776, in time to cast
his vote and break the deadlock between
McKean and George Read. On July 4, he
voted for adoption of the Declaration of

Independence and signed the engrossed copy on August 2, 1776.

On July 22, he was back in New Castle presiding over the last session of the Colonial Assembly which he had summoned for the purpose of fixing a date for assembling a state constitutional convention and of arranging for the election of delegates. The conservatives of Kent County defeated him as delegate to the convention and when the new state constitution went into effect, he also failed to be elected to the first state legislature and was not returned by that body in the autumn as a delegate to the Continental Congress.

Ever patriotic, Rodney turned to military affairs again. In November 1776, he was made chairman of the Kent County branch of the Council of Safety. In January 1777, after George Washington had taken up winter quarters at Morristown, New Jersey, Rodney was placed in command of the post at Trenton for a few weeks of active service. He earned the admiration of George Washington for his good character and complete dedication to the cause of independence. He was commissioned major-general in the Delaware militia. Also in 1777, he was on the board of trustees of the Newark Academy.

In the spring of 1777, the legislature elected him judge of the admiralty, and in December was once again elected as delegate to the Continental Congress. In 1778, he was elected president of Delaware (governor) for a term of three years, to succeed John McKinly who had been captured by the British when they occupied Wilmington. He served as Delaware's war executive seven months beyond the full term, until November 1781. Rodney was a member of the Assembly in 1783, and in 1784 was speaker of the Delaware Senate.

In 1934, Rodney's statue was placed in Statuary Hall, the Capitol Building, representing the State of Delaware.

Additional Information

John Adams met Rodney; his diary entry on September 3, 1774, was "Caesar Rodney is the oddest looking man in the world; he is tall, thin, and slender as a reed, pale; his face is not bigger than a large apple, yet there is sense and fire, spirit, wit, and humor in his countenance."

Rodney's home was Poplar Grove on his Byfield Plantation near Dover. He was an Anglican and a member of Christ Church in Dover.

For some ten years Rodney had a cancerous growth on his nose and was afflicted with asthma. Upon completion of his term as president of Delaware in 1781, he went to Philadelphia to receive several months of treatment and surgery. He returned to Dover with hope but steadily lost strength until his death on June 24, 1784. He was buried at Poplar Grove, but in 1888 his remains were reinterred in Christ Episcopal Churchyard in Dover. A twelve-foot granite monument at his grave was erected by the National Society of the Sons of the American Revolution.

Rodney's will bequeathed most of his real estate to his nephew, Caesar Augustus Rodney. It also made provision for the gradual emancipation of his two hundred slaves. An equestrian statue of Rodney was unveiled on July 4, 1923, and stands in Rodney Square at Wilmington, Delaware.

Genealogy

I. Caesar Rodney was born October 7, 1728, at Dover, Kent County, Delaware, the eldest child of Caesar and Elizabeth (Crawford) Rodney. Rodney never married but apparently remained close to his family. Mary Vining, 1756–1821, born near Dover, was his ward and favorite cousin and became a famous hostess of the Revolutionary period. His brother Thomas Rodney was sent to him about 1762 to assist with the management of his farms, and in 1764 accompanied him to Dover to assist with his official Kent County duties. Rodney also took a special interest in Thomas's son Caesar Augustus Rodney, 1772–1824, and assisted with his education.

CRAWFORD

II. Caesar Rodney, Sr., 1707–1745, married Elizabeth Crawford, 1709–1763. To them were born eight children, the eldest of whom was Caesar Rodney, the signer.

Elizabeth Crawford was the daughter of an Anglican minister, the Reverend Thomas Crawford, born in Scotland, who was the first missionary sent to Dover and environs by the Society for the Propagation of the Gospel in Foreign Parts. He came on January 28, 1703/4, and settled at Lewes, Delaware, St. Peter's Church 1704/5 at Dover, and served Christ Church 1705–1709.

JONES

III. William Rodney, 1652–1708, emigrated to America in 1681/2. He was at Murderkill Hundred, Kent County, Delaware, in 1693. He was first married

to Mary Hollyman and had three children by her. He married second, on February 20, 1693, Sarah Jones, daughter of Daniel and Mary Jones who lived on Jones Creek in Kent County, Delaware, by 1680. By Sarah he had five children, of which Caesar Rodney, Sr., was the youngest. Sarah Rodney married second, George Newell, who died in 1740.

William Rodney was the son of Sir Thomas Rodney and Alice Caesar, daughter of Sir Thomas Caesar. He came with William Penn in 1682.

Daniel and Mary Jones lived on Jones Creek, Kent County, Delaware, by 1680. In 1682, Jones favored the Act of Union with Pennsylvania. He was justice of the peace in 1684, 1689, 1693, and 1694. He was granted 800 acres of land in 1680, and another eight hundred and fifty acres on Jones Creek in 1686. He died in 1694.

IV. William Rodney, sometimes of New York, who married Rachel (maiden name unknown).

CAESAR

V. Sir Thomas Rodney married in England, Alice Caesar, daughter of Sir Thomas Caesar.

SEYMOUR

VI. Sir John Rodney married Jane Seymour, daughter of Sir Henry and Barbara (Morgan) Seymour. Sir Henry Seymour was the son of Sir John and Margery (Wentworth) Seymour. Sir Henry's sister, Jane Seymour, died 1553, was the third wife of King Henry VIII.

Chapter 41

GEORGE ROSS

1730–1779

PENNSYLVANIA

GEORGE ROSS, jurist, patriot, received a classical education, including Latin and Greek. He then read law with his stepbrother, John Ross, in Philadelphia. He was admitted to the bar in 1750 and began the practice of law at Lancaster, Pennsylvania, where he soon had a large clientele. He served as prosecutor for the Crown at Carlisle, Pennsylvania, for twelve years. From 1753 to 1771, Ross was a warden and vestryman at St. James Parish, Lancaster, Pennsylvania.

His political career began in 1768 with his election to the Provincial Assembly. During his seven years there, he gained a reputation for his deep interest in Indian affairs, as well as his support for the rights of the Assembly in its disputes with the royal governor. He gradually gained political influence and was elected to the Provincial Conference at Philadelphia in July 1774. Ross was also in the Pennsylvania delegation to the First Continental Congress on September 5, 1774, although he was regarded as a Tory. As tension with parliament increased in 1775, he became a Whig and served in both the Assembly and on the Pennsylvania Committee of Safety. He signed the Olive Branch Petition on July 8, 1775.

He was not chosen as a delegate to the Second Continental Congress until after the debates had taken place and the vote had been taken on July 2, 1776. He took his seat on August 2, 1776, and signed the Declaration of Independence on that day.

In 1776, as well as being a member of the Pennsylvania Assembly, he was a colonel in the army and served as a congressman. In the same year, he helped negotiate a treaty with the Indians in northwestern Pennsylvania and was vice president of the Pennsylvania Constitutional Convention of 1776 in which he helped draw up the Declaration of Rights.

In 1777 Lancaster County awarded Ross £150 as a testimonial "of their sense of his attendance on public business to his great private loss and of their appreciation of his conduct." He declined to accept it, saying that it was "the duty of every man, especially of a representative of the people, to contribute to the welfare of his country without expecting pecuniary rewards." Ill health forced him to resign in January 1777.

On March 1, 1779, Ross was commissioned judge of the Admiralty Court of Pennsylvania and became involved in a controversy between Congress and the new state government. The controversy would continue for some thirty years, but he died on July 14, 1779, at the age of forty-nine.

Benjamin Rush described him as a man of good humor, wit, and eloquence.

Genealogy

I. George Ross was born May 10, 1730, at New Castle, Delaware, the eldest son of the Reverend George Ross by his second wife, Catherine VanGezel. He married, on August 17, 1751, Anne Lawler, who died May 28 or June 9, 1773. They had two sons and one daughter. Ross died of a severe attack of gout on July 14, 1779, and was buried in Christ Church burial ground in Philadelphia.

The Donegal Chapter of the Pennsylvania Daughters of the American Revolution erected a bronze plaque at Ross's grave site in 1897.

In 1948, a historical highway marker was erected in his honor on Ross Street in Lancaster, Pennsylvania. Another marker honors his memory on Arch Street in Philadelphia.

His children were: George, 1752; James, 1753; Mary, 1765.

LAWLER

Anne Lawler was a beautiful and accomplished lady of Scotch-Irish descent, who was one of Ross's first clients at Lancaster, Pennsylvania. She died May 28 (or June 9), 1773. She was the daughter of Andrew Lawler, 1707–buried April 18, 1752, at Christ Church burial ground, and his wife Mary, born 1709. Mary Lawler's will was dated 1788, in Lancaster County, Pennsylvania.

II. The Reverend George Ross, A.M., was born 1679 at Balbair, Scotland, and died November 22, 1755, at New Castle, Delaware. He was ordained in London in 1700, and was chaplain in the Royal Navy on May 2, 1705. He arrived in Philadelphia August 23, 1705, and settled at New Castle, Delaware, 1705–1708. The Old Church at New Castle is called Immanuel Church, built between 1702 and 1704. The Reverend Ross was their first clergyman, 1705–1708.

The Reverend Ross was a prisoner in France in 1711. Upon his return to Delaware in 1714, he served until he was succeeded by Clement Brooke.

The Reverend Ross married first, Jeanne Williams. He married second, Catherine VanGezel. By his two wives, he had twelve children. The Reverend George Ross was the second son of David Ross, Second Laird of Balblaer of the highland clan Ross, and was descended from the Rosses of Balnagowen, Earls of Ross.

VANGEZEL

Catherine VanGezel, b. 1681, married about 1728, the Reverend George Ross as his second wife. She was the daughter of John and Gertrude VanGezel. John VanGezel was a prominent member of Immanuel Church in 1758, at New Castle, Delaware. Cornelius Vangosell's (VanGezel) will dated November 8, 1717, probated May 22, 1718, names brother Johannes and sister Catherine, and makes his mother, Gertrude Vangosol, executrix. Gertrude VanGezel's maiden name is unknown.

III. David Ross, A.B., from Edinburgh, Scotland. The first record of the Ross surname in Scotland is in Ayrshire, much of the northern part of which, in the twelfth century, was held by a family of Ros or Ross, who came from Yorkshire.

Chapter 42

BENJAMIN RUSH

1745–1813

PENNSYLVANIA

Benjamin Rush

BENJAMIN RUSH, physician, humanitarian, patriot, was placed at the age of eight in the Reverend Samuel Finley's academy at West Nottingham. The Reverend Finley was his uncle by marriage. He entered the College of New Jersey, now Princeton University, and received his A.B. degree in 1760. His friends, and the Reverend Samuel Davies who was head of the college, advised him he should study law. But on the Reverend Finley's advice he chose medicine as his profession.

Rush became a pupil of Dr. John Redman, Philadelphia's leading physician, and lived in his home for four years, during which time he also attended lectures at the College of Philadelphia. Finishing these studies in July 1766, he again took Finley's advice, and in August went to the University of Edinburgh, which had the most renowned faculty in the world. He studied French under a tutor, and on his own, studied Italian and Spanish, and could read in all three languages. After graduating from Edinburgh and receiving his medical degree, he went to London to train at St. Thomas Hospital and to attend medical lectures.

Benjamin Franklin was at that time in London as agent for the province of Pennsylvania. Rush wrote to him, asking for letters of introduction which were generously supplied, and proved helpful in introducing him to English life. In the summer of 1768, he went to Paris, and in the fall returned to America with his doctor of medicine degree and began to practice medicine.

Before his first year ended, he had been called in consultation with some of the eminent physicians of Philadelphia. Two months after his homecoming, Rush was given the professorship of chemistry at the College of Pennsylvania, the first to hold such a chair in the colonies. Within five years, his practice grew to the point where he was making a good income, in spite of his well-known generosity to the poor.

Rush joined in all the patriotic causes. He wrote newspaper articles and became a member of the American Philosophical Society. He was solicited to take a seat in the General Congress of 1775, but declined. He was one of the Sons of Liberty who rode out a few miles to greet the delegates from New England as they arrived to attend the First Continental Congress.

In June 1776, Rush was elected to the Provincial Conference and was a leader in the movement for independence. A month later he was made a member of the Continental Congress when Robert Morris and John Dickinson withdrew from their seats. Rush was not a member when the Declaration of Independence was adopted, but was present on August 2, 1776, and signed the engrossed copy of the document.

Rush was surgeon to the Pennsylvania navy in 1775-76. He wrote *Directions for Preserving the Health of Soldiers*, which was used by the United States Military Medical Department up to the Civil War.

Congress appointed Rush to the post of physician-general of the military hospitals of the middle departments, 1777–1778, for which he would take no pay. In this capacity, he found on investigating the army medical service that it was in very poor condition. He protested to General Washington, accusing Dr. William Shippen of Philadelphia of maladministration. General Washington referred his report to Congress, which decided in Shippen's favor. Rush angrily resigned on January 3, 1778.

General Washington's defeats at Germantown and Brandywine led Rush to express doubt in Washington's ability, and he became associated indirectly with the Conway-Cabal affair, an attempt to remove General George Washington as commander in chief and replace him with General Horatio Gates. Rush wrote an anonymous letter to Virginia Governor Patrick Henry, suggesting that Washington be replaced by Gates or Conway. Governor Henry sent the letter to Washington who recognized Rush's handwriting and accused him of personal disloyalty. This ended his military medical career, and he resumed his private practice.

The new University of the State of Pennsylvania opened in 1778, and in 1780 Rush began to lecture there. He was a member of the staff of the Pennsylvania Hospital from 1783 until his death. In 1785, he established the first free dispensary in the United States. In 1783, he helped the Presbyterians to found Dickinson College and served as one of its trustees. In 1787, he was a member of the Pennsylvania Convention which ratified the United States Constitution and also framed a Constitution for the state of Pennsylvania.

Rush left the only record of the yellow fever epidemic of 1793, but failed to keep accurate records of his cases. Rush worked with desperation while several thousand citizens of Philadelphia, including members of his own family, died of the "yellow monster." When all the known remedies and best medical treatments failed, many physicians feared for their own safety and fled the city. Rush and a few of his pupils and friends remained. He himself had a severe attack of the fever.

He treated one patient who appeared to be near death with a powerful purge, an emetic, and followed by several bleedings. His patient survived the treatments and the disease, and Rush believed that with his treatment, yellow fever "was no more than a common cold."

In 1797, another yellow fever epidemic occurred in Philadelphia, but no longer were Rush's practices accepted by all, and other physicians noted that more died from the treatments than if there were no medical interventions — particularly cited were his use of mercury and bloodletting.

Rush advocated improved education for girls, and encouraged the addition of science and other useful subjects to their studies instead of the traditional Latin and Greek.

He was trustee of the Young Ladies' Academy in Philadelphia in 1786.

Benjamin Rush published several works, among them *A Syllabus of a Course of Lectures on Chemistry*, in 1770 which was reissued in 1773; *Sermons to Gentlemen upon Temperance and Exercise*, London, 1772, which was published anonymously and was one of the first American works on personal hygiene; *An Address to the Inhabitants of the British Settlements in America, Upon Slave Keeping*, 1773; and *Medical Inquiries and Observations Upon Diseases of the Mind*, 1812. In 1810, he had designed a "tranquilizing chair" for treating the mentally ill. His essays on social reform, *Essays, Literary, Moral, and Philosophical*, were collected and published in 1798.

Rush became president of the Pennsylvania Society for the abolition of slavery in 1803. He condemned public and capital punishment.

John Adams' characterization of

Benjamin Rush was, "An elegant, ingenious body, a sprightly, pretty fellow," and "Too much of a talker to be a deep thinker, elegant, not great." As president, John Adams appointed Rush as treasurer of the United States Mint, 1797–1813. During this period, in 1808, the Philadelphia Mint struck two medals in his honor.

Rush received the degree of LL.D. from Yale in 1812. On June 11, 1904, the American Medical Association dedicated a statue of Benjamin Rush in Washington, D.C. Among other honors, in 1948, the Medical Society of Pennsylvania established a Benjamin Rush Award. This is a three inch bronze medallion bearing his profile, to be awarded annually to one layperson and one lay organization for outstanding contributions to the health of the citizens of Pennsylvania.

Genealogy

I. Dr. Benjamin Rush, December 24 O/S, 1745–April 19, 1813, was born at Byberry, near Philadelphia, Pennsylvania. He was the fourth of seven children of John and Susanna Rush, and his father died when he was six years old. He married, on January 11, 1776, Julia Stockton, ca. 1755–July 7, 1848, daughter of Richard and Annis (Boudinot) Stockton. They had thirteen children, four of whom died in infancy, and two others died unmarried. Rush was a professed Christian, but did not adhere to any denomination. He died at Philadelphia and was buried in Christ Church cemetery.

His children were: John, 1777; Ann Emily, 1779; Richard, 1780; Susanna, 1782; Elizabeth, 1783; Mary, 1784; James, 1786; William, 1787 died; Benjamin, 1789 died; Benjamin again, 1791; Julia, 1792; Samuel, 1795; William again, 1801.

STOCKTON
Julia (Stockton) Rush, ca. 1755–July 7, 1848, was a poetess like her mother, Annis Boudinot, daughter of Elias and Catherine (Williams) Boudinot. She is buried with Rush in Christ Church cemetery. (For Julia Rush's Huguenot ancestry, see the genealogy section on Richard Stockton in Chapter 46.)

HALL
II. John Rush, 1712–July 20, 1751, married Susanna (Hall) Harvey, died July 2, 1795. She was the daughter of Joseph and Ann Hall, and the widow of Thomas Harvey, of Tacony, Pennsylvania. John Rush was a gunsmith and farmer. After his death, Susanna moved to Philadelphia and became successful in "commercial pursuits."

PEART
III. James Rush, 1679–March 16, 1727, at Byberry, Pennsylvania, married before 1712, Rachel Peart. Rachel may have been the daughter of Thomas Peart who, on December 31, 1701, sold land to Gabriel Wilkinson at Philadelphia. The land included the wharf, from Front Street, and extended eighty-five feet into the river.

IV. William Rush, July 21, 1652–1688, was born in England and died at Byberry, Pennsylvania. He married first, Aurelia, who died in 1683; her maiden name is unknown. They had three children. He married second, after 1683, but again his wife's name was not found.

V. John Rush, emigrant and yeoman, was born in 1620 in England and died in 1699 at Byberry, Pennsylvania. He married, June 8, 1648, Susanna Lucas, at Horton, Oxfordshire, England, and was commander of a troop of horse in

Cromwell's army. About 1660, he became a Quaker and emigrated to Byberry, Pennsylvania, with a large family. His entire family became followers of George Keith in 1691, but when the Keithians disbanded about 1697, most of them became Baptists.

Chapter 43

EDWARD RUTLEDGE

1749–1800

SOUTH CAROLINA

EDWARD RUTLEDGE, lawyer, patriot, governor of South Carolina, was educated in Charleston, and studied law with his brother John. In 1767, he was admitted as a law student at the Middle Temple of the Inns of Court, University of Cambridge, London. He was admitted to the English bar in 1772 and returned to Charleston.

Rutledge began to practice law in January 1773, and among his earliest clients was Thomas Powell, publisher of the *South Carolina Gazette*. Powell was in prison because he had printed the gazette on unstamped paper. Rutledge was successful in winning Powell's freedom.

On July 7, 1774, Rutledge was elected to the First Continental Congress. He signed the Articles of Confederation October 20, 1774, and in January 1775 he was elected to the first Provincial Congress.

In July 1775, Rutledge was appointed a lieutenant in the South Carolina militia. On August 8, 1775, he was elected to the Second Provincial Congress.

On February 16, 1776, he was elected as a delegate to the Second Continental Congress. He served on the first Board of War from June 12, 1776, which provided for the defense of the country.

He was at Philadelphia to vote in favor of independence on July 2, 1776, and signed the engrossed copy of the Declaration of Independence on August 2, 1776.

At the direction of Congress, on September 11, 1776, Rutledge, Benjamin Franklin, and John Adams met with Admiral Richard Howe and General William Howe on Staten Island concerning Rutledge's proposition for peace. He maintained that nothing short of independence would satisfy the United States. He was again a member of the Continental Congress in 1779, but illness prevented his attendance.

Rutledge served in the South Carolina militia, earning the rank of lieutenant colonel in the Charleston Battalion of Artillery. He commanded an artillery company in 1779, when the British under Major Gardiner were defeated and driven from Port Royal Island. He also took part in the siege of Charleston on May 12, 1780, and was taken prisoner of war at the time of General Lincoln's surrender. He was held eleven months in St. Augustine, Florida, and was exchanged eight hundred miles from home in July 1781.

In October 1781, Rutledge was elected to the South Carolina House of Representatives and reelected in 1782 and in 1786. He was elected a member of the General Assembly which met at Jacksonborough on January 18, 1782, because Charleston was still held by the British. He favored adoption of a federal Constitution, and was a member of the Constitutional Convention of 1790–1791; and of the legislature, 1782–1798.

He drew up the act which abolished primogeniture and gave equitable distribution of the real estate of intestates, February 14, 1791. He opposed the reopening of the African slave trade.

Rutledge declined a seat on the Supreme Court of the United States, May 24, 1794. On December 6, 1798, he was elected governor of South Carolina and was inaugurated governor before a joint session of the South Carolina House and Senate on December 18, 1798. He was a Federalist.

After the Revolution, in partnership with Charles C. Pinckney, who was his brother-in-law, he added to his property by investing in plantations.

During the First Continental Congress

in 1774, John Adams considered "Young Ned Rutledge a peacock who wasted time debating upon points of little consequence." Adams further described him as "a perfect Bob-O-Lincoln, a swallow, a sparrow … jejune, inane, and puerile." Benjamin Rush thought Edward Rutledge was a "sensible young lawyer" and very useful in Congress but also remarked upon his "great volubility in speaking." However, Rutledge later became an orator of great power and eloquence; and a "genial and charming gentleman."

Genealogy

I. Edward Rutledge, youngest child of Dr. John and Sarah (Hext) Rutledge, was born in or near Charleston, South Carolina, on November 23, 1749. He married first, March 1, 1774, Henrietta Middleton, by whom he had three children. He married second, on October 28, 1792, Mary (Shubrick) (Eveleigh), widow of Nicholas. She was born November 15, 1753, died October 22, 1837.

Rutledge died in Charleston while still governor, on January 23, 1800, and was buried in St. Philip's Churchyard Cemetery, in Charleston, South Carolina. In 1969, an historical marker was installed at the entrance to St. Philip's Churchyard by the South Carolina Society of the Daughters of American Colonists. This marker honors both Edward Rutledge and Charles Cotesworth Pinckney, 1757–1824, who is also buried in St. Philip's. In 1974, the National Park Service, U.S. Department of the Interior, designated St. Philip's Church a national historical landmark.

His children were: (by first wife) Henry, 1775; Sarah, 1777; unnamed child, died; (by second wife) none.

MIDDLETON

Henrietta Middleton was the daughter of Henry and Mary (Williams) Middleton; she died April 22, 1792. She was a sister of Arthur Middleton, the signer. (Henrietta Middleton's ancestry can be found in the genealogy section on Arthur Middleton in Chapter 31.)

SHUBRICK

Mary (Shubrick/Eveleigh), November 15, 1753–October 22, 1837, was the daughter of Thomas and Mary (Baker) Shubrick of Charleston, South Carolina, and Savannah, Georgia. Her sister Elizabeth married Thomas Lynch, Jr., and sister Hannah married William, brother of Thomas Heyward, Jr. Thomas Shubrick was one of the largest bondholders of the South Carolina debt, 1776–1780; two loans (estate of Thomas Shubrick February 3–24, 1780), were in the total amount of £136,050. He was a merchant of Charleston and with his brother and others owned several ships.

HEXT

II. Dr. John Rutledge was born ca. 1720 in Ireland, and came with his brother Andrew to South Carolina in 1735. He was married by the Reverend Robert Small on December 25, 1738, to Sarah Hext, born September 18, baptized October 18, 1724, and died April 22, 1792. Sarah was the daughter of Hugh and Sarah (Boone) Hext. Their first child, John Rutledge, 1739–1800, first state governor of South Carolina, was born when Sarah had just turned fifteen years of age. Dr. John Rutledge died on Christmas day, 1750, their twelfth wedding anniversary. He was buried at Charleston on December 27, leaving her with seven young children.

Sarah Hext was the only child of Hugh and Sarah (Boone) Hext, whose marriage was recorded as "Hew Hicks married Sarah Boone, November 21, 1723." The will of Hugh Hext, gentleman, of Berkeley County, was made November 23, 1732, and recorded February 1732/3, giving his wife Sarah Hext for life, use and benefits of all lands given him by the will of Sarah Fenwick, deceased, providing she use the profits arising therefrom to provide for and educate the testator's daughter Sarah Hext, his "dearly beloved and only daughter." Sarah received this and two homes in Charleston, a 550-acre plantation at Stono, and 640 acres on St. Helen's in Granville County. Mr. Hext died and was buried November 29, 1732.

Widow Sarah (Boone) (Rutledge) married second, Andrew Rutledge, Esquire, attorney at law, and brother of Dr. John Rutledge. She was the daughter of Major John and Elizabeth (Paty) Boone. She was buried on Tuesday, October 22, 1743, under her own pew in the church, according to the register of Christ Church Parish.

Hugh Hext, gentleman, who died in November 1732, was the son of Hugh and Mary Hext, who came to South Carolina from Dorsetshire, England, about 1686.

Chapter 44

ROGER
SHERMAN

1721–1793

CONNECTICUT

Roger Sherman

ROGER SHERMAN, lawyer, merchant, writer, statesman, probably received primary education as offered by the circuit schools. He was interested in theology, history, mathematics, and particularly law and politics. It is believed that he was aided in his studies by the Reverend Samuel Dunbar.

Sherman's father William purchased land in Dorchester, Massachusetts, incorporated as Stoughton in 1726. Here Roger learned the trade of cordwainer from his father and worked on his farm. His father died in 1741, and in 1743 Roger moved to New Milford, Connecticut, where his elder brother William had settled. He worked as a cobbler and in a few months opened his own cobbler shop.

About 1745, Sherman began studies to become a self-taught lawyer and was admitted to the Litchfield bar in 1754. In 1745, Sherman was appointed surveyor for New Haven County and continued as surveyor when Litchfield was organized in 1752, serving there until 1758. During this time he had become a "considerable" landowner and had begun taking a large part in civic affairs.

Between 1750 and 1761, Sherman published a series of almanacs based upon his own astronomical calculations. In 1752, he published "A Caveat Against Injustice, or An Inquiry Into the Evil Consequences of a Fluctuating Medium of Exchange."

In May 1755, he represented New Milford in the General Assembly which appointed him justice of the peace. In 1759, he became a justice of the County Court and at subsequent annual elections he was reelected to the legislature. These services prepared him well for legislative duties during the Revolutionary

War, particularly in military finance and supply. He was on a committee in 1755 to consider means of financing Connecticut's part in the Crown Point Expedition. He was appointed commissary for the Connecticut troops in 1759, and his depot was at Albany, New York.

Sherman gave up his law practice about 1761 and moved to New Haven. He began a broad scale of mercantile activities and imported merchandise and books for Yale students. He established another store at Wallingford.

Also in 1761, he contributed liberally to building the College Chapel, and from 1765 to 1776 he was treasurer of Yale College. He received the honorary degree of master of arts in 1768.

One of several offices held by Sherman during this period was judge of the Superior Court of Connecticut beginning May 1766 and continuing for twenty-three years.

In 1766, one of the offenders tried by Sherman was Benedict Arnold, who was accused of riotous conduct.

In 1772, his increasing public duties forced him to retire from business.

Though Roger Sherman belonged to the conservative wing of the revolutionary party, he, with Thomas Jefferson, George Wythe, and James Wilson, were among the first persons to deny the supremacy of Parliament.

Sherman was elected to the First Continental Congress in August 1774 and was present at the first session on September 5, 1774. He was reelected annually until November 1781. He was member of the committee which wrote the Articles of Association; signed the nonimportation agreement; and on May 6, 1776, with others, was appointed to raise ten million dollars. He served with generals Washington, Mifflin, and Gates who were appointed May 25 to lay plans for the ensuing campaign.

On June 11, 1776, he was one of the Committee of Five with Jefferson, Franklin, Livingston, and Adams, chosen to draft a Declaration of Independence. The following day, June 12, he was placed on a committee to prepare Articles of Confederation. On June 13, he was placed on the Board of War and Ordnance.

Sherman voted in favor of independence on July 2 and signed the engrossed copy of the Declaration of Independence on August 2, 1776.

On September 20, 1776, he was on a committee of three to visit headquarters to inquire into the state of the army and the best means of supplying its needs. In 1777, he was the Connecticut delegate to a convention of the New England states and New York concerning depreciation of the paper currency. In the controversy over recognition of Vermont as an independent state, he supported the Green Mountain settlers.

Sherman was a member of the Connecticut Council of Safety, 1777–1779, and in 1782, and was elected to the Constitutional Convention at Philadelphia.

In 1783, Sherman and Richard Law, his associate on the bench of the Superior Court, codified the statute laws of Connecticut. In January 1784, with James Wadsworth he was authorized to convey to the United States all lands claimed by Connecticut west of Pennsylvania, except the "Western Reserve Tract," and to satisfy the officers and privates in the Connecticut army for the lands to which they were entitled by the resolves of Congress.

On May 25, 1787, he offered the Connecticut compromise calling for Congress to have two branches, one with proportional representation and the other with equal representation which satisfied both the large and the small states.

On September 17, 1787, he signed the United States Constitution. Roger Sherman was the only person who also signed all of the other three great national documents: the Articles of Association of 1774, the Declaration of Independence, and the Articles of Confederation.

In 1789, he was elected as a representative of Congress and resigned his post as judge of the Superior Court. In 1790, he assisted with preparation of the Bill of Rights Amendments to the Federal Constitution. In May 1791, he was appointed United States senator and was still a member of the Senate when he died.

In 1872, the state of Connecticut honored Sherman by sending his statue for placement in Statuary Hall, in the Capitol Building, Washington, D.C.

Additional Information

In 1789, Sherman published, "A Short Sermon on the Duty of Self-Examination, Preparatory to Receiving the Lord's Supper." Always greatly interested in theology, he corresponded with a number of New England ministers, which reveals the depth of his religious beliefs.

Though not an eloquent speaker, Sherman spoke often and participated in debates. Contemporaries recorded that his manner was awkward, though he was admired for his devotion to duty, ability, honesty, common good sense, and high morals.

Thomas Jefferson thought him "a man who never said a foolish thing in his life." And John Adams called him "An old Puritan, as honest as an angel and as firm in the cause of American independence as Mount Atlas." Adams also said that "He was one of the soundest and strongest Pillars of the Revolution."

His portrait, painted by Ralph Earl, hangs in the Yale Gallery of Fine Arts. Roger Sherman died at New Haven, Connecticut, and was buried in Grove Street Cemetery.

Genealogy

I. Roger Sherman, April 19, 1721–July 23, 1793, was born at Newtown, Massachusetts, the third son of William and Mehetabel (Wellington) Sherman. He married, first, on November 17, 1749, Elizabeth Hartwell, by whom he had seven children. He married second, May 12, 1763, Rebecca Prescott, and by her had eight children.

His children were: (by first wife) John, 1750; William, 1751; Isaac, 1753; Chloe, 1754 died; Oliver, 1756 died; Chloe again, 1758; Elizabeth, 1760 died; (by second wife) Rebecca, 1764; Elizabeth again, 1765; Roger, 1768; Mehitabel, 1772 died; Mehitabel again, 1774; Oliver again, 1777; Martha, 1779; Sarah, 1783.

HARTWELL

Elizabeth Hartwell, died 1760. She was the first wife of Roger Sherman, and the daughter of Deacon Joseph Hartwell, January 24, 1680–1760. The name of Hartwell's wife was not found. He was probably the son of John Hartwell, February 23, 1641–1703, of Concord, Massachusetts, who married first, on June 1, 1664, Priscilla Wright, who died May 3, 1681. He married second, October 23, 1682, Elizabeth Wright, ca. 1655–1704.

John Hartwell was the son of William Hartwell, ca. 1613–March 12, 1690/1, and his wife Jazen, who died in 1695. William Hartwell arrived in 1636 from Kent County, England, and took the freeman's oath May 18, 1642.

PRESCOTT

Rebecca Prescott, living July 23, 1793, was the second wife of Roger Sherman, whom he married May 12, 1763. She was the daughter of the Reverend Benjamin and Rebecca (Minot) Prescott, of Danvers, Massachusetts.

The Reverend Benjamin Prescott, son of Jonathon, was born September 16, 1687, graduated from Harvard College in 1709, and became a minister at Danvers, Massachusetts. He married Rebecca Minot, born February 9, 1686/7, daughter of James Minot, Jr., born April 2, 1659, who married in 1684, Rebecca Wheeler, 1666–1734, daughter of Timothy and second wife Mary Brooks, daughter of Captain Thomas and Grace Brooks of Concord.

James Minot, Sr., December 31, 1628–March 30, 1676, married first, December 9, 1653, Hannah Stoughton, 1628–March 27, 1670. He married second, May 21, 1673, Hepsibah Corlet, born 1646, daughter of Elijah and Barbara (Cutter) Corlet of Cambridge, Massachusetts.

James Minot, Sr., born 1628, was the son of George Minot, August 4, 1594–December 24, 1671, who was the son of Thomas Minot of Saffron Walden, County Essex, England. George Minot was an early settler, a freeman in 1634, ruling elder for thirty years. His wife was Martha, 1597–March 27, 1657, age sixty, whose surname is unknown.

Israel Stoughton, ca. 1580–1644, first wife unknown, married second on March 27, 1631, widow Elizabeth (Stark)

(Knight), and came from Coggeshall in Essex to Dorchester in 1632. He was opposed to Winthrop's rule and was disfranchised for writing an heretical book. He returned to England and fought under Cromwell in the Civil War, gaining the rank of lieutenant colonel in Rainsborough's regiment. He died at Lincoln in 1644, and his will was proved in London July 17, 1644.

The Reverend Jonathon Prescott, ca. 1645–February 9, 1740, father of the Reverend Benjamin Prescott, married four times. His first wife, Dorothy, married in 1670, had one child Samuel and died in 1674. His second wife, Elizabeth Hoar daughter of John Hoar, was the mother of the Reverend Benjamin Prescott; she died September 25, 1687. His third wife was Rebecca daughter of the Reverend John Jones and widow of Peter Bulkley. His fourth wife was Ruth Brown, who died October 29, 1740, daughter of Joshua Brown of Newbury, Massachusetts. There were no children by wives three and four.

John Prescott, born before 1609–ca. 1683, of Sowerby, Yorkshire, married on January 21, 1629, Mary Platts, a native of Yorkshire. He was a blacksmith. They came to Boston in 1640 and settled at Watertown. He took the oath of allegiance in 1652 and was admitted freeman in 1667. John Prescott was the son of Ralph Prescott, baptized 1571, a resident of Shevington, whose will was proved January 24, 1609.

Ralph Prescott was the son of Roger Prescott of Shevington, Lancashire, whose second wife, whom he married on August 20, 1568, was of Standish. Roger was the son of James Prescott of Standish, Lancashire, in 1564, who with others were required to keep in readiness horsemen and armor.

WELLINGTON

II. William Sherman, July 28, 1692–1741, was born at Cambridge, Massachusetts, ninth of eleven children of Joseph Sherman. He married Mehetabel Wellington, baptized March 4, 1688, daughter of Benjamin and Elizabeth (Sweetman) Wellington. Benjamin Wellington, ca. 1645–January 8, 1709/10, lived at Cambridge; married on December 7, 1671, Elizabeth Sweetman, born January 6, 1647, daughter of Thomas and Isabel Sweetman. Thomas Sweetman, ca. 1610–January 1683, died age seventy-three. Benjamin Wellington's will was dated July 13, 1709. He was the son of Roger Wellington who was at Watertown in 1636, and married about 1637, Mary Palgrave, daughter of Dr. Richard and Anne Palgrave of Stepney, Middlesex, England. Richard Palgrave was baptized at Pulham, St. Mary the Virgin, County Norfolk, on January 29, 1597/8, the son of John and Amy Palgrave, and grandson of Thomas and Christian (Sayer) Palgrave of Pulham.

Richard Palgrave took the oath of fidelity in 1631 and died about 1656. Anna Palgrave, his widow, was buried March 17, 1669, at Roxbury, age seventy-five. Her will named daughter Mary, wife of Roger Wellington.

WINSHIP

III. Joseph Sherman, May 14, 1650–January 20, 1731, of Watertown, was a blacksmith. He married, November 18, 1673, Elizabeth Winship, born April 15, 1652, daughter of Lieutenant Edward Winship of Cambridge who came from Newcastle on Tyne, England, and was a selectman. He married first, Jane, 1618–1649, probably daughter of Isaac and Isabel Wilkinson. He married second, Elizabeth, surname unknown, who died

September 19, 1690, age eighty-five. Lieutenant Edward Winship died December 2, 1688, age seventy-six; he was the son of Lionel Winship of England.

PALMER

IV. Captain John Sherman, ca. 1615–January 25, 1691, died age seventy-six. He was of Watertown in 1636; freeman 1637; captain, selectman, and town clerk many times 1648–1663. He married, by 1635, Martha Palmer who died February 7, 1701, daughter of William Palmer of Watertown in 1636, and at Newbury in 1637. William Palmer came from Long Sutton, South Hampton, England.

Captain John Sherman came to America about 1634 with his cousins Samuel and the Reverend John Sherman. He was a surveyor, a farmer, representative in the general court, and a steward of Harvard College. He assisted Governor Winthrop in establishing the northern boundary of Massachusetts. He was the son of John Sherman of England.

V. John Sherman (wife unknown), son of Edmond and Anne (Cleave) Sherman, was born after 1584 and died after 1615.

PELLATE

VI. Edmond Sherman, ca. 1545–ca. 1600, married first, April 12, 1569, Ann Pellatte. He married second, in 1584, Anne Cleave. This family of Sherman/Shearman was seated at Dedham, Essex, England. It was a family of clothiers. Edmond Sherman founded a school there.

BUTTER

VII. Henry Sherman, died 1589. He married Agnes Butter who died in 1580.

Chapter 45

JAMES SMITH

1713–1806

PENNSYLVANIA

JAMES SMITH, Lawyer, surveyor, patriot, studied Latin, Greek, and surveying at the Reverend Francis Alison's Academy at New London, Chester County, Pennsylvania. He then read law in the office of his elder brother George Smith at Lancaster and was admitted to the bar in 1745. He removed to Shippensburg in Cumberland County where he was a surveyor and there found few chances to practice law. He returned to York where he remained for the rest of his life. Here too he found little business for an attorney. Smith began an iron manufacturing company on Codorus Creek in 1771. By 1778, when he sold out, he had lost £5,000. In 1760, he established a law office in York County, west of the Susquehanna River.

Smith is credited with raising the first volunteer company of associators in Pennsylvania for the revolution in 1774, while he was a delegate to the Provincial Conference. He was chosen captain of the volunteer company which later grew into a battalion. He accepted the honorary title of colonel, but left the active command to younger men. During that year at Philadelphia, Smith was on a committee to draft instructions to the assembly, giving them the order on July 21 to elect delegates to the First Continental Congress. During the Provincial Conference of 1774, he read his essay on "The Constitutional Power of Great Britain Over the Colonies in America," and supported the nonimportation of British goods and a general congress of the colonies.

Smith's speeches included bits of humor. He was an excellent conversationalist and had a large store of anecdotes.

Smith was a delegate to the Provincial Convention at Philadelphia in January 1775. Also, as a delegate to the Provincial Conference June 18–25, 1776, he helped draft resolutions recommending independence, for improving provincial defense, and for securing a new government. During the Constitutional Convention of 1776, he was a member of the committee to draft a new frame of government. Within the first week of the convention, Smith was elected to Congress. Although not present at the July 2 vote for independence, he signed the engrossed copy of the Declaration of Independence on August 2, 1776.

He participated in writing the state constitution, but was opposed to a single chamber assembly which was favored by the dominant party. He served in Congress for two years and four months and was a member in 1777-78 after the fall of Philadelphia. The Board of War held its 1777 meeting in Smith's law office at York. In October 1780, he was chosen to be a member of the assembly, and assisted with reorganization of Pennsylvania under the new constitution. He was appointed to the high court of errors and appeals, November 20, but resigned in May 1781. In 1782, he was made a brigadier general of militia and in 1784, the state made him one of her counsel in the case before the Congressional Court of appeals on the claims of Connecticut to the upper part of Pennsylvania. In 1785, he declined the appointment as delegate to Congress, on account of his age.

Smith retired in 1801, and at the age of eighty-two was probably the oldest practicing lawyer in Pennsylvania. In the fall of 1805, a fire started in the barn of John Hay, Esquire, and destroyed a large number of adjacent buildings including the offices of James Smith. His large library and personal papers were lost.

Smith was a Whig. He was a friend of George Washington, James Wilson, and all those who advocated the federal Constitution.

Genealogy

I. James Smith was born on September 17, 1713 (or 1719?), in Northern Ireland, and died July 11, 1806, at York, Pennsylvania. He was the second son of John Smith, a wealthy farmer, who came to the colony in 1729. Sometime between 1757 and June 1760, James Smith, Esquire, married Eleanor Armor, ca. 1729–1818, of New Castle, Delaware, and York, Pennsylvania. They were the parents of five children; one son and two daughters survived him. His will was dated April 25, 1806.

Smith was described as somewhat eccentric, possessed of a keen sense of humor, lively manner, and an unusually retentive memory. He gained many friends, particularly among the aspiring young lawyers who read law in his office. His personal estate increased considerably between the years 1781 and 1801 while he was chiefly engaged in his practice of the law.

He died July 11, 1806, at the age of ninety-three and is buried in the English Presbyterian Churchyard in York, Pennsylvania, where a Pennsylvania historical highway marker was erected in his honor. The Daughters of the American Revolution's grave marker gives the date of Smith's birth as 1713. If in fact he died at the age of ninety-three in 1806, this would seem to be the correct date.

His children were: Margaret, 1761; Mary, 1763; Elizabeth, ca. 1765; George, 1767; James, 1769.

ARMOR
Eleanor Armor, ca. 1729–July 13, 1818, was the daughter of John Armor of Newcastle, Delaware. She was a niece of Thomas Armor, justice and surveyor of York County, Pennsylvania. For some time prior to the Revolution, Eleanor had lived in Thomas Armor's home. She is buried beside her husband in the English Presbyterian Churchyard cemetery.

II. John Smith, a wealthy farmer from Dublin, Ireland, at the urging of his brothers who were already settled in Chester County, Pennsylvania, brought a large family to Pennsylvania in 1729 and settled west of the Susquehanna River in Lancaster County, which part is now in York County. John Smith died in 1761. The name of his wife is unknown.

Chapter 46

RICHARD STOCKTON

1730–1781

NEW JERSEY

RICHARD STOCKTON, lawyer, patriot, received his preparatory education at the Academy of the Reverend Samuel Finly at Nottingham, Maryland. He attended the College of New Jersey at Newark, and graduated in 1748. He then studied law under the Honorable David Ogden of Newark, later a noted Loyalist. Stockton was licensed as an attorney in 1754 and began his practice at Princeton. In 1758, he was counselor, and in 1764, received the degree of Sergeant-at-Law.

Stockton had, in the first decade of practice, built up a large practice and was recognized as one of the most eloquent lawyers in the middle colonies. One of his legal protégés who studied in his law office was Elias Boudinot, Jr., whose sister Stockton married.

Richard Stockton stated his political view to another of his legal protégés, Joseph Reed, in 1764: "The publick is generally unthankful and I never will become a servant of it, till I am convinced that by neglecting my own affairs I am doing more acceptable service to God and man." He became a charter member of the St. John's Lodge, Free and Accepted Masons, which was organized at Princeton on September 24, 1765. Though there were serious differences between the colonies and Great Britain in 1764, Stockton took a moderate stand. He suggested that some able Americans might be elected to Parliament, but after the Stamp Act was passed he held that Parliament had no authority over the colonies.

Stockton was a trustee of the College of New Jersey (later Princeton), and in 1766, the board requested that he offer the presidency of the college to the Reverend John Witherspoon of Paisley, Scotland. Witherspoon was received in London by the king and the Marquis of Rockingham. He was also given the freedom of the city of Edinburgh, Scotland, at a public dinner. Because of Mrs. Witherspoon's fear of crossing the ocean, Witherspoon declined the invitation. In 1767, Mr. Stockton's future son-in-law, Benjamin Rush, who was then a medical student at Edinburgh, visited the Witherspoons and apparently was able to persuade Mrs. Witherspoon. Witherspoon indicated that if another invitation were forthcoming, he would accept. The College of New Jersey sent their second invitation in 1768, and the Witherspoons sailed for America.

Stockton became prominent in New Jersey's provincial politics, and in 1768, he was appointed to the council and retained his position until the royal government ceased to have power in the colonies. The following year there were riots directed against lawyers because of costs and abuses, and his vigorous stand brought about the resumption of orderly judicial process in Monmouth County, New Jersey. In 1774, he was commissioned one of the justices of the Supreme Court. He presented a plan of self-government for the colonies on December 12, 1774.

Richard Stockton was elected to the Continental Congress June 22, 1776, took his seat on July 12, and heard the closing debates on Richard Henry Lee's resolution leading to the Declaration of Independence. He voted in favor of independence on July 2 and signed the engrossed copy of the Declaration of Independence on August 2, 1776.

During his attendance in the Continental Congress on August 30, 1776, his friends in the legislature put his name on the first ballot as a candidate for governor of New Jersey. Next day, the votes were equally divided between William Livingston and Richard Stockton. William Livingston was chosen governor; Stockton was chosen first chief justice of their new state, but he declined because he desired the more active career in Congress.

He served on numerous important committees during the late summer and autumn of 1776. On September 26, as colonel and inspector, he and George Clymer were appointed to visit General Schuyler's northern army. He reported from Saratoga on October 28 that the New Jersey troops were "marching with cheerfulness, but a great part of the men were barefoot and barelegged.... There is not a single shoe or stocking to be had in this part of the world, or I would ride a hundred miles through the woods and purchase them with my own money."

During his absence on this assignment, he was appointed on November 23 as one of a committee to find ways to aid General Washington and to hinder or obstruct General Howe's army. The British, however, invaded New Jersey before he could get to Princeton. His estate was in the line of their march, and he placed his family in the home of his friend, John Covenhoven, in Monmouth County. While there, he was betrayed by Loyalists, and he and Covenhoven were captured on November 30 by a group of Tory refugees and carried off to jail in Perth Amboy.

Stockton was taken to New York where he was imprisoned in the infamous provost jail in New York City, where he was subjected to indignities and nearly starved. During his imprisonment, General William Howe forced his signing of an "amnesty statement" to avoid even more severe treatment, in which he gave his word he would not meddle in "American affairs." At the direction of Congress, General Washington secured his release by hinting strongly at reprisal.

After his release, Stockton was too disabled to give more than occasional counsel. His beautiful home had been occupied as a military headquarters of the British who destroyed it and burned his books, furniture, and clothes, as well as his writings.

Genealogy

I. Richard Stockton, October 1 or 3, 1730–February 28, 1781, married, on December 12, 1754, Annis Boudinot. They had six children, two sons and four daughters. Their eldest daughter married signer Benjamin Rush on January 11, 1776. In 1763, Stockton received the degree of Sergeant-at-Law at Princeton.

Stockton died at Princeton, New Jersey, and was buried in an unmarked grave in the Stony Brook Quaker Meeting House Cemetery. In 1888, the state of New Jersey placed his statue in Statuary Hall, the Capitol Building, Washington, D.C.

In 1913, the New Jersey Society of the Sons of the American Revolution erected a plaque in his memory near the entrance to the Stony Brook Meeting House Cemetery. On July 30, 1783, Elias Boudinot, Jr., congress president, took up residence at Morven. Morven was willed to the state of New Jersey on October 29, 1956, by Walter Edge, a two-term governor of the state. It became the official residence of the governors of New Jersey.

His children were: Julia, 1759; Mary, 1761; Susan, 1761; Richard, 1764; Lucius Horatio, ca. 1768; Abigail, 1773.

BOUDINOT

Annis Boudinot, died February 6, 1801. She was the daughter of Elias and Catherine (Williams) Boudinot. Elias Boudinot, Sr., LL.D., came from France in 1686 after the revocation of the Edict of Nantz. Annis (Boudinot) Stockton wrote the poem "Welcome, Mighty Chief, Once More" to celebrate the capture of Lord Cornwallis, and sent it to General Washington. He wrote her a letter of thanks.

In 1789, as President Washington passed through Trenton, New Jersey, en route to his inauguration in New York, the young ladies of Trenton threw flowers in his path and sang Mrs. Stockton's poem.

PHILLIPS

II. John Stockton, August 8, 1701–1787, married on February 21, 1729, Abigail Phillips, August 9, 1708, who was the daughter of Philip and Hannah (Stockton) Phillips. John Stockton was chief judge of the Court of Common Pleas of Somerset County, New Jersey. He was also one of the founders of the College of New Jersey, now Princeton.

WITHAM

III. Richard Stockton, 1654–1798, was born in London, England, and died at Princeton, New Jersey. He came with his father from England to Long Island in 1656. In August 1695, he built the Stockton family mansion, Morven, on a tract of 6,000 acres which he purchased from William Penn. He married, on November 8, 1691, Susannah (Witham) Robinson, November 29, 1668–April 1749. She was the daughter of Robert and Ann Witham, and the widow of Thomas Robinson.

IV. Richard Stockton, ca. 1630–September 1707, was born in England and died at Flushing, Long Island, New York. He married in England in 1652, Abigail, whose maiden name is unknown. After he came to America, he settled at Flushing, Long Island, prior to November 8, 1656. He was commissioned a lieutenant of horse, April 22, 1665. He became a Quaker and moved to Burlington, New Jersey, in 1666. He bought 2,000 acres of land and moved to Oneanickon, New Jersey, in 1694.

V. John Stockton was probably the son of Randall Stockton of London, a grandson of John Stockton of Kedington, Cheshire, England, and a descendant of Sir John Stockton, Lord of Stockton Manor, Malpas Parish, Cheshire, England, who was lord mayor of London in 1470-71.

Chapter 47

THOMAS STONE

1743–1787

MARYLAND

THOMAS STONE, lawyer, patriot, received his classical education under a Scottish schoolmaster, following which he studied law at Annapolis in the office of Thomas Johnson. He was admitted to the bar in 1764 and went to Frederick County to practice. In 1771, he returned to Charles County and purchased land near Port Tobacco where he built his home, Habre de Venture.

In 1773, Stone was a member of the Committee of Correspondence for Charles County. In 1774, when the legality of the poll tax for support of the clergy was tested, he was one of the sheriff's lawyers against Samuel Chase, Thomas Johnson, and William Paca.

Stone took his seat in the Continental Congress on May 13, 1775, and signed the Olive Branch Petition on July 8, 1775. He served in the Continental Congress until October 1778, except for part of 1777. His most notable work was on the committee which framed the Articles of Confederation.

A few days prior to the July 2, 1776, vote, Maryland gave her delegates permission to vote as they thought best, and Thomas Stone voted in favor of independence. He signed the Declaration of Independence on August 2, 1776.

In September 1776, Stone was elected a Maryland state senator. He acted as their commissioner, conferring with Virginia concerning jurisdiction of the Chesapeake Bay. In 1777, he participated in the drafting of the Articles of Confederation, and in 1783 was elected to the Confederation Congress. He took his seat on March 26, 1784, and served as its chairman near the end of the session.

Thomas Stone again took up the practice of law in 1785. He was elected as a delegate to the federal constitutional convention on May 25, 1787; however in August he declined to attend.

Stone is the least known of the Maryland signers because he seldom spoke while in Congress or in the Maryland Senate. He was not prominent in debates but served on important committees, including the one for framing the Articles of Confederation.

The National Parks Service, U.S. Department of the Interior, placed a Thomas Stone National Historic Site sign at Habre de Venture. The central portion of the house was destroyed by fire in 1977; the kitchen on the west and Stone's law office on the east survived.

Genealogy

I. Thomas Stone, 1743–October 5, 1787, was born at Poynton Manor, Durham Parish, Charles County, Maryland. He married, in 1768, Margaret Brown, who brought him a dowry of £1,000. He lived in Frederick Town, Frederick County, 1764–1766, then returned to Charles County where he remained for the rest of his life. His home was Habre de Venture, a crescent-shaped, architecturally notable home. He was survived by two daughters and one son. The son, Frederick, died of yellow fever at Princeton, New Jersey, in 1793. Soon after his wife died on June 1, 1787, Stone retired from public service. His own health had failed, and on his doctor's advice he planned a voyage to England. While awaiting a ship at Alexandria, Virginia, he died on October 5, 1787. He was buried in the Stone family graveyard about 200 yards from Habre de Venture, Port Tobacco, Maryland.

On July 4, 1978, the Maryland Society of the Daughters of the American

Revolution placed a Thomas Stone memorial plaque at the foot of his memorial ledger.

His children were: Frederick, 1769; Margaret, 1771; Mildred, date unknown.

BROWN

Margaret Brown, 1751–June 1, 1787, was the daughter of Dr. Gustavus Brown, 1689–1762, and his second wife, Margaret (Black) Boyd, a widow, whom he married after 1744. Brown came from Scotland in 1708 and began a successful medical practice at Nanjemoy, Maryland. He had married, first, in Scotland, Frances Fowke, 1690–1744, daughter of Gerard Fowke, 1662–1734, by whom he had several children.

Brown participated in laying out the town of Charlestown, the county seat, at the head of Port Tobacco Creek. He built their home, Rose Hill, about 1730, which has remained a landmark. He served as an associate judge in 1723, and again in 1755. Margaret Brown had one full brother, born 1747, Dr. Gustavus Richard Brown, who graduated from the University of Edinburgh in 1768 and practiced medicine at Nanjemoy. He was an attending physician of President Washington during his last illness.

JENIFER

II. David Stone, 1709–1773, married first, Mary or Sarah Hanson, both daughters of Samuel Hanson, ca. 1685–1740. Stone married second, Elizabeth Jenifer who died before 1778, daughter of Dr. Daniel Jenifer, d. ca. 1729, and his wife, Elizabeth (Rogers) Jenifer Theobalds Whythill. David Stone was the son of Thomas Stone.

THOMPSON

III. Thomas Stone, 1677–1727, was born in Charles County, Maryland, and married first Christiana, surname unknown. He married second Elizabeth Thompson. He was the son of John Stone, ca. 1648–1697.

WARREN

IV. John Stone, ca. 1648–1697, was born either in Virginia or Charles County, Maryland, as his father migrated from Virginia to Charles County, Maryland, about 1648 or 1649. John Stone married Elizabeth Warren, daughter of Thomas Warren.

SPRIGG (?FOWKE)

V. William Stone, ca. 1603–ca. 1660, married first, Elizabeth Sprigg, sister of Thomas Sprigg (called Miss Fowke), and had several children by her including his eldest son Thomas, John ca. 1648–1697, and Elizabeth who married William Calvert, grandson of George Calvert the first Baron of Baltimore. He married second, on September 1, 1658, Verlinda Graves, who died 1675 in Charles County, Maryland. She was the daughter of Captain Thomas Graves, ca. 1580–1636, and his wife Katherine.

Captain Graves arrived in Virginia in 1608, was a burgess in the first House of Burgesses from Smythe's Hundred in 1619. He purchased 200 acres on the eastern shore of the Chesapeake from Sir Thomas Smith for £25 on March 14, 1628. He was from Accomack County in 1630 and 1632. He later lived in York County and died there in 1636.

William Stone came to Virginia before 1628, bringing four brothers (John, Matthew, Andrew, and Robert) with him to Accomack County, Virginia. There he became a justice of the peace in 1633 and in the same year received a power of attorney to become agent for his uncle

Thomas Stone, merchant and haberdasher of London. He was high sheriff of Hungar's Parish, Accomack County, Virginia, in 1634-35. Stone was called captain in 1637, and was high sheriff of Northumberland County, Virginia, in 1640.

In 1640, he owned 5,250 acres of land in Virginia. He was recognized as a political leader in Virginia with strong ties to the English and Chesapeake Puritan communities in Maryland when Lord Baltimore appointed him governor in 1648. In 1654, he was given Poynton Manor in recognition of his "laudable services," and for transporting himself, his wife, four children, four servants, and others from Virginia. He was a military captain in 1659. Governor Stone's will names children Thomas, Elizabeth (who married a Calvert), Richard, John, Matthew, Mary, and Katharine. He also named his wife Verlinda.

VI. Matthew Stone, haberdasher, late of St. Pancrasse in Soaper Lane, London, left a will dated April 4, 1629. Thomas Stone (the uncle of William Stone) had an eldest brother John Stone as well as brothers Henry, Andrew, Robert, and Matthew whose widow was Ellen Stone.

Chapter 48

GEORGE TAYLOR

(1716?–1781)

PENNSYLVANIA

GEORGE TAYLOR, ironmonger, patriot, came to America about 1736. It was evident that he had received some formal education before indenturing himself to a Mr. Savage to enable him to emigrate to America. He became clerk, then manager, of Savage's foundry in Durham Township, Bucks County, Pennsylvania. He was then clerk at Warwick Furnace and Coventry Forge, in Chester County, and later manager. Savage died sometime before 1742. In 1747, Taylor was a captain in the Chester County Associators.

About 1754, Taylor returned to Durham County where he and a partner leased a furnace in which he retained a business interest for the rest of his life. In 1761, he was justice of the peace for Bucks County. Taylor's political life began about 1763 in Northampton County, where he supervised the construction of the Northampton Courthouse. In October 1764, he was elected to the Provincial Assembly, and reelected five years thereafter. He was a member of the committee which drew up instructions for delegates to the Stamp Act Congress, chairman of a meeting of the principal inhabitants of Northampton County to protest closing of the Boston harbor, and was one of six men named for a committee of correspondence. He favored an intercolonial congress.

By 1774, Joseph Galloway owned the Durham Furnace property; Taylor's lease continued. Taylor attended a conference of deputies at Philadelphia in January 1775. In July he was elected a colonel in the Bucks County militia and though he saw no active service, he retained his title. He helped draft instructions for delegates to Congress in November 1775. He was absent from the radical committees in June 1776, and from the usurping convention which followed. He was appointed by that convention, however, as delegate to the Continental Congress on July 20, 1776, to replace of one of several of the Pennsylvania delegates who refused to approve the Declaration of Independence. He signed the engrossed copy of the Declaration on August 2, 1776, or shortly thereafter, but took no other part in activities of the Congress.

Taylor did represent the Congress, with George Walton, at a conference with the Indians at Easton in 1777. That treaty was not ratified by the Continental Congress.

In March 1777, Taylor was elected from Northampton to the new Supreme Executive Council of Pennsylvania. He served only six weeks because of ill health and then retired from public service.

His furnace manufactured, without profit, ammunition and cannons for the army. In 1778, the state of Pennsylvania confiscated the estates of Joseph Galloway, who was an extreme Loyalist, thereby closing Taylor's furnace. At his death there were no resources with which to pay his debts.

On November 20, 1855, the town of Easton and Northampton County dedicated their first important monument to George Taylor.

Genealogy

Taylor's biographers claim he was born in Northern Ireland in 1716. Among filmed vital records of Antrim, North Ireland, is the birth of one George Taylor on September 15, 1706, to a Reverend Taylor. The mother was not identified.

Taylor married in 1742, Mrs. Ann (Taylor) Savage, widow of Mr. Savage who had brought him to America as a redemptioner. To them were born two children, one son and one daughter. The daughter died in childhood. The son left a large family but predeceased Taylor. Ann Taylor died in 1768. Taylor also had five children by his housekeeper/common law wife, Naomi Smith.

About 1763, Taylor had removed to the East Banks of the Lehigh River, about 15 miles west of Easton in Northampton County. His estate there was called Manor of Chawton. He died at Easton, Pennsylvania, on February 23, 1781, and was buried at the German (St. John's) Evangelical Lutheran Church. His remains were moved to Easton Cemetery on April 20, 1870, and reinterred behind the monument that had been dedicated there in 1855. The monument is made of beautiful Italian marble, twenty-five feet tall, with an American eagle in flight on top.

The George Taylor Chapter, Daughters of the American Revolution, has placed a flag holder in front of the monument.

His children were: (by first wife) James, 1746; Nancy Ann ca. 1748 died; (by Naomi Smith, common law) five children, names not known.

Chapter 49

CHARLES
THOMSON

1729–1824

SECRETARY OF THE CONTINENTAL CONGRESS
AND THE CONFEDERATION CONGRESS
SEPTEMBER 5, 1774–JULY 23, 1789

Cha Thomson

CHARLES THOMSON, teacher, merchant, author, patriot, probably had his primary education at Maghera, Ireland. He was an orphan at the age of ten. After his arrival in Delaware in 1739, he was first placed in the home of a blacksmith in New Castle, but hearing that he would be apprenticed there, he ran away because he desired to become a scholar.

His elder brother placed him in the Thunder Hill Academy of Dr. Francis Allison at New London, Chester County, Pennsylvania. He also lived in Allison's home and was a fellow student of some of the others who would become signers of the Declaration of Independence. For a few years after leaving the academy, he conducted a private school. In 1750, through his friendship with Benjamin Franklin, he was appointed a tutor at the Philadelphia Academy. From 1757 to 1760, Thomson was master of the Latin School which became the William Penn Charter School.

About 1750, Thomson and a few other Philadelphians collected funds and had the first one of Philadelphia's main streets paved. This came about after one of their influential citizens broke his leg when his horse floundered in the mud.

During 1755, Thomson spent most of his time attending to Indian affairs. His friendship with Teedyuscung (Delaware Indian chief 1700–1763) continued for several years. His reputation for fairness and integrity caused him to be chosen by the Indians in 1757 to keep their record of the proceedings at the Treaty of Easton. He was later adopted into the Delaware Tribe. In a solemn ceremony, he was named "Wegh-wu-law-mo-end"— "the man who talks the truth." In 1759, Benjamin Franklin arranged for Thomson's "An Inquiry into the Causes of the Alienation of the Delaware and Shawnees Indians from the British Interest" to be published in London.

Thomson was secretary of several patriotic and literary societies. He organized a junto of twelve young men, patterned after Benjamin Franklin's junto. William Franklin was one of its members.

In 1760, Thomson gave up teaching and became a successful merchant. During the 1760s and early 1770s, he was among the leaders in all the demonstrations against Great Britain's oppressive policies, laws, and taxes. On September 29, 1764, Lord Frederick Grenville's plan for revenue was brought up in Parliament. The proposal called for imposing an excise on certain goods, as well as stamp duties. The Stamp Act was passed by Parliament, and in 1765, the colonies were so opposed to it that it became the most evident of the root causes of the American Revolution.

Franklin, then in England, wrote to Thomson, "The sun of liberty is set; the Americans must light the lamps of industry and economy." Thomson, his friend and neighbor, wrote in reply, "Be assured we shall light torches of quite another sort." Charles Thomson is said to have started the local opposition to the Stamp Act. In 1765, he was on the committee which called for the resignation of the king's new stamp collector, John Hughes.

The Stamp Act was repealed January 16, 1766; however the repeal was preceded by a declaration of Parliament that they had and "of right ought to have power to bind the colonies in all cases whatsoever." By 1767, the favorite project of the British ministry, taxing the colonies, persisted. An act was passed imposing duties on tea, glass, paint, and other items. A custom house was established; a board of commissioners was appointed; and two regiments of soldiers were sent to be stationed at Boston to sustain the parliamentary act. In January 1769, New York and Massachusetts began to enforce their nonimportation resolves and Pennsylvania followed their example. This was extremely detrimental to their mercantile businesses.

Charles Thomson discontinued his mercantile trade. To augment his income, he established a rum distillery at Kensington, near Philadelphia. His rum was either sold at the distillery or at his home.

Thomson was secretary of the American Philosophical Society from 1769 to 1780. He took the lead in resistance to the collection of duties on tea at Philadelphia.

By 1774, Thomson had become an adept and active liberal politician. In April he was elected president of the Liberty Party. In May, he appealed to the Quakers to support the Boston Resolves of May 13, 1774, and Paul Revere left bearing Philadelphia's declaration of support. On October 3, 1774, Charles Thomson was elected a member of the Pennsylvania Assembly.

John Adams was probing the minds of all present at the First Continental Congress on the vital questions. He had "much conversation with the delegates." Adams wrote, "This Charles Thomson is the Sam Adams of Philadelphia, the life of the cause of liberty, they say."

No minutes were taken on September 5, 1774; therefore, John Adams' notes are the only valid record. The delegates to the First Continental Congress convened at Philadelphia and chose Carpenters' Hall as their place to meet, and elected officers. Thomas Lynch, Sr., of South Carolina, nominated the Honorable Peyton Randolph, Esquire, of Virginia, to be their president. He was unanimously chosen. Lynch then proposed that "Mr. Charles Thomson, a gentleman of family, fortune, and character, in this city, should be appointed secretary," which was done without opposition. Thomson served without pay. He was not in Carpenters' Hall at his election but a messenger was sent to advise him that the Congress requested his presence.

Joseph Galloway was surprised and chagrined that Charles Thomson, whom he called "one of the most violent of the Sons of Liberty in America" was chosen by Congress to be its secretary. Thomson became the sole secretary of the Continental Congress and the Confederation Congress, from this first session on September 5, 1774, to its last session July 23, 1789.

As secretary of the Continental Congress, Thomson listened to the debates and recorded the minutes. He witnessed the progress of the American Revolution more fully than any other person could have.

John Hancock, as president, was the only member of Congress who signed the July 4, 1776, broadside copy of the Declaration of Independence. Thomson witnessed Hancock's signature and attested that the broadside draft as sent to the printer was correct.

On July 5, 1776, copies of the broadside draft of the Declaration of Independence were delivered to the Congress by John Dunlap, the printer. Thomson sent a copy to each state, military command, and others. The Declaration of Independence was first published on July 6, 1776, in the *Pennsylvania Evening Post*, and was publicly proclaimed in the yard of the State House on July 8, 1776, when it was read by John Nixon.

On December 1, 1778, Henry Laurens made a charge of insubordination against Charles Thomson but did not supply evidence to back his charge and Congress declined to act upon it.

On March 2, 1781, Thomson was elected secretary of the Congress of the Confederation. On May 25, 1787, the Confederation Congress met in Independence Hall to revise the Articles of Confederation. The federal Constitution was submitted to Congress on September 17, 1787, and Thomson prepared, signed, and distributed the resolution to the thirteen states for its ratification.

From 1784, Richard Henry Lee had advocated putting an end to slavery. While Lee was president of the Confederation Congress in 1784, Thomson agreed with him that "slavery is a cancer that we must get rid of."

After adoption of the Constitution, Charles Thomson helped to organize the new government. He was chosen to carry the news to George Washington that he had been elected president of the new United States government. He arrived at Mount Vernon on April 14, 1789, and with David Humphries, who had served as aide-de-camp to General Washington, accompanied him from Mount Vernon to New York City for his inauguration. Thomson took no part in the inaugural ceremonies.

Although President Washington did not offer Thomson a post in his new government, he sent a testimonial letter to him concerning the conduct of his duties during his years as secretary of the Congresses. He wrote, "Posterity will find your name so honorably connected with the verification of such a multitude of astonishing facts…. Your services have been as important as your patriotism was distinguished."

Thomson had hoped for an appointment in the new government. On July 23, 1789, he submitted to George Washington his resignation of the office of secretary of the Confederation Congress and custodianship of its records. He presented the records of his office to a deputy clerk on June 25, 1789, thus ending his association with the government, and left New York. In January 1793, President Washington requested that Thomson head a delegation to meet with the western Indians, but he declined the honor.

Thomson retired to his estate Harriton in Merion Township, Montgomery County, Pennsylvania, where he devoted many years to translating the Septuagint and the New Testaments. Translated from Greek, they appeared in four volumes in 1808, under the title *The Holy Bible Containing the Old and New Covenant, Commonly Called the Old and New Testament.* He published *A Synopsis of the Four Evangelists* in 1815.

Thomson received an honorary M.A. degree from the College of New Jersey for services as one of the founders of the college. In 1784, Thomson received an LL.D. degree from the University of Pennsylvania. He also received the degree of LL.D. from Princeton College in 1822.

Genealogy

I. Charles Thomson, November 29, 1729–August 16, 1824, was born at Maghera, Derry, Ireland. The Thomson home in Ireland was Gorteade Cottage. He married, first, Ruth Mather, ca. 1734–ca. 1770, of Chester County, Pennsylvania. They were the parents of twin sons who died in infancy. He married second, September 1, 1774, Hannah Harrison.

Thomson was one of four orphaned sons of John Thomson who were put ashore at New Castle, Delaware, in 1739. On arrival the master of the ship confiscated all his father's possessions as well as his "substantial sum" which he had placed in the ship's safe, in payment of the voyage to America.

The two youngest Thomson children, Matthew and Mary, were left in Ireland and came to America later. The mother probably died in 1738 or 1739 as can be calculated from the fact that sister Mary Thomson was living in 1822 when Charles Thomson wrote his will and she died at age eighty-four.

The 1790 Census of Pennsylvania lists the Charles Thomson household as: four males above sixteen; no males under sixteen; three females; four other free persons; and no slaves.

On September 13, 1824, the will of Charles Thomson was proved. Thomson died at Harriton on August 16, 1824, and was buried in the Harriton Family Cemetery. In 1838, he and his wife Hannah were reinterred in the Laurel Hill Cemetery in Philadelphia.

His children were: by first wife, twin sons, ca. 1770 (died); by second wife, none.

MATHER

Ruth Mather, ca. 1734–ca. 1770, was the daughter of John Mather and Mary Hoskins, who were married February 27, 1730/1 at St. Paul's Episcopal Church, Chester, Pennsylvania.

Mary (Hoskins) Mather was the daughter of John Hoskins who died December 28, 1774, at Chester County, now in Delaware.

John Mather was a well-known citizen of Chester County. Some items gleaned from the *Pennsylvania Gazette*:

on April 20, 1738, a parcel of servants just imported in the brigantine *Charming Sally* to be sold by John Mather at Chester, and Robert Barton, opposite the post office in Philadelphia. On February 9, 1748, John Mather was chosen captain of a regiment of associators for Philadelphia County. April 3, 1755, Keeper of the workhouse of Chester County is lately deceased; person desiring said position is to apply to John Mather or Thomas Morgan, Esquires, at Chester.

John Mather probably died in 1768. Charles Thomson was executor of his estate.

HARRISON

Hannah Harrison, December 23, 1728–September 6, 1807, was the daughter of Richard and Hannah (Norris) Harrison of Harriton, in Merion Township, Philadelphia County (Quakers). She was married to Charles Thomson on September 1, 1774, four days before he was elected secretary of the Continental Congress, and was expelled from the Society of Friends for marrying a non–Quaker.

She was a niece of John Dickinson. She was also a great-granddaughter of Provincial Governor Thomas Lloyd.

Hannah's Fairhill home was burned by orders of General Howe in November 1777. She died at Harriton and was buried there.

Richard Harrison, who died March 2, 1747, was a Maryland planter. He came to Pennsylvania and in 1719 acquired Bryn Mawr, a home built in 1704 on a 700 acre estate. He renamed it Harriton and founded Harriton Family Cemetery in 1719. His second wife was Hannah Norris.

Hannah (Norris) Harrison was the daughter of Isaac Norris, 1671–1735, of

Norristown which was settled in 1712. In 1704, Isaac Norris purchased Norris Plantation (Norrington), in Philadelphia County, from William Penn's son Thomas. It is now Norristown in Montgomery County, Pennsylvania. Norris also purchased a tract from Samuel Carpenter which became part of Norrington Plantation East and adjacent to his Fairhill land.

Isaac Norris was the son of Thomas Norris who was in Jamaica, British West Indies, in 1678. He came to Philadelphia in 1693 and established Fairhill. He was a member of the Governor's Council for more than thirty years; judge of the Court of Common Pleas; mayor of Philadelphia 1724; trustee under William Penn's will, and attorney for Hannah Penn. In 1694, he married Mary daughter of Thomas Lloyd, the first provincial governor.

Thomas Lloyd, 1640–1694, came from Wales on the *Fortune* with William Penn's colonists. He sailed June 10, 1683, and arrived August 18 in Delaware Bay,

and was in Philadelphia August 20, 1683. He and eighty other persons came with William Preston. He was chief magistrate, 1684–1693, during William Penn's absence; master of the rolls; and keeper of the great seal. He married Mary Jones who died in 1680, daughter of Roger Jones of Wales. He was in correspondence with William Penn in 1684 and in that year, as president of the council, he became acting governor for Holme (6 month, 18 day, 1684). Thomas Lloyd was provincial governor of Pennsylvania, 1690–1693.

II. John Thomson, d. 1739, was emigrating from Maghera, Derry, Ireland, with several of his children. He died as the ship bringing them to America entered the Delaware Harbor and was buried at sea. Thomson's wife had died in Ireland, probably in 1738 as their daughter Mary was born ca. 1738.

Thomson had a prosperous linen trade in Northern Ireland. His home, Gorteade Cottage, is now an historic site.

Chapter 50

MATTHEW
THORNTON

1714–1803

NEW HAMPSHIRE

MATTHEW THORNTON, physician, Loyalist turned patriot, received his early education at Worcester, Massachusetts. He studied medicine in Leicester, Massachusetts, with Dr. Grout, a relative. He qualified as a doctor in 1740 and removed to Londonderry, New Hampshire, where he established his medical practice.

Thornton accompanied Sir William Pepperell in the expedition against Louisburg in 1745, acting as under-surgeon in King George's War.

In 1758, he was a member of the legislature from Londonderry and became prominent in provincial and state politics. In 1765, he was active in the opposition to the Stamp Act. In June 1775, he held a commission as colonel of militia under the royal government.

In 1775, Thornton denounced the "unconstitutional and tyrannical Acts of the British Parliament." He was chief justice of Hillsboro County, and president of the Provincial Convention of 1775. In January 1776, he was elected speaker of the assembly.

On September 12, 1776, he was elected to the Continental Congress. On taking his seat November 4, 1776, he signed the Declaration of Independence though he had taken no part in its framing. In December 1776, he was reelected to the Continental Congress for a year.

From 1776 until 1782, Thornton was a judge of the Superior Court of New Hampshire. He moved to Exeter, Merrimack County, about 1780 and gave up the medical profession. Thereafter, he wrote newspaper articles and a treatise on sin that was never published.

In 1783, he resigned his commission in the New Hampshire militia. He was a member of the state senate during 1784-85.

On May 22, 1892, New Hampshire dedicated a monument honoring Thornton's memory which is located at the entrance to the Thornton Ferry Cemetery in Merrimack. The Matthew Thornton Chapter of the Daughters of the American Revolution placed a bronze marker at his grave, which reads, "Revolutionary Soldier, Matthew Thornton, 1775–1782."

Genealogy

I. Matthew Thornton was born March 3, 1714, in Ireland, of Scottish descent. He was a successful practicing physician from 1740 to 1780 at Londonderry, New Hampshire. About 1760, he married Hannah Jack. In 1761, Andrew Jack, his father-in-law, bought property from him located in New Chester and Alexandria. Matthew and Hannah had five children, three sons and two daughters. Thornton, New Hampshire, was named in his honor. Thornton died at Newburyport, Massachusetts, on June 24, 1803, at the home of his daughter Hannah (Mrs. John McGrath). He was buried in Thornton's Ferry Cemetery near his home in Merrimack County, New Hampshire. His original gravestone was inscribed "An Honest Man." In 1887, New Hampshire legislature provided $1,000 for a new monument.

His children were: James, 1763; Andrew, 1765; Mary, 1768; unnamed child, 1770; Matthew, 1771.

JACK
Hannah Jack, 1742–December 5, 1786, was the daughter of Andrew and Mary (Morrison) Jack of Chester, New Hampshire. Andrew Jack's will, dated November 12, 1773, leaves to his daughter Hannah, wife of Matthew Thornton,

one lot of land in Thornton, New Hampshire, and her equal share of stock and cash and notes with her three sisters Jane, Ann, and Mary. Matthew Thornton and widow Mary Jack to be executors. The will was proved January 12, 1774.

MORRISON

Mary (Morrison) Jack was the daughter of John Morrison whose will was dated May 14, 1743. In 1743, Andrew and Mary Jack sold to Samuel Morrison 10 acres in Londonderry which was their share of John Morrison's estate.

II. James Thornton, born probably about 1690, married Elizabeth Jenkins. They emigrated to America, having lived at Lisburn, County Antrim, in 1718 and first settled at Wiscaset, Maine, but soon moved to Worcester, Massachusetts. James Thornton's name was in a list of "Merrymeeting Bay Scotch-Irish Settlers 1718–1722."

Chapter 51

GEORGE
WALTON

1741–1804

GEORGIA

GEORGE WALTON, lawyer, patriot, governor of Georgia, was largely self-taught. Orphaned at an early age, he was apprenticed to a carpenter who recognized Walton's intelligence, ambition, and character, and released him from the apprenticeship. He gave him part of his wages so that he might attend a local school. In 1769, he went to Savannah, Georgia, and read law with Henry Young while working as surveyor assistant to Matthew Talbot.

Walton was admitted to the bar in 1774 at the age of thirty-three. He also became a Master Mason in 1774, a member of Solomon's Lodge F and AM, Savannah. Two Masonic Lodges have been named in his honor: Walton No. 200, Jasper County, and George Walton Lodge No. 699, Augusta, Georgia. He was one of the founders and a trustee of Richmond Academy, and a member of the committee to locate Franklin College, now the University of Georgia, at Albany.

In Savannah, Walton attended the first meetings called by the patriots, and condemned British colonial policies. He was one of the group which called a meeting at the Liberty Pole at Tondee's tavern, where the Georgia Provincial Congress began, with George Walton being chosen its first secretary. He was also elected president of the newly formed Council of Safety.

At a meeting of the Provincial Congress, he was elected to be a delegate to the Second Continental Congress. He probably was in Philadelphia in late June and present to vote in favor of independence on July 2. However, the journals of the Congress first mention his presence there on July 17. He signed the Declaration of Independence on August 2, 1776, and continued as a delegate to the Continental Congress until October 1781.

Walton's elder brother, John Walton, was a delegate to the Continental Congress in 1778 and signed the Articles of Confederation. George Walton had been the leader of the opposition to Button Gwinnett, and a friend of General Lachlan McIntosh. In 1779, as governor of Georgia, he forwarded a forged letter to Congress which brought about McIntosh's transfer from Georgia. In 1783, the legislature censured George Walton and ordered the attorney general to bring suit against him, but on the day before it had elected him chief justice of the state of Georgia.

Captain William McIntosh, son of the general, had threatened that if Walton took his seat as chief justice, he would be "pulled off" the bench. An account of Walton's horsewhipping by William McIntosh is contained in the *Collections of the Georgia Historical Society, Volume XII.* In 1783, Captain William McIntosh was being tried before a general court-martial.

On January 9, 1778, Walton was commissioned colonel of the Georgia militia's first regiment. During the siege of Savannah, his leg was broken by a cannonball. He fell from his horse and was captured by the British. He was exchanged in September 1779, sent home, and was elected governor but served only two months. The Tory legislature confiscated his property in 1781.

He was commissioned in 1783 to negotiate a treaty with the Cherokees in Tennessee, then served six years as chief justice of Georgia. In 1789, he was a presidential elector and was again elected governor. During this term, a new constitution for Georgia was adopted, Augusta became the capital, and the Creek

Indians were pacified. He retired in 1790, but was called back to public service as judge of the Supreme Court of Georgia.

Walton was a U.S. senator in 1795. From 1799 to 1804, he was judge of the Middle Court of Georgia.

In 1818, Walton County, Georgia, was created from a portion of Cherokee lands and was named in honor of George Walton. He is also honored by the Signers Memorial at Augusta which was dedicated in July 1848.

The Georgia Hall of Fame was founded in 1955. Walton, Lyman Hall, and Button Gwinnett were the first three Georgians admitted. Their busts were placed in the rotunda of the Georgia Capitol Building.

Additional Information

George Walton was a politician who kept his promises. He had a violent temper but was warm in his friendships. He was described as of small stature, handsome, and appearing haughty, dignified, and stern.

His residence Meadow Garden was built in 1789. In 1795, he built College Hill, which was his home until his death. He died February 2, 1804.

Walton was buried in Rosney Cemetery in Augusta. For an Independence Day celebration July 4, 1848, the citizens of Georgia erected a monument to their three signers of the Declaration of Independence, and his remains were reinterred beneath the monument.

During the 1970s, Meadow Garden was a restoration project of the National Society of the Daughters of the American Revolution (NSDAR). The home is owned by the Georgia Society of NSDAR, and is a national historic monument.

Genealogy

I. George Walton was born in 1741 near Farmville, Prince Edward County, Virginia, the son of George and Mary (Hughes) Walton. He married, in 1777, Dorothy Camber, and they had two sons.

George Walton, Jr., became secretary of state under General Andrew Jackson when he was governor of the territory of West Florida. The other son, Thomas Camber Walton, died in Georgia October 3, 1804.

His children were: Thomas Camber, 1776; George, Jr., 1786.

CAMBER
Dorothy Camber, born ca. 1759, was the daughter of Thomas Camber, Esquire, and mother not known. Though her father was a loyalist, she supported the patriots' causes. She had four sisters who married into families of Habersham, Brisbane, Walker, and Butler.

Thomas Camber was in New Hanover County, North Carolina, in 1755. His will in probate records of South Carolina, January 15, 1774, was administered by John Lewis Bourquin and Adrian Meyer.

Dorothy (Camber) Walton is buried in a brick-walled lot with a plaque in St. Michael's Cemetery. The plaque reads "In Memory of Dorothy Walton, Wife of George Walton, a Signer of the Declaration of Independence. Placed by the Pensacola Chapter, DAR and Pensacola Chapter SAR—1929"

On a flat stone within the wall, another plaque reads:

"Died in Pensacola 12 September 1832, Age 73 Years. Mrs. Dorothy Walton, a Native of the State of Georgia, A Matron of the Revolution, Consort and Relict of George Walton, A Signer of the Declaration of American Independence."

HUGHES

II. George Walton, Sr., was living at Farmville, Prince Edward County, in 1741. He was the son of the emigrant, Robert Walton, who came from England to Virginia in 1682. Mary Hughes married George Walton, Sr., before 1730. She was the daughter of Jesse and Sarah (Sally Tarlton) Hughes. Sally Hughes named Mary, wife of George Walton, in her will which was proved in Goochland County May 19, 1730.

Robert Hughes' will dated July 13, 1750, was proved in Cumberland County, October 25, 1752. He names a wife Martha and children including Mary Walton, second in the list, wife of George Walton.

WILLIAM WHIPPLE

1730–1785

NEW HAMPSHIRE

WILLIAM WHIPPLE, seaman, merchant, patriot, received a good public school education at Kittery, Maine. His tutor, 1738–1746, was Robert Elliott Gerrish, a 1730 graduate of Harvard College. He went to sea on a merchantman when he was very young. At twenty he was in command of a vessel and made several voyages to Europe and the West Indies. It has been alleged, but never quite proven, that he was engaged in the slave trade.

In 1759, William Whipple and his brothers went into the mercantile business at Portsmouth, New Hampshire. He was of the Popular party in disputes during the pre–Revolution era, and was on a committee in 1764 to prevent the landing of tea at Portsmouth, New Hampshire.

In 1775, he entered upon his public career and relinquished his share of the mercantile business to his brother, Joseph Whipple. Whipple was a member of the 1775 Provincial Congress of New Hampshire; a member of the Council in 1776; and of the New Hampshire Committee of Safety.

On January 23, 1776, he was elected to be a delegate at the Second Continental Congress, where he took his seat February 29, 1776. He voted "yes" for independence on July 2 and signed the engrossed copy of the Declaration of Independence on August 2, 1776.

Whipple served on committees of marine, commerce, secret correspondence, military affairs, and finances. He served in the Congress until 1779, with the exception of some occasions of military service.

On July 17, 1777, the General Court divided the whole militia of New Hampshire into two brigades and gave the commands to William Whipple and John Stark. In August following, Brigadier-General William Whipple marched with a large number of his brigade and a number of volunteers to the northern armies to oppose General John Burgoyne. On September 27, 1777, he commanded New Hampshire troops in Vermont and New York. These troops fought in the Battle of Saratoga and witnessed the British surrender on October 17, 1777.

At the surrender of Burgoyne, General Whipple was one of two representatives of General Gates who arranged the terms of capitulation. In 1778, he accompanied General Sullivan in his unsuccessful campaign in Rhode Island.

Whipple advocated "spirited measures" against speculators and Loyalists. In a 1779 letter to Josiah Bartlett, he wrote concerning the Loyalists, "I think it high time they were all hung or banished."

He retired from Congress in 1780 and declined the appointment as commissioner of the Board of Admiralty. He served several sessions in the New Hampshire legislature, and from 1782 was also an associate justice of the Superior Court. He was president of the commission appointed to arbitrate the land dispute between Pennsylvania and Connecticut called the Yankee-Pennamite War. Also in 1782, he was made receiver for New Hampshire by Robert Morris, superintendent of finance, who persuaded him to remain in that office until 1784, when he resigned.

In 1784, he became justice of the peace and quorum throughout New Hampshire and died suddenly while on circuit.

On the street near North Cemetery at Portsmouth, New Hampshire, is an historical marker stating that William Whipple, Governor John Langdon, and

Captain Thomas Thompson of the Continental ship *Raleigh* are among the noted citizens buried there.

Genealogy

I. William Whipple, January 14, 1730–November 28, 1785, was the eldest of five children of William and Mary (Cutt) Whipple. He married his cousin, Catharine Moffatt, and with her had two children who died in infancy. During his last three years of life, Whipple was an associate justice of the Superior Court, though in poor health. He died suddenly of "ossification of the heart" while on circuit. He was buried in Union (now North) Cemetery, at Portsmouth, New Hampshire.

Whipple's original memorial ledger was replaced by the Rockingham Bicentennial Committee on October 10, 1976.

His children were: unnamed child, 1751; William, 1772.

MOFFATT

Catharine Moffatt, was the daughter of the Honorable John Moffatt, 1694–1786, died age ninety-two. John Moffatt's wife was Catharine Cutt, September 30, 1700–December 1769; they were married on August 20, 1723. Catharine Cutt was the daughter of Robert Cutt.

The Honorable John Moffatt was the grandfather of Governor John Langdon, 1784–1785, of New Hampshire. Another daughter, Elizabeth, married the Reverend Joseph Whipple.

CUTT

II. William Whipple, January 28, 1695/6–August 17, 1751, was born at Ipswich and died at Kittery, Maine. He was a maltster. On May 14, 1727, he married

Mary Cutt, daughter of Robert Cutt II, and granddaughter of Robert Cutt who came from Bristol, England, to Portsmouth, New Hampshire. Robert Cutt, son of Robert, died September 18, 1734, in his sixty-ninth year. His will was dated on the day of his death. He married Dorcas Hammond, daughter of Joseph and Catharine (Frost) Hammond of Kittery. Her father Joseph was carried to Canada in 1695 by the French. Catharine Frost Hammond died August 1, 1715. She was the daughter of Nicholas Frost, ca. 1595–July 20, 1663, from Tiverton in Devon, England. Dorcas Hammond Cutt died November 17, 1757, age eighty-two. Her will was dated May 26, 1749.

Robert Cutt, Sr., shipwright, came from Bristol, England, to Portsmouth, New Hampshire. He went to Barbados but returned about 1663 and lived at Kittery, Maine, where he built several ships. His first wife's name is unknown, but he had a second wife, Mary, by whom he had a daughter Mary and others children. His will, dated June 18, 1674, was probated July 6 following. Mary Cutt, his widow, married second, Francis Champernoon, nephew of Sir Ferdinando Gorges.

DENISON

III. Matthew Whipple, December 24, 1658/9–January 28, 1738/9, born and died at Ipswich, was the posthumous child of Matthew Whipple, ca. 1630–1658. He married first, Joanna Appleton, born about 1660, daughter of Samuel Appleton, Jr., who was baptized in 1624 at Little Wallingford. He married second, Mary Oliver. Samuel Appleton, Sr., born 1586, came to America in 1635 with his wife Mary Everard. He was the son of Thomas Appleton of Little Wallingford, County Suffolk, England. Matthew

Whipple married second, Martha (Denison) Rindge, b. 1668–September 12, 1728, daughter of John Denison who graduated from Harvard in 1684 and was a minister at Ipswich. John Dennison married Martha Symonds, daughter of Deputy Governor Samuel Symonds of Ipswich who came from Yeldham, County Essex, England, in 1637, as deputy governor.

Samuel Symonds married about 1620, Deborah Harlakenden. Deputy Governor Samuel Symonds died October 12, 1678, during a session of the General Court. John Denison died January 9, 1671, and his widow married Richard Martyn of Portsmouth, New Hampshire.

John Denison was the only son of Major General Daniel Denison who was at Cambridge in 1633. Daniel Denison was the son of William Denison of Roxbury. He married Patience Dudley who died in 1690. Daniel Denison died September 19, 1682, age seventy. His will was dated July 18, 1673, with codicils added in 1679 and 1680.

Patience Dudley was the daughter of Governor Thomas Dudley, third governor of Massachusetts Bay Colony.

Thomas Dudley was the son of Captain Roger Dudley born in 1576 at Northampton, England.

BARTHOLOMEW

IV. Matthew Whipple, ca. 1630–October 20, 1658, married on December 24, 1657, at Gloucester, Mary Bartholomew, born 1632, daughter of William Bartholomew who arrived from London in September 1634, in the ship with the Reverend John Lothrop, Zachary Symmes, and Mrs. Hutchinson. He was admitted freeman March 4, 1635, was a merchant at Boston in 1660, at Marblehead in 1674, and died January 18, 1681. The name of his wife is unknown.

V. Matthew Whipple, 1590–1647, of Bocking, England, came to Ipswich, Massachusetts, before February 21, 1638/9. He had a land grant in 1638. He married first, in England; married second, Rose (maiden name unknown).

VI. Matthew Whipple, ca. 1560–September 19, 1616, married in 1582, Joan, who was buried May 19, 1612. He was a clothier of Bocking, England. His will was proved on January 28, 1618.

Chapter 53

WILLIAM
WILLIAMS

1731–1811

CONNECTICUT

WILLIAM WILLIAMS, merchant, patriot, graduated from Harvard College in 1751. He began to study theology under his father's guidance, but this study was abandoned after 1755.

In 1775, during the French and Indian War, he participated in the operations at Lake George. He was a member of the staff of Colonel Ephriam Williams, a cousin, who was killed there. At the conclusion of the campaign, Williams returned to Lebanon, Connecticut, and went into the mercantile business.

Williams became an ardent participant in the struggle for American independence, both in financial support and in his writings. He presented the claims of the colonists in the press, and helped compose many of the Revolutionary state papers of the distinguished Royal Governor Jonathon Trumbull, the only British colonial governor who supported the colonies during the Revolutionary War.

Williams held many public offices in Lebanon, Connecticut. He was a colonel in the Connecticut militia, 1773–1775. He was clerk, 1752–1796; selectman 1760–1785; a member of the lower house of the state legislature, 1757–1776 and 1781–1784; and a member of the Governors Council, 1784–1803. He was repeatedly elected clerk, also Speaker of the House. During the mid–1760s he served on committees that considered the Stamp Act, the Connecticut claims to the Susquehanna lands, the case of the Mohegan Indians, and settlement of the boundary disputes between Connecticut and Massachusetts.

In 1775, on Williams' promissory note, money was raised to defray the cost of sending Connecticut troops to aid in the capture of Ticonderoga. He was appointed to represent Connecticut at various conferences of delegates from the New England states held to study matters of common interest.

Williams took the seat of Oliver Wolcott when he left the Continental Congress in June 1776, due to illness. He voted in favor of independence, and signed the engrossed, parchment copy of the Declaration of Independence on August 2, 1776.

He was a member of the Continental Congress, 1777–1778 and 1783–1784. He was elected to the Board of War in 1777, and served on the Committee of Safety. He assisted in framing of the Articles of Confederation in 1778.

In 1779, it was impossible to purchase the necessary supplies for the army because of the depreciated value of the Continental currency. Williams accepted paper money, nearly worthless, for $2,000 in coin. He was said to have remarked that if independence were established he would get his money back; if not, the loss would be of no account to him.

He had been criticized for resigning his colonelcy of the Twelfth Militia Regiment at the outbreak of the Revolution, in order to accept election to the Continental Congress. However, his courage was evidenced in 1781, when word arrived in Lebanon of Benedict Arnold's raid upon New London. He immediately mounted his horse and rode twenty-three miles in three hours to offer his services as a volunteer. On his arrival the town was already in flames.

William Williams was judge of the Windham County Court, 1776–1805, and judge of the Probate Court for Windham District, 1775–1809. Williams was a delegate to the convention that met at Hartford in 1788 to consider the adoption, by Connecticut, of the Constitution of the

United States. He voted for it, but objected to the clause forbidding religious tests.

Genealogy

I. William Williams, born April 8, 1731, was the son of Pastor Solomon Williams, D.D., and Mary Porter. He married, on February 14, 1771, at Lebanon, New London, Connecticut, Mary Trumbull, and they were the parents of three children. He died on August 2, 1811, and was buried in the Trumbull Vault in Trumbull Cemetery at Lebanon, Connecticut.

His children were: Solomon, 1772; Faith, 1774; William Trumbull, 1777.

TRUMBULL

Mary Trumbull was born at Lebanon, Connecticut, on July 1, 1745. She was the daughter of Governor Jonathon and Faith (Robinson) Trumbull who were married December 9, 1735. Mary (Trumbull) Williams' genealogy contains examples of the interrelationships between some of the signers and their wives: She was related to President John Adams, descended from John and Priscilla (Mullins) Alden; Ann Remington, first wife of William Ellery; descended from Nicholas and Elizabeth (Symmes) Danforth; Oliver Wolcott, descended from William and Philippa (Denys) Drake. (Refer to chapters 1, 2, 9 and 56 for early details, as they are not repeated in the Williams genealogy.)

Governor Jonathon Trumbull, October 12, 1710–August 17, 1785, was born at Lebanon, Connecticut. He graduated from Harvard College in 1727 and married on December 9, 1735, Faith Robinson. He

was the son of Joseph Trumbull, born January 16, 1679, and Hanna Higley, the daughter of John and Hannah (Drake) Higley of Windsor, who were married on November 9, 1671.

Hannah Drake was the daughter of John and Hannah (Moore) Drake of Windsor. John Higley removed to Simsbury after 1679 and died there. It is believed that he came from Frimley, in Surry, England.

Governor Trumbull was preparing for the ministry, but family difficulties obliged him to enter his father's mercantile business. He studied law, and was sent to the General Assembly in 1733; from 1740 to 1750 he was assistant to the royal governor of Connecticut. He was appointed deputy governor of Connecticut and chief justice of the Connecticut Supreme Court, both in 1766. In 1769, he was elected by the assembly to the governorship of Connecticut and held the position until 1784. As the "Rebel Governor of Connecticut," he frequently corresponded with General Washington and helped supply materials for the Continental Army.

Faith Robinson, born 1718 at Duxbury, Massachusetts, wife of Governor Trumbull, was the daughter of the Reverend John Robinson and Hannah Wiswall. The date of her death is unknown. Faith auctioned off her scarlet cloak to purchase food for the colonial soldiers.

The Reverend John Robinson graduated from Harvard College in 1695, was minister of Duxbury, and ordained November 13, 1702. He died November 14, 1745, at Lebanon, Connecticut, in the home of Governor Trumbull. His wife, Hannah Wiswall, February 22, 1682–September 22, 1722, drowned at Nantasket, Massachusetts. She was the daughter

of the Reverend Ichabod Wiswall, 1637–
July 20, 1700, agent of the Plymouth
Colony in London.

The Reverend Ichabod Wiswall entered Harvard College in 1654, but did
not graduate. He took the Oath of Fidelity in 1674, and was ordained at Duxbury
in 1676. He married on December 24,
1677, Priscilla Peabody, January 15, 1653–
May 3, 1724.

The Reverend Ichabod Wiswall was
the son of Thomas Wiswall, who with
his wife Elizabeth, settled at Dorchester
in 1635. Thomas was a freeman in 1653;
died December 6, 1683. Priscilla Peabody
was the daughter of William Peabody of
Duxbury who married on December 26,
1644, Elizabeth Alden, eldest daughter of
John and Priscilla (Mullins) Alden. William Peabody died December 13, 1707,
age eighty-eight; Elizabeth died May 31,
1717, age ninety-three.

John Alden, ca. 1600–September 12,
1687, age eighty-four or eighty-eight, was
the last male survivor of the *Mayflower*.
He married, in 1623, Priscilla Mullins,
born ca. 1600 — living in 1650, when it
was recorded that they had eleven children. Priscilla was the daughter of
William Mullins (or Molines) who came
to Plymouth on the *Mayflower* and died
February 21, 1621. His wife, Alice, died a
few days before or after her husband.
John Alden was hired at Southampton as
a cooper on the *Mayflower* and had the
right to stay or return to England. He
was a representative in 1641 and had been
chosen an assistant to Governor Winslow
in 1633, in which position he served for
forty-two years.

The Reverend John Robinson was
the son of Samuel Robinson of Dorchester, baptized June 14, 1640; he was
constable 1667, selectman 1688, freeman
1690, and representative 1701–1702.

He died September 16, 1718. He married the eldest daughter of Richard Baker
of Dorchster in 1639. Baker was a freeman May 18, 1642; was in the artillery
company in 1658. His will was dated October 7, 1689, and he died October 25,
1689. His wife was Faith Withington,
daughter of Henry Withington; she died
July 15, 1673. Henry Withington came to
Dorchester about 1636 and was one of the
six who founded a church for Richard
Mather on August 23, 1636. He brought
his wife Elizabeth and five children. His
wife Elizabeth died February 16, 1661, and
he married in 1662 Margaret, widow of
Richard Paul. He died February 2, 1667,
age seventy-nine. His will was dated January 8, 1665.

Samuel Robinson was the son of
William Robinson of Dorchester in 1636.
William Robinson was in the artillery
company in 1643; freeman May 18, 1642;
and died July 6, 1668. His widow, Ursula,
not the mother of Samuel Robinson, had
been widow of Stephen Streeter and of
Samuel Hosier.

Joseph Trumbull, born 1679, was the
son of Joseph Trumbull born ca. 1655,
who was of Suffield, Connecticut, in 1677
and was a freeman at Rowley in 1681.
Joseph Trumbull, born ca. 1655, was the
son of John Trumble/Trumbull, who was
of New Castle-Upon-Tyne, England. He
was at Roxbury in 1639. He married first,
in England, July 7, 1635, Elinor Chandler;
married second, June 1650, at Rowley,
Ann (Swan) Hopkinson, widow of
Michael Hopkinson who died in 1648.
Ann was the daughter of the first Richard
Swan in America.

Richard Swan joined the Boston
church January 6, 1630. His wife was
Ann; her surname is unknown. He was
dismissed to Rowley, November 24, 1639,
to form a church for Richard Mather. He

was a freeman May 13, 1640; representative in 1666; and died 1678.

II. The Reverend Solomon Williams, D.D., June 4, 1700–February 28, 1776, was born at Hatfield, Massachusetts. He was graduated from Harvard College in 1719, A.B., A.M.; and from Yale in 1773. He was ordained December 5, 1722, and died at Lebanon, Connecticut, age seventy-six. He married in 1726, Mary Porter, November 4, 1703, born at Hadley, Massachusetts, the daughter of Samuel Porter and Joanna Cooke. Joanna was the daughter of Aaron Cooke (the third), February 21, 1640–September 16, 1716, married May 30, 1661, to Sarah Westwood, 1644–1730, daughter of William and Bridget Westwood. Aaron and Sarah Cooke moved to Hadley, Massachusetts, where he was a captain for thirty-five years.

Aaron Cooke the third was the son of Aaron Cook the second, who was baptized March 20, 1613, and died September 5, 1690, at Northampton, Massachusetts. He was the son of Aaron Cook and Elizabeth Chard who were married September 2, 1610, at Thorncombe, Dorset, England. His father was buried at Bridgport, December 28, 1615, and his mother married on June 19, 1616, Thomas Ford, whose first wife, Joan Waye, had died leaving a daughter Mary. Aaron Cook second married his stepsister, Mary Ford, born 1612. About 1637, they moved to Windsor, Connecticut. He became a civil and military leader and helped settle the towns of Northampton, Westfield, and Hadley, Massachusetts. In 1688, Governor Andros promoted him from captain to major. Mary (Ford) Cook died in 1645, and Aaron Cook the second subsequently had three wives. Thomas Ford's ancestry has been traced (ten generations) to John de Forde who died

1315, son of Simon de Forde of Abbey Field and his wife Agnes.

Samuel Porter, 1660–1722, was the son of Samuel Porter, baptized at Felsted, County Essex, England, on June 1, 1635, and died at Hadley, Massachusetts, September 6, 1689. He married Hannah Stanley, daughter of Thomas and Benett Stanley; she died December 18, 1708. Samuel Porter was the son of John Porter, an early settler at Windsor in 1638 with a second wife Rose. He died April 21, 1648; Rose died twenty days after he did.

III. The Reverend William Williams was born at Cambridge Village, Massachusetts, on February 2, 1665, and was buried at Hatfield, Massachusetts, August 29, 1741. He graduated from Harvard in 1683. He married, second, April 23, 1699, Christian Stoddard, who was born at Northampton, Massachusetts, August 23, 1676, and died April 23, 1764. Christian was the daughter of the Reverend Solomon Stoddard, born at Boston October 4, 1643. He was graduated from Harvard in 1662 and died February 11, 1729. The Reverend Stoddard married on March 8, 1670, Esther (Warham) Mather, baptized at Windsor, Connecticut, December 8, 1644. She died February 10, 1736.

The Reverend Solomon Stoddard was the son of Anthony Stoddard, born Ireland in 1617. He married first Mary Downing who died June 16, 1647, and he died at Boston, Massachusetts March 16, 1686/7. Mary Downing was the daughter of Emanual Downing, who died between September 1653 and August 4, 1656; he married in England, April 10, 1622, Lucy Winthrop, baptized Groton, England, January 27, 1601, died after August 4, 1656. Lucy Winthrop was the daughter of Adam Winthrop and sister of the first governor of Massachusetts, John

Winthrop. Adam Winthrop was buried at Groton, England, March 28, 1623.

Esther Warham, baptized December 8, 1644, married first, Eleazer Mather, and married second, the Reverend Solomon Stoddard. She was the daughter of the Reverend John Warham and his second wife, married in 1637, Jane Dabinott who died at Norwalk on April 23, 1655; Jane was the widow of Thomas Newberry. Jane Dabinott was the daughter of Christopher Dabinott of Chardstock, Devon, England. The Reverend John Warham died April 1, 1670.

The Reverend John Warham was ordained May 23, 1619, at Silverton, Devon, by the bishop of Exeter; then was minister at Crewkerne, Somerset. Because he was a Puritan, he was forced to resign by Laud, then bishop of Bath and Wells. He then lived at St. Sidwell's until 1630, when he joined with the *Mary and John* passengers at Plymouth, England. He was first at Dorchester with the Reverend John Maverick. Religious dissension occurred among members of the company, and he led a large body of the group to Connecticut where they founded the city of Windsor.

IV. Isaac Williams, born at Roxbury, Massachusetts, September 1, 1638, died at Newton, Massachusetts, February 11, 1707. He married first, at Roxbury, in 1660, Martha Park, March 12, 1642–October 12,

1676, died about age thirty-four. Martha was the daughter of William Park baptized Semer, England, June 21, 1607, and died at Roxbury, Massachusetts, May 11, 1685. William Park married Martha Holgrove, born England ca. 1614, died at Roxbury, Massachusetts, August 25, 1708. She was the daughter of John Holgrove, freeman November 5, 1633; representative at the first assembly May 14, 1634–1635. After 1640, he resided at Gloucester and died at Salem, Massachusetts, after 1656. John Holgrove's first wife was Lydia, his second, Elizabeth, surnames unknown.

William Park was the son of Robert Park who died at New London, Connecticut in 1664/5. He married in England, 1601/2 Martha Chaplyn, daughter of William. She was baptized February 4, 1583/4.

V. Robert Williams, born at Great Yarmouth, England, about 1593, died at Roxbury, Massachusetts, September 1, 1693. He married first, in England, Elizabeth Stratton, who was born in England and died at Roxbury, July 28, 1674. He married second, November 3, 1675, Margaret Fearing, widow of John Fearing from Cambridge who came with Matthew Hawke of Hingham, England. Robert Williams came to Roxbury from Norwich, Norfolk County, England, in 1637. He was a freeman May 2, 1638.

Chapter 54

JAMES
WILSON

1742–1798

PENNSYLVANIA

James Wilson

JAMES WILSON, congressman, Supreme Court justice, speculator, attended the University of St. Andrews, 1757–1759, probably studied for some period of time between 1759 and 1763 at the University of Glasgow, and attended the University of Edinburgh, 1763–1765, but did not receive a degree.

In June 1765, he began the study of accounting, but abandoned it quickly and left for America. He arrived in New York amid the Stamp Act disturbances.

He was well educated and brought letters of introduction, one of them to the provincial secretary and trustee of the College of Pennsylvania, where in February 1766, he became a Latin tutor. He petitioned for an honorary M.A. degree which was granted on May 19, 1766.

Wilson soon realized that there were more promising opportunities for advancement in law than in tutoring, and he entered the law offices of John Dickinson to study. He was admitted to the bar in November 1767. He practiced law briefly at Reading and Cheerlessly, then returned to Philadelphia in 1770. His success was rapid and brilliant. In 1770, he became a member of the bar of the Supreme Court.

In 1769, he coauthored *The Visitant* with William White, later Bishop White of Christ Church for fifty years, and wrote a pamphlet "Considerations on the Authority of the British Parliament over the Colonies" in 1774. By 1773, he had begun borrowing capital to make speculative land purchases. His law practice was prospering, which occasionally took him into New York and New Jersey. Most of his practice involved land disputes. During six years of this early period, he lectured on English literature at the College of Philadelphia.

On July 12, 1774, he was made head of a committee of correspondence at Cheerlessly, and was elected to the first Provincial Conference at Philadelphia. He was nominated, but not elected to the legislature as a delegate to the First Continental Congress. He then began revising his manuscript, which was published and distributed to the members of Congress as *Considerations on the Nature and Extent of the Legislative Authority of the British Parliament.* Wilson had concluded that Parliament had no authority over the colonies in any instance. In 1774, he was still on the extreme Whig left; thereafter, he moved progressively to the right.

In January 1775, he was a member of the Convention of the Province and in May 1775, a member of the Continental Congress, where he served to the end of 1777. James Wilson was an active and prominent member of the Continental Congress as a speaker and a member of committees. In addition, he was colonel of militia and commissioner to treat with the Indians.

On May 3, 1776, he was elected colonel of the Fourth Battalion of Cumberland County Associators. He was never in active service, as on May 6, 1776, he was elected to the Second Continental Congress. He took a cautious stand on independence and, with Rutledge, Livingston, and Dickinson, on June 8, succeeded in getting a three-week delay on the vote for independence. Richard Henry Lee's resolution was debated the same day; when the debate ended, Pennsylvania and five other colonies voted in the negative, seven voted in the affirmative. On June 11, a committee of five was chosen with Thomas Jefferson as chairman, to prepare a declaration.

On July 2, 1776, James Wilson was one of the three out of seven Pennsylvania delegates who voted in favor of independence. He signed the Declaration of Independence on August 2, 1776.

During 1776-77, most of Wilson's time was required by the Board of War and with his quasi-judicial duties as chairman of the standing committee on appeals. He opposed the constitution of Pennsylvania of 1776, which brought about his removal in February 1777. He was reinstated on February 22 when no replacement could be found. He continued his opposition and was removed from Congress on September 14, 1777. He spent the winter of 1777-78 in Annapolis, Maryland, because political opinion had turned against him in Pennsylvania.

He once again took up residence at Philadelphia and resumed his law practice in 1778, becoming a corporation counselor. Where once he was an extreme Whig, he now became a leader of the Republican Society. His church affiliation also changed, from Presbyterian to Episcopalian. From 1779 to 1782, Wilson was advocate general for France in America. Being counsel to Loyalists, plus his interest in commercial enterprises and his continued interest in privateering, he became more unpopular with the public.

During 1779, food shortages and high prices brought about rioting in Philadelphia against profiteers, Loyalists, and their sympathizers. On October 4, 1779, a handbill appeared calling for the militia to "drive off from the city all disaffected persons and those who supported them." After securing some persons, they sought Wilson "who had always plead for such." He gathered some friends and barricaded his home, defending himself against the mob. There were a few casualties on both sides before Wilson was rescued by the First City Troop and President Reed. His home became known as "Fort Wilson." He went into hiding for a few days, but appeared on October 19 to post a bond of $10,000. On March 13, 1780, the legislature passed an act of oblivion for all concerned in the affair of Fort Wilson.

In July 1780, Wilson acted as legal adviser to Robert Morris when he formed the Bank of Pennsylvania, drawing up plans for the private agency for purchasing army supplies. In 1785, he published his *Considerations on the Power to Incorporate the Bank of North America.*

The conservatives were in power again in 1782, and James Wilson was once more elected to Congress, and he also served in 1785–1787. In 1784, he was one of the thirty-nine members of the Pennsylvania convention to adopt a constitution for the United States, held at Independence Hall with George Washington as president.

Wilson's most important contribution in public service was probably his work in framing the federal Constitution. He was "the best read lawyer," and chairman of the committee which submitted the first draft of the Constitution on August 6, 1787. In the state convention he urged its ratification as "the best form of government ever offered to the world." He stated there were "some parts of it, which if my wish had prevailed, would certainly have been altered," but he signed the Constitution and pressed for its adoption.

The Pennsylvania Constitution of 1790 was part of a reactionary movement following the Revolution, and Wilson was credited with being its author. He modeled it after the federal Constitution.

Also in 1790, he received an honorary

degree of LL.D. from City College and became its first professor of law. He continued in the position for a time after the combining of City College with the University of Pennsylvania.

Having abandoned his own private enterprises for the three years he devoted to framing the two constitutions, Wilson probably expected appointment to a high office in the new federal government. He recommended himself to Washington for chief justice, but Washington appointed him associate justice on September 29, 1789.

Wilson again began vast land speculations. In 1792 and 1793, he became involved with the Holland Land Company in unwise purchases of several hundred thousand acres in Pennsylvania and New York. In 1795, he bought a large interest in one of the ill-famed Yazoo Companies.

In the summer of 1797, he removed to Burlington, New Jersey, to avoid arrest for debt. Nevertheless, he was arrested for drunkenness and debt, and was released from prison in December 1797. Early in 1798, suffering from acute mental distress and fearing prosecution and pursuit, he exchanged circuits with his friend, Judge Iredell of Edenton, North Carolina.

Additional Information

In 1776, Dr. Benjamin Rush thought James Wilson

> An eminent lawyer, an enlightened statesman, a profound and accurate scholar. Mr. Wilson's personal appearance made his eloquence even more impressive. He stood six feet tall with a large frame and erect bearing, and his fiery energy went into his declamations. Though his voice was not melodious, it

was powerful, and his blue eyes gleamed through heavy spectacles rimmed in metal.

Wilson died at Edenton, North Carolina, of a "violent nervous fever" and was buried there. His remains were reinterred in Christ Church cemetery at Philadelphia on November 22, 1906. In 1948, Pennsylvania historical highway markers were installed at Cheerlessly, Pennsylvania, and at Christ Church in Philadelphia.

Genealogy

I. James Wilson, September 14/21, 1742–August 28, 1798, was born at Carskerdo, near St. Andrews, Scotland, Fife. He married first, on November 5, 1771, Rachel Bird and they had six children. He married second, in 1793, Hannah Gray of Boston, they had one son who died in infancy.

His children were: (by first wife) Mary, 1772; William, 1775; Bird, 1777; James Bird, 1779; Emily Bird, 1782; Charles Bird, 1785; (by second wife) Henry, 1796 died infant.

BIRD

Rachel Bird, 1750–April 19, 1786, was the daughter of William Bird. Among her siblings were Mark Bird who married Mary Ross, a sister of signer George Ross. Her sister, Mary Bird, married George Ross, Jr., third son of the signer. William Bird, 1707–November 26, 1761, born in England, was married on October 28, 1735, to Brigetta Huling (Hewling) by the Reverend Alexander Murray. They are buried at St. Gabriel's Church, Douglassville, Pennsylvania.

Brigetta Bird was descended from the Marquis Jean Paul Frederick de

Hulingues, a Huguenot nobleman of the Province of Bearn, attached to the court of Henry of Navarre. Hulingues was in Paris in 1572 during the massacre of St. Bartholomew and fled with his betrothed, Isabella du Portal, a lady in waiting to Catherine de Medici. They were married at Dieppi, then settled in Sweden. They had one son (given name not seen), who had sons Marcus and Lars.

Marcus Huling, 1687–1757, married Margaret Jones, daughter of Mouns (Mons, Moses) Jones, the emigrant, who died in 1727, and his wife Ingeborge. Mouns Jones was in Douglas Township, Berks County, before 1704 and with other Swedes received land grants. He built a stone house at Morlatton. Its date stone is 1716, and bears the initials of Mouns and Ingeborge Jones.

GRAY

Hannah Gray, born 1774, was the second wife of signer James Wilson. She was the daughter of the Reverend Ellis Gray, 1716–January 17, 1753, who died before his father. Ellis Gray graduated from Harvard College, 1734. He was a minister at Boston and half-brother of Harrison Gray, the Loyalist treasurer of the Province.

Edward Gray, an apprentice at Boston in 1686, came from Lancashire, England. In 1699, he married first, Susanna Harrison. He married second in 1714, Hannah Ellis, and died after January 1753.

LANDALE

II. William Wilson married Aleson Landale in Scotland. They came to America from Carskerdo, Scotland, in 1755.

Chapter 55

JOHN
WITHERSPOON

1722/3–1794

NEW JERSEY

THE REVEREND DOCTOR JOHN
WITHERSPOON, educator, clergyman, writer, patriot, began his preparatory education in 1728 at the Haddington
Grammar School. He entered the University of Edinburgh at the age of thirteen and remained for seven years. He
received his master of arts degree in 1739
and the master of divinity degree in
1743. During his years at Edinburgh he
was a member of literary clubs for students and businessmen, and became
proficient in debate and public speaking.

Witherspoon was licensed to preach
by the Haddington Presbytery, September 6, 1743; he was ordained at Beith, in
Ayrshire, on April 11, 1745. He was the
Presbyterian minister of the Parish of
Beith from 1745 to 1755. He observed the
battle of Falkirk, January 17, 1746, and
was arrested with other onlookers and
imprisoned in Donne Castle. He joined
in the religious controversies of the day
on the side of the extreme orthodoxy, at-
tacking the moderates under the leadership of Dr. William Robertson.

Witherspoon's satire *Ecclesiastical
Characteristics* in 1753 was followed by
Serious Apology, *Essay on Justification* in
1756; and *Inquiry into the Nature and
Effects of the Stage*, which was aimed at
John Home, author of *Douglas* who was
later driven from the ministry.

Witherspoon was installed as minister of the Low Church at Paisley, January 16, 1757. In 1758 he became moderator of the Synod of Glasgow and Ayr. In
1762, he was prosecuted and fined for
naming certain offenders in a sermon. In
1764, he published three volumes of essays and a work called *Regeneration*, and
received a degree of D.D. from the University of St. Andrews, in recognition of
his leadership and ability.

In November 1766, he was presented
a letter of invitation to become president
of the new College of New Jersey (now
Princeton University). He received similar offers from Dundee, Rotterdam, and
Dublin in 1768. He refused all of them.

Benjamin Rush, then studying medicine in Scotland, persuaded Witherspoon to reconsider. A second invitation
was presented and Witherspoon and his
family sailed for America in May 1768.
Witherspoon delivered his inaugural address as the fifth president of the College
of New Jersey on August 17, 1768.

Witherspoon said he had become an
American the moment he landed. He
found the college in great need of money
and he worked to raise funds to procure
books. During the years 1768–1776, he
introduced the Scottish system of lecture
and the study of history, oratory, French,
and philosophy. He insisted upon a mas-
tery of the English language. The faculty,
student body, and the endowment
steadily increased. But the college was
destroyed when the British invaded New
Jersey; the student body was dispersed,
and the college could not be used for ed-
ucational purposes.

At the start, Witherspoon thought
ministers should not be involved in politics, but in 1774 his interest in the controversies with Great Britain grew. He
was a county delegate, serving on committees of correspondence, and at
provincial conventions.

At the convention which met to
frame a New Jersey constitution, he displayed much legal knowledge and urged
the omission of religious tests. He played
an important part in the removal and
imprisonment of Royalist Governor
William Franklin.

On June 22, 1776, he was appointed
as a delegate to the Continental Congress,

and arrived in Philadelphia as the Congress had come to the point of adopting a resolution of independence and drafting the Declaration. On July 2, 1774, Witherspoon assured Congress that the country "had been for some time past loud in its demand for the proposed declaration," and "it was not only ripe for the measure but in danger of rotting for want of it." He signed the engrossed copy of the Declaration of Independence on August 2, 1776.

He served in Congress from June 1777 until November 1782, except in 1780, when he declined reelection and made an attempt to revive the college and gather its dispersed students. As a member of the Congress of the Confederation, he was appointed to more than one hundred committees and was a member of two standing committees of great importance, the Board of War and the Committee of Secret Correspondence. He was active in the debates on the Articles of Confederation; assisted in organizing the executive departments; shared in forming the new government's foreign alliances; and was a leader in drawing up instructions for the American peace commissioners.

In 1781, he wrote many papers for Congress, seeking to give them the power to regulate commerce. His "Essay on Money" and various papers in *The Druid* in 1781 were his last published works. Witherspoon's active career closed in 1782, and he tried to rebuild the college. In 1783-84, his attempt to collect funds from England for Princeton (as the College of New Jersey was beginning to be called) was opposed by John Jay and Benjamin Franklin as "not merely unpromising but undignified," and proved unsuccessful. He did not live to see Princeton fully recover from the Revolution.

In 1783, he returned to the New Jersey legislature, and again in 1789. In 1787 he was a member of the New Jersey Ratifying Convention of the United States Constitution. From 1785 to 1789, he was engaged in a plan to organize the Presbyterian Church along national lines, and was elected in 1788 as moderator of the first general assembly of the Presbyterian Church in America.

Genealogy

I. The Reverend Doctor John Witherspoon, February 5, 1722/3–November 15, 1794, was born at Yester, near Edinburgh, Scotland. He was the son of the Reverend James and Ann (Walker) Witherspoon. He married first, September 2, 1748, Elizabeth Montgomery, by whom he had ten children. He married second, Anne Marshall Dill, widow of Dr. Armstrong Dill, on May 30, 1791, by whom he had two daughters. His son James was killed at the Battle of Germantown. Only two daughters survived him. He came from Yester, East Lothian, Scotland, to New Jersey, in 1768, and settled at Princeton. Witherspoon was blind during the last two years of his life, caused by an injury from a fall off a horse.

Witherspoon died at his farm, Tusculum, and was buried in the Presidents' Lot at Princeton. His statue was erected at Fairmont Park, Philadelphia, in 1876.

His children were: (by first wife) Anne, 1749; Christian, 1750; James, 1751; Robert, 1753; Barbara, 1756; John, 1757; Frances, 1759; David, 1760; George, 1762; (by second wife) Frances, 1792 died; Marianne, 1794.

MONTGOMERY
Elizabeth Montgomery, born about 1721, died October 1, 1789. She was the first wife of Dr. John Witherspoon, and

was the daughter of Robert Montgomery of Craighouse, Scotland.

MARSHALL

Ann (Marshall) Dill, born about 1768, was the widow of Dr. Armstrong Dill. At the time of her marriage to Dr. John Witherspoon, she was only twenty-three and he was sixty-eight. One of their two daughters died in infancy.

WALKER

II. The Reverend James Witherspoon, born at Gifford(?), Scotland, married Ann Walker, and was residing at Yester at the birth of their son John. Early biographers claimed Ann Walker was a descendant of John Knox (ca. 1505–November 24, 1572). She was not a direct descendant, though possibly a relative.

Chapter 56

OLIVER
WOLCOTT

1726–1797

CONNECTICUT

Oliver Wolcott

OLIVER WOLCOTT, lawyer, judge, patriot, graduated from Yale in 1747, having led his class for four years. Before leaving college on January 21, 1747, he was commissioned by Governor George Clinton of New York to raise a company and serve as captain, in connection with the ill-fated Louisburg expedition to Canada during the French and Indian War.

Wolcott then studied medicine with his uncle, Dr. Alexander Wolcott, intending to practice at Goshen, Connecticut. His father owned property in Litchfield and when the county was organized in 1751, he moved there and took up law. He was Litchfield's first sheriff and held the office for twenty years. He was a deputy for Litchfield in 1764, 1767, 1768, and 1770; was elected assistant in 1771 and reelected concurrently until 1786. He was judge of the Probate Court for Litchfield, 1772–1781, and judge of the County Courts, 1774–1778.

He became a major in the militia in 1771; colonel in 1774. Wolcott was active in the military throughout the Revolutionary War. In April 1775, the assembly sent him to Boston to interview General Gage, and he was appointed commissary to supply stores and provisions for the troops. In July 1775, the Continental Congress appointed him as one of the commissioners of Indian affairs for the northern department. He met with representatives of the Six Nations at Albany in 1775 and assisted in the settlement of Wyoming Valley, Pennsylvania-Connecticut and the New York–Vermont boundary disputes.

Wolcott was elected as a delegate to the Continental Congress in October 1775 and served from three to six months of every winter/spring session until 1783, except in 1779. He participated in the 1776 activities preceding the Declaration of Independence, but became ill and left Philadelphia at the end of June. His substitute, William Williams, signed in his absence. He returned to the Continental Congress on October 1, 1776, and was allowed to sign the Declaration of Independence. In July, as he traveled from Philadelphia through New York, he transported the lead equestrian statue of King George III to Litchfield where it was melted into bullets at Wolcott's home by his wife and daughter.

In August 1776, he commanded as brigadier-general the fourteen militia regiments sent to New York to reinforce General Putnam on the Hudson River. In December he commanded the Sixth Militia Brigade in northwestern Connecticut, and in September 1777, he led several hundred volunteers from his brigade to join General Gates' army against Burgoyne. As a major-general in 1779, he defended the Connecticut seacoast against New York Governor William Tryon's raids on Fairfield and Norwalk. In May 1780, he became a member of the Council of Safety, which was the executive committee for prosecution of the war.

Wolcott resigned from Congress in 1783 after the Treaty of Paris was signed. He served as commissioner at the Treaty of Fort Stanwix in 1784 to make peace with the Six Nations, then resigned that post in 1785. In 1789, he helped conclude a treaty with the Wyandotte Indians, thus extinguishing their title to the western reserve.

He was said to be "a man who spoke his mind," and described by Thomas Rodney as "a man of integrity, is very candid in debate and open to conviction and does not want abilities, but does not appear to be possessed of much political knowledge."

At Samuel Huntington's death, Wolcott succeeded to the governorship. He was elected to the office in May 1796, and died on December 1, 1797, before completing his term. Oliver Wolcott received an M.A. degree from Yale College in 1765. He was president of the Connecticut Society of Arts and Sciences, and received an honorary LL.D. degree from Yale in 1792.

Genealogy

I. Oliver Wolcott was born November 20, 1726, at Windsor, Connecticut, the fourteenth of fifteen children of Roger and Sarah (Drake) Wolcott. He graduated from Yale College in 1747, and on January 21, 1755, married Laura Collins. They had five children.

Wolcott has been described as tall, erect, dark-complexioned, dignified, and a man of integrity and deep Puritan faith. He died December 1, 1797, and was buried in the Wolcott Plot in the Litchfield Old Cemetery.

His children were: Oliver, died before 1760; Oliver again, 1760; Frederick, 1767; Laura, 1761; Mary Ann, 1765.

COLLINS

Laura Collins, January 1, 1732/3–April 19, 1794, was the daughter of Captain Daniel Collins, June 13, 1701–February 4, 1768, of Guilford, Connecticut, and Lois (Cornwall) Collins, baptized in 1701 at Middletown, Connecticut. Daniel Collins and Lois Cornwall were married on March 25, 1725; at the time of the marriage, Lois Cornwall and her sister Jemima were "of Long Island." They were the daughters of William Cornwall, born at Middletown, Connecticut, January 22, 1672/3, died December 25, 1704, whose wife was Esther. William Cornwall was the son of Samuel Cornwall, born at Hartford, Connecticut, September 1642, died December 6, 1728. He married, on January 15, 1667, Rebecca Bull, born August 27, 1644, daughter of William and Blythe Bull of Cambridge, Massachusetts. William Bull's will was dated May 21, 1687, probated October 12, 1688. His widow died September 23, 1690, age seventy-two. Samuel Cornwall's will was dated July 3, 1722, and mentions his granddaughters Jemima and Lois, daughters of his deceased son William Cornwall. Samuel was the third son of Sergeant William Cornwall, the emigrant, who came with wife Joan in 1633, probably from Hertfordshire, England. They were members of the Roxbury Church and Joan died soon after their arrival.

William Cornwall was a soldier in the Pequot War in 1637. He removed to Hartford, Connecticut, in 1639, where his wife was Mary and was the mother of his children. He went to Middletown, Connecticut, with the earliest settlers in 1650; was representative in 1654 and again in 1664-65. He died "an old man" on February 21, 1678.

Captain Daniel Collins was the son of John Collins, 1665–January 24, 1751, who married, in 1696, Ann (Leete) Trowbridge, widow of John Trowbridge. She was born August 5, 1671, and died November 2, 1724, at Guilford, Connecticut.

Ann Leete was the daughter of John Leete, 1639–November 25, 1692, who was married at Guilford, on October 4, 1670, to Mary Chittenden, 1647–1668. Mary was the daughter of William Chittenden of Guilford who died February 1, 1661, and Joanna Sheafe, daughter of Dr. Jacob Sheafe of Cranbrook, in Kent, England.

William Chittenden came from East Guilford, County Sussex, adjoining Rye on the British Channel, arriving at Boston in 1638. He soon moved to New Haven and was founder of the church at Guilford on June 1, 1639, and was also trustee of land purchase from the Indians. He had been a soldier in the Netherlands, attaining the rank of major. His widow married second, May 1, 1665, Abraham Cruttenden and died August 16, 1668.

John Leete, 1639–1692, was the son of Governor William Leete, ca. 1611–April 16, 1683, and his first wife Anna Payne, 1621–buried September 1, 1688. Anna was the daughter of the Reverend John Payne of Southhoe, England; she and William were married in England August 1, 1638. William and Anna Leete came to America from Hail Weston, Huntingdon, on the *St. John* in 1639, and lived at Guilford and Hartford.

Leete married second, in 1671, Sarah, widow of Henry Rutherford who died February 10, 1674. He married third, Mary (maiden name unknown), widow of the Reverend Nicholas Street and formerly widow of Governor Francis Newman. Mary (Newman) (Street) Leete was the great-great grandmother of Lyman Hall, another signer of the Declaration of Independence.

Governor Leete had signed the Plantation Covenant of June 1, 1639; was assistant of the New Haven Colony, 1643–1657; deputy governor, 1658; governor, 1661–1665. After the New Haven Colony united with Connecticut, he became an assistant in 1669; and deputy governor until 1676 when Governor Winthrop died. He was elected governor of Connecticut 1676–1683, by annual election, until his own death on April 16, 1683.

John Collins, 1639–1692, was the eldest son of John Collins, Boston, a shoemaker. In 1640, John Collins, Sr., had a grant for a lot at Braintree (now Quincy). In 1644, he was in an artillery company. He died March 29, 1670.

PITKIN

II. Roger Wolcott, January 4, 1679–May 17, 1767, was the youngest son of Simon Wolcott and his second wife, Martha Pitkin. Wolcott married at Windsor, December 3, 1702, Sarah Drake, May 10, 1688–January 21, 1747. He commanded the Connecticut troops at the siege of Louisburg in 1745, and was second in command under Sir William Pepperell. He was colonial governor of the colony of Connecticut, 1751–1754. Sarah Drake was the daughter of Job Drake, baptized March 28, 1651–after 1688, who married September 13, 1677, Elizabeth Clark born October 28, 1651, widow of Moses Cook, who was killed in King Philip's war in 1676. Elizabeth was the daughter of Daniel Clark, ca. 1623–August 12, 1710, of Windsor.

Clark came in 1639 with the Reverend Ephriam Huet, married first on June 13, 1644, Mary Newberry, daughter of Thomas. Mary died August 20, 1688, and Clark married second, late in 1688, Martha (Pitkin) Wolcott, widow of Simon Wolcott, 1625–1686, and mother of Roger Wolcott, 1679–1767. Martha Pitkin was a sister of William Pitkin of Hartford in 1660, who was a son of Roger Pitkin of London in 1666.

Job Drake, baptized March 28, 1652, died after 1688, was the son of Job Drake, ca. 1623–September 16, 1689, who married, on June 25, 1646, Mary Wolcott, ca. 1622, born at Tolland, Somersetshire, England, sister of Simon Wolcott, and daughter of Henry and Elizabeth

Saunders Wolcott. Job Drake, 1623–1689, was the son of John and Elizabeth Drake who came on the *Mary and John* in 1630, bringing three sons and a daughter Mary.

John Drake, 1585–August 17, 1659, was from Wiscombe, Devon, England. He was first at Dorchester, then at Windsor, Connecticut, by 1639. He married second, Elizabeth Rogers, who died October 7, 1681, age 100. John Drake was the son of William Drake, died 1625, and Philippa Denys, who died 1647. William Drake's lands in Wiscombe, Devon, England, were called Wiscombe Park.

The Drake line traces from William Drake-8, (i.e., William Drake is eighth in line of descent from progenitor of Drake line, John Drake-1), Robert-7, John 6-5-4-3-2-1. John Drake-1 married Christian Billett, daughter of John Billett. He lived in Exmouth, in Devon, in 1360, and acquired lands called Ashe.

III. Simon Wolcott, 1625–September 11, 1686, was the son of Henry Wolcott the emigrant to America. He married first, on March 19, 1656, at Windsor, Joanna Cook, baptized August 5, 1638–April 1657, daughter of Aaron and Mary Ford (both *Mary and John* passengers). He married second, at Hartford, October 17, 1661, Martha Pitkin, died October 13, 1719. She was the mother of Roger Wolcott; she married second, as his second wife, in 1688, Daniel Clark. Simon Wolcott was representative for Simsbury in 1671 and 1675.

SAUNDERS

IV. Henry Wolcott, ca. 1578–May 30, 1655, was baptized in the Parish of Lyiard, St. Lawrence, Somersetshire, England, on December 6, 1578. He lived in Somersetshire at or near Wellington near the border of Devonshire. He came on the *Mary and John* in 1630, bringing his family. He married in England, January 19, 1606/7, Elizabeth Saunders, born 1582, baptized December 20, 1584–July 5, 1655. Elizabeth Saunders was the daughter of Thomas Saunders of Lyiard, St. Lawrence, Somerset, England, who had died by 1650.

V. John Wolcott of Gladon, Tolland, Somerset; his will was dated November 10, 1623.

VI. John Wolcott, clothier, who died 1589.

VII. Thomas Wolcott, Jr. tacker, died 1572. He married Alice (maiden name unknown). His will was dated November 4, 1572.

VIII. Thomas Wolcott, Sr., tacker, 1487–June 5, 1554; was living at Tolland, Somerset, in 1552. His wife was Alice.

IX. William Wolcott, 1463–1502, was buried at Dalverton, Somerset. He married Elizabeth Whethill, who died in 1514, at Lydiard, St. Lawrence, Somerset. William Wolcott's will was dated 1500 A.D.

The Wolcott line continues; however, it may be fictitious before William Wolcott, 1463–1502.

X. William Wolcott, who settled in Tolland, Somerset.

XI. Roger Wolcott of Wolcott, Esquire, who married Margaret, daughter of David Lloyd, Esquire.

XII. John Wolcott of Wolcott, who married Matilda, daughter of Sir Richard Cornwall of Bereford, Knight.

XIII. John Wolcott.

XIV. Thomas Wolcott.

XV. Sir John Wolcott, Knight, 1382 A.D.

XVI. John Wolcott of Wolcott, who married Alice, daughter of David Lloyd, Esquire.

XVII. Sir Philip Wolcott of Wolcott, who married Julian, daughter of John Herle.

XVIII. Roger Wolcott of Wolcott, who married Edith, daughter of Sir William Donnes, Knight.

XIX. Jeran Wolcott of Wolcott, married Anna, daughter of John Mynde of Shropshire.

XX. Sir John Wolcott.

Chapter 57

GEORGE
WYTHE

1726–1806

VIRGINIA

George Wythe

GEORGE WYTHE, lawyer, educator, patriot, "learned little at school," but was carefully taught by his well-educated mother. He attended the College of William and Mary for a very short time, but left to study law in the office of Stephen Dewey in Prince George County, Virginia, through a family connection. He was admitted to the bar in 1757. Wythe became associated in law practice with John Lewis, a prominent lawyer in Spotsylvania County.

In 1754, while Peyton Randolph, attorney general of the Virginia Colony, was in England on a mission, Governor Dinwiddie appointed Wythe to the office until Randolph's return. At the death of his brother in 1755, he inherited Chesterville, the large Wythe estate. Having represented Williamsburg in the House of Burgesses in 1754-55, he established his residence there. He then studied law in earnest, mastered the classics and liberal sciences, and was admitted to the bar of the General Court.

In 1758, Wythe's life and his career were enriched by his friendships with Governor Francis Fauquier, an educated, cultured gentleman, a fellow of the Royal Society, and William Small, professor of math and natural philosophy, at the College of William and Mary. In 1760, he was a vestryman of the Bruton Parish Church. He represented the College of William and Mary in the House of Burgesses from 1758 to 1761 and Elizabeth City County from 1761 to 1768. In June 1762, he began instructing Thomas Jefferson in his study of the law. He was mayor of Williamsburg in 1768, and was a member of the Board of Visitors for William and Mary in 1769; also, clerk of the House of Burgesses, 1769–1775. He was George Washington's attorney in 1769.

In the meantime, relations with England had been deteriorating. Wythe recommended that Virginia set up a full-time army instead of a part-time volunteer militia, and when the conflict began he volunteered his services. He was, however, sent to the Continental Congress where he served until the end of 1776, having signed the Declaration of Independence on August 27, 1776.

Wythe was a member of a committee to create a seal for the State of Virginia, which was adopted in 1776. It is thought that Wythe designed it. In November 1776, Thomas Jefferson, Edward Pendleton, and George Wythe served as a committee assigned to revise the laws of Virginia. Wythe's portion of the resulting report covered the years from the Revolution to American Independence. One hundred twenty-six bills were submitted to the General Assembly in 1779 as a result of the committee's work. A few had already been adopted, but most of the bills were adopted in 1785 under the leadership of James Madison.

In 1777, Wythe was Speaker of the House of Delegates. In 1778, he became one of the three judges of the new Virginia High Court of Chancery and thereafter was known as Chancellor Wythe. The Board of Visitors of the College of William and Mary, led by his friend and former student, Thomas Jefferson, governor of Virginia and also a member of the Board of Visitors, on December 4, 1779, established the Professorship of Law and Police. This was the first chair of law in an American college, established just twenty-one years after the Vinerian Professorship of English law at Oxford.

George Wythe became its incumbent and was regarded as the pride of the college. He was credited with charting the way in American jurisprudence. In 1787, he was a law professor at William and Mary and also taught Latin and Greek.

Wythe assisted in organizing the Constitutional Convention but the press of other duties called him away. In 1788, he represented Williamsburg at the Virginia Convention which ratified the U.S. Constitution. He presided over the committee and offered the resolution for ratification.

When the Virginia judicial system was reorganized in 1788, Wythe became sole chancellor and held the position until 1801. Three chancery districts were then created, and he continued to preside over the Richmond district until his death.

He had suffered great losses during the Revolutionary War, and his appointment as chancellor in 1789 brought income that was quite welcome. In 1790, William and Mary awarded him an honorary degree. That same year he resigned his professorship at William and Mary, moved to Richmond, and established his own small law school. Among his students was Henry Clay, who was clerk of the court. In 1791, he wrote the citation for William and Mary's honorary degree which was bestowed upon Thomas Jefferson.

In May 1793, Wythe, in the Virginia High Court of Chancery, ruled that payments into the Virginia loan office did not discharge debts due British creditors. In 1795, he published *Decisions of Cases in Virginia by the High Court of Chancery, with Remarks Upon Decrees by the Court of Appeals Reversing Some of Those Decisions.*

Benjamin Rush thought George Wythe "a profound lawyer and able politician," and wrote, "I have seldom known a man who possessed more modesty or a more dove-like simplicity and gentleness of manner."

Wythe County, Virginia, was created from a part of Montgomery County on December 1, 1789, named in George Wythe's honor.

Additional Information

George Wythe was of medium height, well proportioned, unostentatious in appearance and habits, polite and courteous in address.

Wythe died at the age of eighty, of arsenic poisoning, murdered by his grandnephew, George Wythe Sweeney, son of his sister Margaret. He had manumitted and provided for his slaves in his will dated April 20, 1803. Sweeney read the will, discovered a legacy to Benjamin Broadnax, whom Wythe was giving a thorough education. Benjamin was the son of Lydia, the black cook. Sweeney was the principal heir but if Benjamin died his legacy would also go to Sweeney. Sweeney was tried for murder, but the only witness to his actions was Lydia Broadnax. Her testimony was not admissible in the courts of Virginia at that time, and Sweeney was acquitted.

Wythe lived three days, during which time he disinherited the nephew. His death occurred on June 8, 1806, and he was buried in the St. John's Churchyard cemetery, at Richmond, Virginia. A simple monument was placed at his grave by the citizens of Virginia in 1922.

Genealogy

I. George Wythe, 1726–June 8, 1806, was born near Hampton, Elizabeth City County, Virginia. His father died when he was three. His elder brother, under the primogeniture law, inherited his father's estate. His mother was left in moderate circumstances, but she cared for him and taught him Latin, Greek, grammar, rhetoric, and logic. However, his mother also died while he was quite young, and his brother became his guardian.

Wythe, having been admitted to the bar in 1746, became an associate in the law practice of Attorney John Lewis of Spotsylvania County. In 1747, he married Lewis's sister Ann. She died eight months later. Wythe remained in Spotsylvania County until about 1754 when he became a member of the House of Burgesses and moved to Williamsburg. His brother died in 1755.

About 1755 he married Elizabeth Taliaferro. They had one son who died in infancy.

His children were: (by first wife) none; (by second wife) an unnamed son who died as an infant.

LEWIS

Ann Lewis, who died in 1748, was the daughter of Zachary Lewis of Spotsylvania County, Virginia. The date of her birth or the name of her mother, is unknown.

TALIAFERRO

Elizabeth Taliaferro, who died in 1787, was the daughter of Richard and Elizabeth (Eggleston) Taliaferro, of Powhattan, James City County, Virginia. Richard Taliaferro's will was dated 1775, proved 1779. Wythe "supposed" the emigrant ancestor to be Lawrence Taliaferro, and perhaps of Italian origin. *Genealogies of Virginia Families* states Elizabeth's emigrant ancestor was Robert, gentleman, who came from England and married

Sarah Grymes, daughter of Charles Grymes of Brandon, Virginia.

WALKER

II. Thomas Wythe, born before 1695 and died 1729, married in 1719 Margaret Walker, daughter of George Walker, a Quaker "of learning and of good fortune." She was also the granddaughter of George Keith, who was a "well-known scholar and divine." Thomas Wythe was a member of the House of Burgesses.

SHEPHARD

III. Thomas Wythe, Jr., gentleman, died before July 1795. He married Ann (Shephard), daughter of John Shephard. Her brother, Baldwin Shephard, was a justice of the peace of Elizabeth City. Ann Wythe married second, on July 11, 1695, the Reverend James Wallace, who was forced to leave Scotland during the rebellion of 1645. He was born at Errol, Scotland, came to America and settled on Back River, in Elizabeth City County.

The Reverend James and Ann (Sheppard) (Wythe) Wallace had children among which were three daughters who married into the Ball, Dandridge, and Wythe families. Although not descended from the Reverend Wallace, George Wythe was related by marriage to both President George Washington and his wife Martha (Dandridge) (Custis) who were descendants of James Wallace.

IV. Thomas Wythe, Sr., gentleman, emigrated to America from England, before June 19, 1676, when he was seated in Elizabeth City, Virginia, at the head of Little Poquoson Creek. He was a landowner and leading magistrate of Elizabeth City. He died early in 1693/4 and his will was probated March 19, 1693/4. His widow Anne, married second, on September 7, 1695, Thomas Harwood.

APPENDIX I
INTERRELATIONSHIPS AMONG SIGNERS AND THEIR FAMILIES

There were numerous interrelationships among the families of the signers. Such relationships are contained in the individual genealogy sections of the chapters. A few highlights and special facts are given here:

John and Samuel Adams were second cousins.

John Adams and his wife Abigail Adams were cousins (Boyleston line).

Josiah Bartlett married his first cousin, Mary Bartlett.

Carter Braxton's mother, Mary Carter, Benjamin Harrison's mother, Anne Carter, and Thomas Nelson's grandmother, Elizabeth Carter, were sisters.

Carter Braxton's wife, Elizabeth Corbin, was a cousin of Elizabeth Bassett Harrison, wife of Benjamin Harrison.

Elizabeth Corbin Braxton was also a cousin of Francis Lightfoot and Richard Henry Lee.

Charles Carroll of Carrollton and his wife Mary Darnall were cousins.

Abraham Clark and his wife Sarah Hatfield were cousins.

William Ellery and his second wife, Abigail Carey were second cousins.

Elbridge Gerry's wife, Ann Thompson, was a niece of Lewis Morris's wife, Mary Walton.

Lyman Hall's great-great grandfather the Reverend Nicholas Street married third, Mary (maiden name unknown) (widow of Governor Francis Newman); Mary Newman Street married third, as his third wife, John Leete (step-) great-great grandfather of Laura Collins, wife of Oliver Wolcott.

Stephen Hopkins and his second wife, Ann (Smith) Smith were cousins.

Francis Hopkinson and Thomas McKean married sisters, Mary and Anne Borden.

John Hancock's wife, Dorothy Quincy and Abigail Quincy Adams were cousins.

Benjamin Harrison and his wife, Elizabeth Bassett, were cousins.

Thomas Jefferson and Lucy (Grymes) Nelson, wife of Thomas Nelson were cousins.

Benjamin Harrison's brother married Thomas Jefferson's aunt Susanna Randolph, sister of Jane Jefferson.

Benjamin Harrison's sister Elizabeth married Peyton Randolph, brother of Jane Randolph Jefferson, mother of Thomas Jefferson.

Francis Lightfoot Lee and his wife, Rebecca Tayloe, were cousins. Therefore

Rebecca Tayloe was also a cousin of Richard Henry Lee.

Thomas Nelson's wife Lucy Grymes was the daughter of Philip Grymes and his wife Mary Randolph, sister of Peyton Randolph; Lucy was also a niece of Isham Randolph who was the father of Jane (Randolph) Jefferson, mother of Thomas Jefferson.

Robert Treat Paine and Roger Sherman were cousins.

George Read married Gertrude (Ross) Till, sister of signer George Ross.

Benjamin Rush married Julia Stockton, daughter of signer Richard Stockton.

Edward Rutledge married first, Henrietta Middleton, sister of Edward Middleton;

he married second, widow Mary Shubrick Eveleigh.

Mary (Shubrick) (Eveleigh) Rutledge's sister Elizabeth married signer Thomas Lynch, Jr. Another sister, Hannah Shubrick, married William Heyward, brother of signer Thomas Heyward, Jr.

William Whipple and his wife, Catharine Moffat, were first cousins.

William Williams' wife Mary (Trumbull) Williams was related to John Adams, Oliver Wolcott; also, to William Ellery's first wife, Ann Remington.

James Wilson married Rachel Bird of Birdsboro, Pennsylvania; her brother married signer George Read's sister.

APPENDIX II
THE DECLARATION OF INDEPENDENCE

In Congress, July 4, 1776,
THE UNANIMOUS DECLARATION OF THE
THIRTEEN UNITED STATES OF AMERICA

When in the Course of human events, it becomes necessary for one people to dissolve the political bands which have connected them with another, and to assume among the powers of the earth, the separate and equal station to which the Laws of Nature and of Nature's God entitle them, a decent respect to the opinions of mankind requires that they should declare the causes which impel them to the separation.

We hold these truths to be self-evident, that all men are created equal, that they are endowed by their Creator with certain unalienable Rights, that among these are Life, Liberty and the pursuit of Happiness.

That to secure these rights, Governments are instituted among Men, deriving their just powers from the consent of the governed.

That whenever any Form of Government becomes destructive of these ends, it is the Right of the People to alter or to abolish it, and to institute new Government, laying its foundation on such principles and organizing its powers in such form, as to them shall seem most likely to effect their Safety and Happiness. Prudence, indeed, will dictate that Governments long established should not be changed for light and transient causes; and accordingly all experience hath shewn that mankind are more disposed to suffer, while evils are sufferable, than to right themselves by abolishing the forms to which they are accustomed. But when a long train of abuses and usurpations, pursuing invariably the same Object evinces a design to reduce them under absolute Despotism, it is their right, it is their duty, to throw off such Government, and to provide new Guards for their future security.

Such has been the patient sufferance of these Colonies; and such is now the necessity which constrains them to alter their former Systems of Government. The history of the present King of Great Britain is a history of repeated injuries and usurpations, all having in direct object the establishment of an absolute Tyranny over these States. To prove this, let Facts be submitted to a candid world.

He has refused his Assent to Laws, the most wholesome and necessary for the public good.

He has forbidden his Governors to pass Laws of immediate and pressing importance, unless suspended in their operation till his Assent should be obtained; and when so suspended, he has utterly neglected to attend to them.

He has refused to pass other Laws for the accommodation of large districts of people, unless those people would relinquish the right of Representation in the Legislature, a right inestimable to them and formidable to tyrants only.

He has called together legislative bodies at places unusual, uncomfortable, and distant from the depository of their public Records, for the sole purpose of fatiguing them into compliance with his measures.

He has dissolved Representative Houses repeatedly, for opposing with manly firmness his invasions on the rights of the people.

He has refused for a long time, after such dissolutions, to cause others to be elected; whereby the Legislative powers, incapable of Annihilation, have returned to the People at large for their exercise; the State remaining in the mean time exposed to all the dangers of invasion from without, and convulsions within.

He has endeavoured to prevent the population of these States; for that purpose obstructing the Laws of Naturalization of Foreigners; refusing to pass others to encourage their migrations hither, and raising the conditions of new Appropriations of Lands.

He has obstructed the Administration of Justice, by refusing his Assent to Laws for establishing Judiciary powers.

He has made Judges dependent on his Will alone, for the tenure of their offices, and the amount and payment of their salaries.

He has erected a multitude of New Offices, and sent hither swarms of Officers to harass our People, and eat out their substance.

He has kept among us, in times of peace, Standing Armies without the Consent of our legislatures.

He has affected to render the Military independent of and superior to the Civil power.

He has combined with others to subject us to a jurisdiction foreign to our constitution, and unacknowledged by our laws; giving his Assent to their Acts of pretended Legislation:

For quartering large bodies of armed troops among us:

For protecting them, by a mock Trial, from punishment of any Murders which they should commit on the Inhabitants of these States:

For cutting off our Trade with all parts of the world:

For imposing Taxes on us without our Consent:

For depriving us in many cases, of the benefits of Trial by Jury:

For transporting us beyond Seas to be tried for pretended offences:

For abolishing the free System of English Laws in a neighbouring Province, establishing therein an Arbitrary government, and enlarging its Boundaries so as to render it at once an example and fit instrument for introducing the same absolute rule into these Colonies:

For taking away our Charters, abolishing our most valuable Laws and altering fundamentally the Forms of our Governments:

For suspending our own Legislatures, and declaring themselves invested with power to legislate for us in all cases whatsoever.

He has abdicated Government here, by declaring us out of his Protection and waging War against us.

He has plundered our seas, ravaged our Coasts, burnt our towns, and destroyed the Lives of our people.

He is at this time transporting large Armies of foreign Mercenaries to compleat the works of death, desolation and tyranny, already begun with circumstances of Cruelty & perfidy scarcely paralleled in the most barbarous ages, and totally unworthy the Head of a civilized nation.

He has constrained our fellow Citizens taken Captive on the high Seas to bear Arms against their Country, to become the executioners of their friends and Brethren, or to fall themselves by their Hands.

He has excited domestic insurrections amongst us, and has endeavoured to bring on the inhabitants of our frontiers, the merciless Indian Savages, whose known rule of warfare, is an undistinguished destruction of all ages, sexes and conditions.

In every stage of these Oppressions We have Petitioned for Redress in the most humble terms: Our repeated Petitions have been answered only by repeated injury. A Prince, whose character is thus marked by every act which may define a Tyrant, is unfit to be the ruler of a free people. Nor have We been wanting in attentions to our British brethren. We have warned them from time to time of attempts by their legislature to extend an unwarrantable jurisdiction over us. We have reminded them of the circumstances of our emigration and settlement here. We have appealed to their native justice and magnanimity, and we have conjured them by the ties of our common kindred to disavow these usurpations, which would inevitably interrupt our connections and correspondence. They too have been deaf to the voice of justice and of consanguinity. We must, therefore, acquiesce in the necessity, which denounces our Separation, and hold them, as we hold the rest of mankind, Enemies in War, in Peace Friends.

We, therefore, the Representatives of the united States of America, in General Congress, Assembled, appealing to the Supreme Judge of the world for the rectitude of our intentions, do, in the Name, and by Authority of the good People of these Colonies, solemnly publish and declare, That these United Colonies are, and of Right ought to be, Free and Independent States; that they are Absolved from all Allegiance to the British Crown, and that all political connection between them and the State of Great Britain, is and ought to be totally dissolved; and that as Free and Independent States, they have full Power to levy War, conclude Peace, contract Alliances, establish Commerce, and to do all other Acts and Things which Independent States may of right do.

And for the support of this Declaration, with a firm reliance on the protection of divine Providence, we mutually pledge to each other our Lives, our Fortunes and our sacred Honor.

SELECTED BIBLIOGRAPHY

Books

Adams, Nathaniel. *Annals of Portsmouth, New Hampshire.* Bowie, Md.: Heritage Books, 1989 reprint.

Austin, Jeannette Holland. *Georgia Intestate Records.* Baltimore, Md.: Genealogical Publishing Company, 1986.

_____. *Virginia Bible Records.* Riverdale, Ga.: Austin, 1987.

Austin, John Osborn. *The Genealogical Dictionary of Rhode Island.* Albany, N. Y.: Printed by Joel Munsell's Sons, 1887.

Bakeless, John, and Katherine Bakeless. *Signers of the Declaration.* Boston, Mass.: Houghton-Mifflin, 1969.

Baldwin, Agnes Leland. *First Settlers of South Carolina, 1670–1700.* Easley, S. C.: Southern Historical Press, 1985.

Banks, Charles Edward. *Bank's Topographical Dictionary of 2885 English Emigrants to New England, 1620–1650.* Philadelphia, Pa.: Southern Book Company, 1937.

_____. *English Ancestry and Homes of the Pilgrim Fathers.* New York, 1929. Baltimore, Md.: Genealogical Publishing Company, 1989 reprint.

_____. *Immigrants to America Before 1650.* Philadelphia, Pa.: Southern Book Company, 1930.

_____. *The Winthrop Fleet of 1630.* Baltimore, Md.: Genealogical Publishing Company, 1983 reprint.

Barnes, Robert and Catherine, indexers. *Genealogies of Virginia Families* (5 Volumes). Extracted from the *William and Mary College Quarterly.* Baltimore, Md.: Genealogical Publishing Company, 1982.

Beard, Alice L. *Concord Monthly Meeting (Quaker).* Chester County, Pa.: 19th Day, 4th Month, 1769.

Bender, Bruce A. *Colonial Delaware Assemblymen 1682–1776* (1989).

Boatner, Mark Mayo. *Encyclopedia of the American Revolution.* New York: David McKay, 1966. 3rd edition.

Bolton, Charles Knowles. *The Scotch-Irish Pioneers in Ulster and America.* (Boston, 1911). Baltimore, Md.: Genealogical Publishing Company, 1981.

Bowie, Effie Gwynn. *Across the Years in Prince George's County, Va.* Richmond, Va.: Garrett and Massing, 1947.

Brandow, James C. Indexed by Robert and Catherine Barnes. *Genealogies of Barbadoes Families*. Baltimore, Md.: Genealogical Publishing Company, 1983.

Burke, Arthur Meredyth. *The Prominent Families of the United States of America* (London 1908). Baltimore, Md.: Genealogical Publishing Company, 1991 reprint.

Burke, Sir John Bernard (1814–1892). *American Families with British Ancestry*. Originally published 1939, Burke's Peerage, London. Baltimore, Md.: Genealogical Publishing Company, 1983 reprint.

Church of Jesus Christ of Latterday Saints (Filmed by). *Connecticut Original Probate Records Film*.

Clapham, Blanche Adams. *Wills and Administrations of Elizabeth City, Virginia, 1688–1800* (1941). Baltimore, Md.: Genealogical Publishing Company, 1980 reprint.

Clemens, William Montgomery. *American Marriages Before 1699*. Baltimore, Md.: Genealogical Publishing Company, 1967 reprint.

Coldham, Peter W. *The Bristol Register of Servants Sent to Foreign Plantations, 1654–1686*. Baltimore, Md.: Genealogical Publishing Company, 1988.

Colket, Meredith B., Jr., *Founders of Early American Families: Emigrants from Europe 1607–1657*. Published: Cleveland: General Court of Order of Founders and Patriots of America, 1912. Distributed by Founders Project in 1975.

Cote, Richard N., and Patricia H. Williams. *Dictionary of South Carolina Biography*. Easley, S. C.: Southern Historical Press, 1985.

Currer, Noel-Briggs. *Virginia Settlers and English Adventurers*. Baltimore, Md.: Genealogical Publishing Company, 1969.

Daughters of the American Revolution Patriot Index. Washington, D.C.: Centennial Edition, 1990.

Davis, Bailey Fulton. *The Wills of Amherst County, Virginia, 1761–1865*. Easley, S. C.: Southern Historical Press, 1985.

Delaware Reconstructed Census 1790; including estate settlements.

des Cognets, Louis, Jr. *English Duplicates of Lost Virginia Records* (1958). Baltimore, Md.: Genealogical Publishing Company, 1981 reprint.

Dubin. *Five Hundred First Families in the United States*. Fourth edition, 1972–3.

Early Delaware Census Records 1665–1697.

Faber, Doris. *The Mothers of American Presidents*. New York, N. Y.: New American Library, 1968.

_____, and Harold Faber. *Great Lives, American Government*. New York, N. Y.: Charles Scribner's Sons–Macmillan Publishing, 1988.

Farmer, John. *Genealogical Register of the First Settlers of New England* (1829). Lancaster, Mass. Baltimore, Md.: Genealogical Publishing Company, 1989 reprint.

Fay, Bernard. *Franklin, the Apostle of Modern Times*. New York: Little Brown, 1929.

Ferris, Benjamin (1780–1867). *Original Settlements on the Delaware*. Wilmington, Del.: Wilson and Heald, 1846.

Ferris, Mary Walton. *Dawes-Gates Ancestral lines, a Memorial Volume*, and *Allied Families*. Private printing, Milwaukee, Wis.: Cunro Press, 1931–43. Volume 1, 1943.

Freeman, Frederick. *History of Cape Cod, the Annals of the Thirteen Towns of Barnstable County*. Boston: George C. Rand & Avery & Cornhill, 1862.

Galsberg, Henry et al., eds. *The American Guide*. Printed in the U.S.A. by H. Wolf, New York City: Hastings House, 1949.

Greer, George Cabell. *Early Virginia Immigrants 1623–1666*. Richmond, Va.: 1912. Baltimore, Md.: Genealogical Publishing Company, 1989 reprint.

Groves, Joseph Asbury. *The Alstons and Allstons of North Carolina and South Carolina*. Atlanta, Ga.: The Franklin Printing and Publishing Company, 1830.

Gwathmey, John H. *Historical Register of Virginia Men in the Revolution*. Baltimore, Md.: Baltimore Publishing Company, 1938.

Gwynn, Zoe Hargett. *Abstracts of the Wills and Estate Records of Granville County, North Carolina, 1746–1808*. Rocky Mount, N. C.: Joseph W. Watson, 1973.

Hardy, Stella Pickett. *Colonial Families of the Southern States of America*. Baltimore, Md.: Genealogical Publishing Company, 1981 reprint.

Hatfield, Abraham. *The Descendants of Matthias Hatfield*. New York Genealogical and Biographical Society, 1954.

Hendricks, J. Edwin. *Charles Thomson and the Making of a New Nation*. Cranberry, N. J.: University Press, 1979.

Hess, Stephen. *American Political Dynasties from Adams to Kennedy*. Garden City, N. J.: Doubleday Company. First edition, 1966.

Hoff, Henry B. *English Origins of American Colonists*. Baltimore, Md.: Genealogical Publishing Company, 1991.

_____. *Long Island Source Records* (Excerpted from New York Genealogical and Biographical Record). Baltimore, Maryland: Genealogical Publishing Company, 1987.

Holcomb, Brent. *Probate Records of South Carolina, Vol. 2*. Easley, S. C.: Southern Historical Press, 1977.

Holmes, Frank R. *Heads of New England Families 1620–1700*. New York: 1923. Baltimore, Md.: Genealogical Publishing Company, 1989 reprint.

Hotten, John Camden. *Hotten's Original Lists of Persons of Quality, 1600–1700*. (Originally published in London, 1874). Baltimore, Md.: Genealogical Publishing Company, 1974–1983 reprint.

Hutton, Mary Louise Marshall. *Seventeenth Century Colonial Families*. (Members of the National Society, Colonial Dames of the United States of America. XVII 1915–1975). 1976, 1983.

Huxford, Judge Folks. *Genealogical Material from Legal Notices in Early Georgia Newspapers*. Easley, S. C.: Southern Historical Press, 1989.

_____. *Marriages and Obituaries from Early Georgia Newspapers*. Easley, S. C.: Southern Historical Press, 1989.

Jacobus, Donald Lines. *History and Genealogy of the Families of Old Fairfield, Connecticut*. (For DAR, Fairfield, Connecticut, 1930–1932.) Baltimore, Md.: Genealogical Publishing Company, 1991 reprint.

Jester, Annie Lash. *Adventures of Purse and Person 1607–1624/5*. Third Edition. Princeton, N. J.: Deitz Press, 1956.

Johnston, H. P. *The Record of Connecticut Men During the American Revolution*. 1889.

Jordan, John W. *Colonial and Revolutionary Families of Pennsylvania* (1911). Baltimore, Md.: Genealogical Publishing Company, 1978 reprint.

Kenan, Alvaretta. *State Census of North Carolina 1784–1787* (*Granville County*). Norfolk, Va.: 1971. Genealogical Publishing Company, 1983 reprint.

Laird, Archibald. *Profitable Company*. Norwell, Mass.: The Christopher Publishing House, 1987.

Landis, John T. *Mayflower Descendants and Their Marriages for Two Generations After the Landing*. Baltimore, Md.: Genealogical Publishing Company, 1985.

Linn & Egle. *Pennsylvania Marriages before 1790*. (1890). Baltimore, Md.: Genealogical Publishing Company, reprint.

Lodge, Henry Cabot. *A Short History of the English Colonies in America*. Franklin Square, N. Y.: Harper and Brothers, 1881.

Lossing, Benson John. *Biographical Sketches of the Signers to the Declaration of American Independence*. New York: Derby & Jackson, 1848.

McGee, Thomas Darcy. *History of the Irish Settlers in North America from the Earliest Period to the Census of 1850*. Boston, Mass.: P. Donahoe, 1855.

Mackenzie, George Norbury. *Colonial Families of the United States* (7 Volumes), 1912. Baltimore, Md.: Genealogical Publishing Company, 1966 reprint.

Maddox, Joseph T. *Information on Some Georgia Pioneers*. Privately published by Maddox, 1982.

Malone, Dumas. *The Story of the Declaration of Independence*. New York, N. Y.: Oxford University Press, 1954.

Mather, Frederick Gregory (1824–1925). *The Refugees of 1776 from Long Island to Connecticut*. Albany, N. Y.: J. B. Lyon Company, 1913.

Montgomery-Massingberd, Hugh, ed. *Burke's Presidential Families of the United States of America*. London, England: Burke's Peerage Limited, 1975.

Moss, Bobby Gilman. *Roster of South Carolina Patriots in the American Revolution*. 1983.

National Society of the Colonial Dames of the United States of America. *Ancestral Records and Portraits*. New York: The Grafton Press, ca. 1910.

_____. *Lineages of Members of the National Society of the Sons and Daughters of the Pilgrims*. Baltimore, Md.: Genealogical Publishing Company, 1988 reprint.

New Jersey Biography and Genealogy.

New York Endorsed Land Papers 1643–1803.

Noyes, Sybil, Charles Thornton Libby, and Walter Goodwin Davis. *Genealogical Dictionary of Maine and New Hampshire*. Baltimore, Md.: Genealogical Publishing Company, 1972.

Nugent, Nell Marion *Cavaliers and Pioneers*. (Abstracted for Virginia State Library.) Richmond, Va.: 1977 and 1983.

Papenfuse, Edward C., Alan F. Day, and David W. Jordan. *A Biographical Dictionary of the Maryland Legislature 1635–1789*. Baltimore, Md.: Johns Hopkins University Press, 1985.

Pennsylvania Genealogy and History. *Genealogies of Pennsylvania Families*. 3 Volumes. 1982.

Pope, Charles Henry. *Pope's Pioneers of Massachusetts*. Boston, Mass., 1900. Baltimore, Md.: Genealogical Publishing Company, 1986 reprint.

Ratcliff, Clarence E. *North Carolina Tax Payers, 1679–1790*. Baltimore, Md.: Genealogical Publishing Company, 1987.

Riker, James. *Annals of Newtown in Queens County, Long Island, New York*. Lambertville, N. J.: Hunterdon House.

Roberts, Gary Boyd, in cooperation with the NEHGR. *Ancestors of American Presidents*. Boston, Mass., 1989.

_____, in cooperation with the NEHGR. *Connecticut Genealogies, 4 Volumes*. Baltimore, Md.: Genealogical Publishing Company, 1983.

_____. *Royal Descent of 500 Immigrants to the American Colonies of the United States*. Baltimore, Maryland: Genealogical Publishing Company, 1993.

Ross, George Edward. *Know Your Declaration of Independence and the Fifty-Six Signers*. Chicago, Ill.: Rand McNally, 1963.

Rupp, Israel Daniel. *Names of Immigrants in Pennsylvania 1727–1776* (1876). Baltimore, Md.: Genealogical Publishing Company, 1985 reprint.

Salter, Edwin, and George C. Beekman. *Old Times in Old Manmouth, New Jersey* (1887). Frehold, N. Y. Baltimore, Md.: Genealogical Publishing Company, 1980 reprint.

Saltonstall, William G. *Ports of Piscataqua, New Hampshire*. Bowie, Md.: Heritage Books, 1987.

Sanderson, John, and Robert Waln, Jr. *Biography of the Signers to the Declaration of Independence* (6 Volumes). 1824.

Savage, James. *Genealogical Dictionary of New England, 1860–1862* (4 Volumes). Baltimore, Md.: Genealogical Publishing Company, 1981 reprint.

Scharf, Turner. *Sussex County Probate and Land Records*. HSD Files.

Scott, Kenneth. *Genealogical Data from Colonial New York Newspapers*. Baltimore, Md.: Genealogical Publishing Company, 1982.

_____, and Janet R. Clarke. *Abstracts from the Pennsylvania Gazette, 1748–1755*. Baltimore, Md.: Genealogical Publishing Company, 1977.

Smith, Ellen Hart. *Charles Carroll of Carrollton: A Biography*. Cambridge, Mass.: Harvard University Press, 1942.

Smyth, A. H., ed. *The Writings of Benjamin Franklin* (10 Volumes). Princeton, N. J.: 1905.

Society of Colonial Wars in the State of Connecticut. *The Register of Pedigrees and Services of Ancestors*. Hartford, Conn.: Case, Lockwood, & Brainard, 1941.

Spear, Burton W. *Search for the Passengers of the Mary and John of 1630 and Their Children*. Toledo, Oh.: B. W. Spear, 1985.

Stewart, Frank H. & Gloucester County, New Jersey, Historical Society. *Notes on Old Gloucester County, New Jersey Volume I*. (1917). Baltimore, Md.: Genealogical Publishing Company, 1977.

Talcott, Alvan. *Families of Early Guilford, Connecticut*. Baltimore, Md.: Genealogical Publishing Company, 1984.

Tepper, Michael, ed. *Emigrants to Pennsylvania 1641–1819*. Baltimore, Md.: Genealogical Publishing Company, 1979.

Torrence, Clayton, ed. *Edward Pleasants Valentine Papers* (4 Volumes). Baltimore, Md.: Genealogical Publishing Company, 1979.

_____. *Old Somerset on the Eastern Shore of Maryland*. 1935. Baltimore, Md.: Regional Publishing Company, 1979 Reprint.

Torrey, Clarence Almon. *Marriages Prior to 1700*. Baltimore, Md.: Genealogical Publishing Company, 1985.

Virkis, Frederick Adams. *The Abridged Compendium of American Genealogy* (7 volumes). Baltimore, Md.: Genealogical Publishing Company, 1987 reprint.

Wagner, Frederick. *Robert Morris Audacious Patriot 1734–1806*. New York: Dodd-Mead, 1976.

Walker, Joseph B. *New Hampshire's Five Provincial Congresses*. Concord, N. H.: Rumford Printing Company, 1905.

Walker-Yardley (indexed by Gary Parks). *Genealogies of Virginia Families* (4 volumes). Baltimore, Md.: Genealogical Publishing Company, 1981. (Extracted from *Tyler's Quarterly*.)

Weis, Frederick L. (Published by the Society of the Descendants of the Colonial Clergy). *Colonial Clergy of New England and the Colonial Churches*. 1936/1977.

_____. *Colonial Clergy of Maryland, Delaware and Georgia*. Baltimore, Md.: Genealogical Publishing Company, 1978.

Weston, Frances W., and Mrs. Herman E. (National Society of Daughters of Founders and Patriots of America). *Founders and Patriots of America*. Published by the Society, 1975.

Whitney, David C. *Colonial Spirit of '76: The People of the Revolution: The Lives of Members of the Continental Congress and Other Prominent Persons*. Chicago, Ill.: J. G. Ferguson Publishing Company, 1974.

Wildman, Edwin. *The Founders of America in the Days of the Revolution*. Boston, Mass.: L. C. Cage & Company, 1924.

Wilson, Emily S. *Inhabitants of New Hampshire in 1776*. Lambertville, N. J.: Hunterdon House, 1983.

Withington, Lothrop. *Virginia Gleanings in England* (extracted from NEHGR and from *Virginia Magazine of History and Biography*). Baltimore, Md.: Genealogical Publishing Company, 1980.

Young Washington: A Biography. New York, N. Y.: Charles Scribner's Sons, 1948.

Periodicals, Archival Sources, Encyclopedias and Annuals

The Boston Transcript. (Newspaper) 1850–1930.

Calendar of Virginia State Papers.

Collier's Encyclopedia, various volumes and dates.

Daughters of the American Revolution Lineage Books (NSDAR).

Daughters of the American Revolution Patriot Index, Bicentennial Edition, 1990 (NSDAR).

Dictionary of American Biography, 1928–1946.

Georgia Historical Society Collections.

Georgia Genealogical Magazine.

Hennings Statues at Large.

Maryland Archives, various volumes.

Massachusetts Historical Collections.

National Cyclopedia of American Biography.

New England Historic Genealogical Record (NEHGR), volumes 1 through 50.

New York Genealogical and Biographical Record, various volumes, years.

Original Records, Filmed by the Church of Jesus Christ of the Latterday Saints: Birth, Marriage, Death, Estates, Wills, Land and Property, Cemeteries, The International Genealogical Index, etc.

Pennsylvania Archives, various volumes.

Pennsylvania Magazine of History and Biography.

South Carolina Historical Society's Historical and Genealogical Magazine.

United States Census Records, 1790 through 1830.

Who's Who in America, various years.

World Almanac and Book of Facts, various years.

World Book Encyclopedia, various volumes and years.

INDEX

Names in **bold** indicate signers of the Declaration of Independence. A hyphen (-) appearing after women's names indicate proven ancestors whose parents have not been identified.